A None's Story

A None's Story

*Searching for Meaning Inside Christianity,
Judaism, Buddhism, & Islam*

CORINNA NICOLAOU

Columbia University Press

New York

This is a work of nonfiction. It depicts events faithfully rendered to the best
of the author's ability. Some names and identifying characteristics have been
changed to protect the privacy of others. In very few instances, a sequence of
events has been modified for clarity and brevity.

The author is grateful to the *Los Angeles Times*, *Salon*, and *Gawker*, where
some of the material in this book first appeared in a different form.

Columbia University Press
Publishers Since 1893
New York   Chichester, West Sussex
cup.columbia.edu
Copyright © 2016 Corinna Nicolaou

Library of Congress Cataloging-in-Publication Data
Names: Nicolaou, Corinna, author.
Title: A None's story : searching for meaning inside Christianity, Judaism,
    Buddhism, and Islam / Corinna Nicolaou.
Description: New York : Columbia University Press, 2016.
Identifiers: LCCN 2015032283| ISBN 9780231173940 (cloth : alk. paper) | ISBN
    9780231541251 (e-book)
Subjects: LCSH: Nicolaou, Corinna. | Spiritual biography. | Christianity. |
    Judaism. | Buddhism. | Islam.
Classification: LCC BL73.N53 A3 2016 | DDC 200—dc23
LC record available at http://lccn.loc.gov/2015032283

Columbia University Press books are printed on permanent and durable acid-
free paper.
This book is printed on paper with recycled content.
Printed in the United States of America

c 10 9 8 7 6 5 4 3 2 1

Cover & interior design by *Martin N. Hinze*

References to websites (URLs) were accurate at the time of writing. Neither
the author nor Columbia University Press is responsible for URLs that may
have expired or changed since the manuscript was prepared.

For my grandmothers, Irene Nicolaou and Betty Bentley, and their grandmothers

Also in memory of Joan Gruen, Marilyn Nicolaou, Barbara Boster, and Barbara Drabkin—moms we lost too soon

Contents

Introduction

I'm a "None." When I say this out loud, people think I've said "I'm a nun," as in a habited woman who lives in a convent, which I find both funny and a little ironic because I'm actually sort of the opposite of that kind of nun. I'm one of the Americans who on recent national surveys claim no religious affiliation, who answer "none" to the question about what religion they are (this is why pollsters call us "Nones").

I have not had the opportunity to declare such an affiliation on an official document as I have yet to be randomly selected to participate in one of the few national surveys that measures religious attitudes. One such study is the American Religious Identification Survey, which has been conducted periodically since 1990, allowing for scientific monitoring of change over time. Because the U.S. Bureau of the Census is constitutionally prohibited from inquiring about religion, it relies on these results and has included them in the Statistical Abstract of the United States since 2003. If you are selected to participate in the study, a pollster will ask you a slew of questions by telephone. For example, on the "religious screener" portion of the form, you will be asked, "What is your religion, if any?" The list of possible responses is exhaustive and includes such options as Rastafarian, Wiccan, and Druid. Way down at the bottom (option number 95) is the one I would select: "No religion / None." Apparently this answer has become one of the most popular in recent years.

The number of religious services I attended growing up could fit on the fingers of one hand with enough left over for a peace sign. I never officially learned about the Bible, I did not study religion, and I was not baptized. I did not marry my husband in a church. My parents didn't teach me anything biblical—save, perhaps, for a secular version of the "Golden Rule." I managed to go through life almost completely ignorant of the specifics of religion besides what I picked up on in popular culture or through schoolyard gossip. Until recently I hardly knew a Catholic from a Protestant, let alone the belief systems of other world religions. Schools are, after all, legally required to avoid most aspects of the subject.

Granted, not all Nones are so uninformed about religion. Some grew up attending church but distanced themselves from their faiths as adults. Others may still attend religious services but do not identify as members of any one religion. Then there are those, like me, whose lack of religion was inherited. Both of my parents were raised with a Christian affiliation but were Nones by the time I entered the picture.

I married a fellow None, though you could say we are a "mixed-faith" None couple: my broken affiliation is with Christianity, and my husband's is with Judaism. Phil's parents were both raised attending synagogue; his father even participated in the Jewish coming-of-age ritual of the bar mitzvah. But both his mom and dad were leaning toward Noneness by the time Phil was born—though, officially, his parents would have still identified as Jewish. Like a lot of None couples today, Phil and I feel a greater affinity with Noneness than our seemingly divergent religious backgrounds.

Phil and I don't have children, but if we did, in all likelihood we would raise them as Nones. It's not uncommon today to find third- and fourth-generation Nones—kids whose understanding of religion may be more meager than my own. A None friend of mine told me not long ago that when her seven-year-old asked, "What happens in church?" she was stumped for a few seconds as she searched for an answer that seemed age-appropriate. Yes, what are they doing in there? Singing about love? Celebrating friendship? Practicing kindness? She offered a medley of honorable intentions, which seemed to satisfy her little None—for now.

According to the Pew Research Center, the ranks of the Nones have ballooned in recent years, making "no religious affiliation" the fastest-growing category among religious affiliations. Between 1972 and 1989, about 7 percent of Americans identified as having no formal religious affiliation. However, between 1990 and 2012, that figure jumped to 19.6 percent. Among people under age thirty, just over 30 percent say they have no religious affiliation. At the same time, the percentage of the U.S. population that identifies as Christian has experienced a steady decline, and other faiths have had modest growth at best.

One might assume that Nones are atheists, a categorization known for its denial of deity; for the most part, this is not the case. Growth in atheism has not kept pace with the rise in Nones. Less than 15 percent of the country's 46 million unaffiliated adults go on to claim atheism as their viewpoint of choice, a number that has remained relatively stable over the last decade or so.

In fact, most Nones agree that churches and other religious institutions benefit society and that they personally feel religious or spiritual in some way. A special study by the Pew Research Center's Forum on Religion and Public Life, conducted with the PBS television program *Religion and Ethics News Weekly* in 2012, found that 68 percent of Nones say they believe in God. More than a third (37 percent) classify what they feel as "spiritual," and over half (58 percent) say they often feel a deep connection with nature and the earth. Perhaps most surprising is the number of Nones who report communing with a higher power: 41 percent say they pray at least once a month, and half of this group says they pray every single day.

Robert Putnam and David Campbell, who discuss religious trends and attitudes in their book *American Grace: How Religion Divides and Unites Us*, characterize the sudden rise of the Nones as the most significant trend in our country's religious landscape in the last fifty years. They find that, for the most part, Nones mirror the population at large in terms of education, social standing, gender, and race.

So what is causing this seemingly sudden religious disassociation among a large subset of the American population? The only explanation that seems to make sense, the authors suggest, is political. The one characteristic many Nones share is that they lean left politically.

Putnam and Campbell state that the rise in Nones appears to be tied to the perception that religion and conservative politics go hand in hand—and I have to admit, this sounds about right to me. On a national survey, Nones report disassociating from organized religion at least in part because "they think of religious people as hypocritical, judgmental, or insincere." Many also report feeling that religious organizations "focus too much on rules and not enough on spirituality." In general, Nones believe that religious leaders do not treat certain social issues, particularly those regarding sexuality, with enough acceptance. We can't wrap our heads around a God who is more concerned with our private parts than with the content of our hearts.

But by disassociating with religion, are Nones missing out? I'm told religion has helped people be happier, kinder, more inclined to see "the big picture." It's been credited with keeping believers grounded, reducing anxiety and the compulsions that often lead to self-destructive behavior. In times of great difficulty, it may be the only thing that keeps a person afloat until things get better. Religion is touted as a doorway to the eternal, helping us understand our role in the cosmos.

I wished to know what the faithful knew, but I was scared.

Eventually I had this thought: What if I conquered my fear and walked into those places of worship and attended the services and maybe even communed with believers? What divine wisdom would I gather along the way? What, if anything, would I get from these experiences that I'm not getting by staying firmly planted in a secular world? I was also interested in how religions are practiced in the United States and what this says about our country and the citizens who inhabit it. The account presented here wasn't initially conceived as a "journey," but it picked up steam along the way. Early on I happened on a quote by Max Müller, a German-born scholar who lived in the 1900s. He advocated for the study of comparative religion, famously stating: "He who knows one, knows none." I took his words to heart.

According to the 2008 American Religious Identification Survey, 76 percent of Americans identify as Christians. The next most numerous religious identifications (aside from "none") are Judaism, Buddhism, and Islam, which collectively make up as much as 5.5 percent of the adult population in the United States. While this percentage seems relatively small, when you consider the world as a whole, the significance of these religions becomes clearer. Christianity has around 2.1 billion believers globally, and Islam is a close second with roughly 1.5 billion followers. Both of these were built on the foundation of Judaism, so even though only about fourteen million people around the world identify as Jewish, the theological influence of the faith is far greater than this number might indicate. The inhabitants of the planet who call themselves Buddhist number 376 million. All told, almost four billion of the Earth's seven billion inhabitants claim an affiliation with one of these four religions, which suggests that even if the followers of these belief systems do not account for huge portions of the U.S. population, they are tapped into a way of thinking so pervasive on a global scale that it transcends quantification.

In this book I make my way through four of the world's greatest wisdom traditions—Christianity, Judaism, Buddhism, and Islam—which also happen to be the most practiced religions in the United States. I let demographics and availability shape my work. Most of the U.S. population is Christian, and, within this segment, a majority is Protestant. Therefore, I started my churchgoing with Lutheranism, as Martin Luther is credited with being the "father" of the Protestant Reformation. From there, I roughly follow the chronological order in which denominations developed. Within the other faiths, my visits to places of worship were shaped by what is most readily available to faith consumers. For example, Zen is the most popular version of Buddhism in the United States, Reform Judaism is the most widely practiced in Judaism, and most followers of Islam within the United States (and in the world) are Sunni. Therefore, I grounded my explorations in the most prevalent traditions while also including within each faith category as many variants as were available to me.

Despite my efforts to visit as many places of worship as possible and to place each in a theological context, I would not characterize this book as "academic." Never once did I think of it as a "study." Nor would I characterize it as "investigative journalism." I never attempted to conceal my identity or act like someone I wasn't. I did not feel any reason to do so because, throughout, I considered this a personal quest to acquaint myself with religion. I said as much to anyone I met along the way. I shared all the real particulars of my life, including my ignorance about religion. However, while I did share that I was a writer, I never told anyone I was working on a book because, at the time, I wasn't. I may have dreamed of such a thing, but no such offers were on the table. To the extent any of this was "research," it was all a private effort to learn as much as possible. If anything, its scale and scope are evidence of a deep desire to know more.

Because I've come to see the importance of starting any journey right where you are, I began my explorations near my current home, which is a relatively small town in the Pacific Northwest. I also returned to the places I'd lived in the past—California, Texas, and Washington, D.C.—for additional experiences and to further enrich my understanding of the various religions. I've selected these cities in part because, for the particular faith I explore there, they offer a healthy range of options. More importantly, each played a part in my "None story": from my introduction to Christianity in Texas, my first encounters with Judaism in Los Angeles, and the full embrace of my Noneness as a college student in the San Francisco Bay Area to the aching that started to tug on my heart as a young professional in Washington, D.C., which led me to the Pacific Northwest and, ultimately, on this path.

A None's Story

Christianity

Like a lot of stories, this one begins on impact. Specifically, American Airlines Flight 77 slamming into the Pentagon. Counting the terrorists, 189 people were incinerated there: 59 passengers and 125 employees for whom it was a normal morning until a Boeing 757 ripped open their workplace.

That day I was not far from where the plane hit—about two miles as the crow flies. I was in another sturdy behemoth nearer to the Capitol. At the time I worked for the federal government in a branch of the U.S. Congress. My desk was part of a vast bank of cubicles next to windows. Here's how that particular morning unfolded: My coworkers and I gathered in a conference room to watch on a television the collapse of the towers in New York City. In a state of disbelief, I returned to my cube. My mother called from Austin, Texas. She told me about the Pentagon. I hadn't heard about that, so I told her she must be mistaken. Then we received orders from higher-ups to shut the blinds.

With the blinds closed, it was hard to do anything other than speculate about why we had been told to shut them. They were thick Levolors, and they were always open, streaming in daylight. Now a hundred pools of light emanated from individual desk lamps, but above was a thick layer of dark. Was closing the blinds meant to protect us in some way? I hated to think our best defense was window treatments.

Next we were told it was up to us: remain at work or go home. Up to us? It was only noon. I really wanted to stay because I thought doing so might make the day normal. So I told myself I would continue working, and as soon as I made that decision, I left.

A couple days later, I craned my neck from the passenger seat of my friend's car to get a look at the damaged Pentagon. I felt compelled to see it in person, and my usual form of transport—the Metro—was underground, so I asked my friend if she'd drive. Turns out she wanted to see it too and was glad for the company. We managed to stay upbeat on the way there, but neither of us was prepared for the sight of that blackened hole. Our squat, durable superhero was bleeding from a still-gaping wound.

During those next weeks, the experience of living in the District of Columbia changed. The airspace over the city was shut to commercial flights. I had never realized how integral the muffled roar of far-off jetliners was to the symphony of city noise. Now the most soothing of the background sounds was replaced by the disturbing chop-chop of helicopter propellers. Residents were encouraged to stockpile enough provisions for several days in case we were ordered to remain indoors or quickly flee. My roommate and I gathered a mound of necessities, which we kept in an out-of-the-way corner of our living room, growing like some hungry goblin we fed protein bars and jugs of water.

After 9/11 the popular discourse about faith shifted noticeably. In this country's short history, I don't think there's ever been so fierce and public a takedown. On a national scale, people felt emboldened to criticize religion. Between 2004 and 2007, a slew of books railing against faith took the best-seller lists by storm. Collectively they added up to a cultural trend given the nickname "New Atheism," and their authors became the movement's spokesmen. Perhaps the most prominent of the New Atheists was the journalist and professional curmudgeon Christopher Hitchens, a Brit who claimed D.C. as his honorary hometown and whose penthouse was a short walk from my apartment.

Hitchens was not so much presenting a new argument as giving an old one fresh fight. He claimed that atheism in itself did not imply hostility toward religion. Rather, as a statement of disbelief, it was neutral: no evidence suggests the existence of God. An atheist might privately hope for such confirmation. Hitchens preferred his atheism with a bit more bite. He hoped to popularize the term "antitheist" to refer to a nonbeliever who is grateful for this lack of evidence. In his book *God Is Not Great: How Religion Poisons Everything*, he insists we are all better off without religion, which he decries as "violent, irrational, intolerant, allied to racism, tribalism, and bigotry."

The youngest and perhaps most eager of the New Atheists was Sam Harris, an American. His book, *The End of Faith: Religion, Terror, and the Future of Reason*, was the first out of the gate in 2004. He began writing it in the days after 9/11, inspired and horrified by those events. In its pages, he lashes out at all faiths for being "pervasive sources of conflict in the world," but it seems to me he reserves his most pointed barbs for Islam. He writes that one cannot believe what a good Muslim is supposed to believe and not perpetrate violence. Islam, he claims, is not compatible with a civil society.

I assumed the New Atheists must be very knowledgeable about religion. These were well-educated men (all were men) making claims in public forums. Hitchens had been raised with religion: first within the Church of England and later at a Methodist boarding school. He says he knew by age ten it was all untrue; I figured he must have gained enough familiarity with the Bible and its teachings to speak with such authority. Harris claims a secular upbringing, but apparently he had absorbed enough understanding along the way. He holds a Ph.D. in neuroscience from UCLA; certainly he wouldn't say such things without a thorough understanding of the subject matter. His was a world where one didn't make claims without convincing proof.

What is a good Muslim supposed to believe? I had no clue. I didn't even know what a good Christian or Jew might believe. I had gone through a phase several years earlier when I called myself an atheist; I thought it was the only alternative to thinking the world was run by a giant grandpa sitting on a cloud. Later I realized I knew too little to rightfully claim atheism; to reject something, it's necessary to have a working knowledge of what you reject. I had no such knowledge. Perhaps many religious people conceived of God as a much more complex entity than I imagined. Who was I to say evidence to prove them right didn't exist? Perhaps everything is evidence.

Jesus Is a Start

Ten years later, and for the first time, I feel it: not the presence of Jesus, but a stirring in my heart that tells me I'm beginning to sense his purpose. I'm sitting in the sanctuary of a Methodist church a couple miles from my house when it happens. I've been at this churchgoing thing for several months now. So far I have attended the Sunday services of a handful of Christian denominations that include Lutheran,

Presbyterian, Reformed, Episcopalian, and Baptist—almost all of what I've come to understand are the "mainline" Protestant denominations whose theological roots can be traced directly to Europe—and while I have picked up bits and pieces of wisdom from each, I have not until now felt anything. On the contrary, I have maintained my stance as passive and wide-eyed observer, unable or unwilling to let any aspect of the strange concoction of music, ceremony, and prayer reach the sturdy enclosure of my heart.

Why am I, an individual about as alienated from religion as they come, sitting in this church? Here is the short answer: I realized I am a fragment, and that's why the panic has returned.

Let me explain.

A few years earlier, I had moved to a small town in the Pacific Northwest. This happened because I answered in the affirmative to a series of life-altering questions.

"Will you marry me?"

"Yes!"

"Will you quit your job, sell your condo, and move to the middle of nowhere?"

Oh. Hmmm. Wait, let's think this through.

Ultimately, I was willing, happy even, to make these changes because it seemed like life was handing me what I needed at just the right time. Hadn't I been secretly longing to step off the hamster wheel of worldly ambition? Then the events of 9/11 had sent me into an existential tailspin. I was exhausted and mildly depressed, wondering, "Is this all there is?" But I wasn't bold enough to plan an escape route, and then along came Phil: Ph.D. student, wonderful man, soon-to-be professor in a remote college town, and, suddenly, fiancé.

As I made the transition from old life to new, I felt like an archaeologist brushing away layers of dirt and grime to get at some prized artifact: the "real" me. Away went the city, the bustle, and the endless distractions. I cleared the need to be at a specific location for ten hours a day working hard at something that was not necessarily my passion—along with the paycheck that went with it.

What remained was unscheduled time and a stillness to my days I had never known. No tall buildings divided the air; no city blocks organized the land; no regular job structured my day. The more irrelevant crud I removed, the more evident it became that what I had hoped would be the complete and pristine vessel of my true self was actually a jagged little edge, curved just so and embedded in the earth so that it only appeared to be whole. I would find myself standing at a window, looking out on the wheat fields that surrounded my little neighborhood and wishing desperately for a crazy, active city to materialize so I could lose myself in it. A tight squeeze of panic would rise in my chest, and I would need to lie down and repeat a collection of short sentences: You are okay. Everything is fine. You are not dying.

It wasn't that I was unhappy with the direction my life had taken. I was content with my decision to leave the big city. Even quitting my good job, while difficult, felt right. The problem lay deeper, I realized, because all of these changes, while easing one kind of suffering, had uncovered another. As an adolescent and then again in college I suffered a frequent low-grade anxiety that occasionally peaked in bouts of panic. I had thought these were gone for good, but now I realized whatever caused them had simply been buried under layers of distraction. Which is why this churchgoing project has taken on such significance: I'm on a desperate search for the bits and pieces that might make my pot whole.

o

When I arrive at the Methodist church this morning, I'm several Sundays into this adventure and Jesus is about the farthest thing from my mind. I am preoccupied with having left the house at what seems like an unreasonably early hour for a Sunday. I feel a little nervous, as I always do before entering a new place of worship. I wonder how long the service will last and if there will be snacks afterward.

In sermons and readings over the last few months, Jesus has appeared in one of two guises: as a sweet man walking the earth or as an interchangeable component of the Holy Trinity, a synonym for God or the Holy Spirit. I've heard preachers call him "our savior," saying that he "died for our sins." But why or what this means, I wasn't quite sure—and no one had yet to elaborate. I'm hoping to find out because this information might shed light on my personal struggles.

At the door to the sanctuary, an elderly gentlemen in a brown corduroy blazer, his full head of white hair neatly coiffed, welcomes me politely and hands me the day's program: one eight-and-a-half-by-eleven piece of paper folded in half. From the outside, this church looks like a ski chalet circa 1970, the kind where the roof reaches all the way to the ground, but inside it is more of a cavernous barnlike space with a raised altar/stage at one end. As expected, decorations are minimal—a couple of chunky wooden candelabras affixed to the walls on either side of the room, a big shiny cross hanging against a row of golden organ pipes at the back of the altar, a funny little bowl-on-a-pedestal contraption that I guess is the baptismal font. Two big fans turn slowly where the ceiling reaches its most dramatic height. Mesmerized by the long steel blades, I keep glancing skyward, which makes me feel pious.

A choir of about ten strong wearing ordinary clothes is practicing as I take a seat in a row of chairs near the back. Several voices soar like doves and help the unremarkable ones reach greater heights. They are going over the day's hymns as people trickle in.

Two raised, flat screens on either side of the altar display an image of a painting of Jesus in what appears to be a post-crucifixion moment of reflection. He's sitting hunched and naked except for a strategically draped loincloth. His knocked-over crucifix lies nearby. His back is a mess of ripped flesh; a halo backlights his head, gently illuminating his somber profile and the twist of thorny brambles crowning him.

The heading reads: "Torture and Humiliation: Man of Sorrows." Uh oh. I think, "It's time to face the grim aspect of this Jesus thing."

One afternoon when I was a kid visiting my great-grandmother's house in Cockrell, Texas, my cousins taught me the words to the song "Jesus Loves the Little Children," and we marched up and down the driveway belting it out. They showed me an illustration of Jesus. He had rosy cheeks, a gentle smile, and the same long, wavy locks Grandma and Grandpa hated on my dad. I didn't understand why the look was okay on Jesus but dad needed a haircut.

As little as I've thought about Jesus since then, I must admit there have been times in my adult life when I have loudly cried out for him. This has usually occurred following a night of too much alcohol, when I find myself curled up on the bathroom floor or hugging the toilet for dear life. I have misjudged my tolerance for mixed drinks, and now I am violently sick and it's my own damn fault and I really, really, really do not want to die, although death is surely imminent, and, much to my surprise and that of anyone who may be within earshot, I shout, "Oh, Jesus!" or "Jesus, help me!" Which may indicate that some barely conscious, even primal, part of me trusts in this notion of Jesus and automatically reaches for it at times of great need.

So it is with heartfelt curiosity that I approach the story of Jesus now. The main event is so ubiquitous that one need never step foot in church to know the basics: Jesus is nailed to a cross and killed. The image of him hanging up there is almost too pervasive for me to actually feel anything in response.

A bloody young man drooping from planks of wood? Just Jesus.

It is Lent. Before this, what I knew of Lent came from my elementary and middle school years, when a classmate would proudly announce she was "giving something up for Lent." It might be chocolate or video games or, if she was super hardcore, television. I thought this was a fascinating and impressive endeavor, especially as it seemed to come out of nowhere, like a little personal challenge of willpower. My secret feelings about my own worthiness lent a certain logic to the notion that people might deny themselves something they loved: a self-inflicted punishment for whatever deep badness lay hidden inside.

I've recently learned that the purpose of Lent is to move past the desensitization about Jesus's death, to dive deeper into the painful aspects of the story. In fact, in some cultures a decadent party is thrown before Lent to help sweeten the bitterness of this "Season of Grief." Carnival in Brazil is an example, as is Mardi Gras in New Orleans—just think of all those partying Nones participating in the preparations for an ancient Christian ritual without even knowing it.

The Methodist minister seems as good a guide as any to lead us into the storm. He is an absent-minded-professor type with a trim beard and a lazy eye: one looks at us, the other is trained forever on the unknown. In his sermon he explains that when Jesus was summoned to Jerusalem to stand trial for his crime, which was his supposed claim of divinity, he was greeted as a hero. The crowd adored him and knew he had never been anything but exceptionally kind to everyone; he had lived his days practicing the love he preached. The people lined the streets and cheered as he entered the city. They spread palm fronds on the ground so that the hooves of the donkey he was riding wouldn't touch the ground. But after his conviction, they spit on him, kicked him, ripped at his clothes. They clapped when he was lashed and cheered as the spikes were driven through his palms and feet.

I knew Jesus was crucified, but I hadn't realized the abuse he suffered beforehand from his "friends." How would I have felt to be in Jesus's shoes? I believe I would have been terrified and pissed; I would have been furious at those people; I would have gone down with the bitterest anger in my heart and the worst expletives spewing from my mouth. But Jesus goes willingly, with nothing but love for every one of those jerks. Then I think, what if I were one of the crowd? Would I have stood up for Jesus? Doubtful. All my information would have been through the grapevine: this man says he's God. I wouldn't buy such a claim now; what makes me think I would have bought it then? Even some of his most loyal followers turned their backs on him. In every person exists the same capacity for cruelty. Jesus knew it, but he said he loved everyone anyway.

I think about the many public examples of greed in our culture, the CEOs who take million-dollar bonuses when their businesses have just been bailed out by taxpayers and all the smaller versions of self-ishness we perpetrate, and how Jesus's actions and message were the antithesis of this behavior. I glance at the whirring fans, hoping to blink away whatever this is rising in my chest.

In his ultimate act, Jesus was so painfully vulnerable—and yet he demonstrated amazing courage. Here, in these little outposts of devotion, something similar is happening: people show up to search their hearts and confront their own frailties. Perhaps they find ways to turn weaknesses into assets. I don't know. But I sense that some-where in Jesus's story is a message I desperately need and that each time I conquer my fear and enter a new place of worship I get closer to understanding what that lesson might be.

This moment feels like a victory—a small step, but forward movement nonetheless. I can't possibly understand the essence of Christianity unless I get Jesus. I have yet to tackle the biggest challenge: how to wrap my mind around God. But Jesus is a start.

o

I dab my eyes with my shirt sleeve to absorb the few tears threatening to travel down my cheek. I don't want anyone to get the wrong idea about me. I'm not having one of those ridiculous "coming to Jesus" moments you hear about—I don't think. I am just moved, that's all.

The minister invites us to return later in the week to go through the "stations of the cross," which he says he'll be setting up throughout the sanctuary over the next couple of days. I have never heard of "stations of the cross," so at home I look it up. It's a Catholic tradition of erecting "shrines" (usually fourteen), each dedicated to one event in the last twenty-four hours of Jesus's life. The idea is for the faithful to experience step-by-step that fateful day. It's not a Methodist custom, but the minister said it's something "he's trying out." I've read that a trend is afoot in which mainline Protestants are embracing elements of Catholic tradition they once distanced themselves from, and I suppose this is an example of just that. I decide to return on Good Friday, the day Jesus's crucifixion is traditionally recognized, to walk through the stations.

I spend several days obsessing over Jesus like I need to prep for a blind date with him. By all accounts, he was a real man, a carpenter and a Jew who was interested and knowledgeable enough in religion to be called rabbi. Just from the Bible snippets I've been hearing over these last several weeks, I know he preached love and equality, even stopping to talk with individuals considered so lowly that his friends wondered what he was doing. All of which makes me like him very much. Yet I've never quite come to terms with his claims of divinity. Why is he exalted as the Son of God when others making similar declarations are locked away in loony bins? When I was twelve, my friend Julie confided in me a painful secret. We were walking home from school and I could sense something was wrong. She was the first good friend I had made since mom and I moved to Dallas. Finally she spat it out. She said, "My dad is in the mental hospital." I knew she was referring to her biological father, a talented artist whom she saw infrequently. She called her stepdad by name.

Her face scrunched up. It looked like she was in physical pain, like the time we stepped barefoot in cactus needles. "He went crazy. He thinks . . ." She couldn't say it, whatever it was—it was too horrific. Her face was a map of agony. She took a deep breath and closed her eyes. "He thinks he's Jesus!"

I didn't know how to react. Judging by her face, it was about the worst thing imaginable, and I got the sense it wasn't the crazy part that so disturbed her—it was the Jesus part. Her misery was apparent, and I wished for something to say to make it go away. She made me promise not to breathe a word to our school friends. I wouldn't dare. I had my own angst to worry about. My dad had left for California, which was the reason mom and I moved to Dallas. We needed to be closer to my grandparents. That vague sense of unworthiness I felt as a kid in

Austin, the sense that made the denials of Lent sound reasonable, had blossomed into full-blown shame.

So why have so many people over the last two thousand years accepted the actual historical Jesus as the Son of God? I decide it is time: I must to go back and read every word Jesus said. It sounds like an enormous task, but really it isn't. All the dialogue he is purported to have spoken would fit in fewer than a hundred pages and, by some accounts, would take a person about two hours to recite if she were to perform it as an enormous, disjointed, and somewhat repetitive monologue. But it can't possibly be exact quotes can it? The words attributed to Jesus were written down fifty or more years after he died and, then, not necessarily by the original guys to whom he spoke them. After that, copies of the originals were made by hand until the printing press was invented; the texts also went through translations into modern tongues—all of which can make it seem like some epic game of telephone has been played between the original source and us contemporary folks.

I pore over the Gospels of Mathew, Mark, Luke, and John, the books of the New Testament where the bulk of the Jesus story is told. It's amazing what I learn. Again and again, Jesus lets others draw their own conclusions about his identity. He asks his disciples, "Who do you say that I am?" and they're the ones who say "messiah." He asks several times, "Who say the people that I am?" When rulers call him "King of the Jews," he says, "If you say so." I find it truly remarkable that I've gone through life thinking that Jesus went around saying, "I'm the messiah," which has colored my impression of him despite his many good qualities. I just bought what other people said about Jesus as words he said about himself.

One quote stands out. He's giving advice, like loving neighbors and avoiding false prophets, when he implies that our obligation to make these morally responsible decisions stems from the simple fact that we are among the living despite odds too slim to imagine. He says, "Because strait the gate, and narrow the way, which leadeth unto life, and few there be that find it" (Matthew 7:14).

I read the line again, and the truth of it hits like a lightning bolt to my heart.

Think of all the human pairings that had to occur since the dawn of human pairings and then within those couplings all the millions of potential seedling combinations. If just one of those had gone a different way: no you. Being alive is like winning the cosmic lottery, he's saying. I think each of us recognizes the truth of this, even if just subliminally. But our default setting isn't gratitude. Instead we are fearful, somewhere deep inside, of not being good enough, of being unworthy of this life we've been given.

I had been trying to figure out why I carried around such a heavy burden of shame as a perfectly normal kid. I had always attributed my feelings to my situation, as if my lack of goodness were exactly proportional to the difference between a conventional family and mine. But now I wonder if my shame didn't stem from a more universal source, if I would have smuggled the sense of being not quite good enough into a perfect nuclear family if those had been my circumstances. The more I talk to people from various backgrounds, the more I realize how others struggled with similar feelings that began around the same time. Perhaps it's the greater self-awareness that occurs between the ages of, say, eight and twelve that brings with it a dawning comprehension of one's own potential shortcomings. I've known some people who, exposed to religion and hoping to please God, became fervent during those years. Others, like me, pinned their nascent feelings of insufficiency on whatever scraps they could find. This phase marks the onset of a general level of anxiety, manifested in errant behaviors such as random bed-wetting or compulsive handwashing or other small acts of self-admonishment. Who didn't announce at least once during those years, "I wish I was never born!" (Interesting tidbit: the American Religions Identification Survey measures a respondent's religious affiliation at two points: current and at age twelve.)

Could these feelings go hand in hand with what Christians call "original sin"? Technically defined as the guilt all humans carry due to the disobedience of Adam and Eve, I'm beginning to wonder if this concept speaks to the widespread sense of shame written into the human condition. That it is tied to the Bible's first man and woman seems to indicate this feeling is a birthright and that each of us, by virtue of having been born, suffers to some degree. It's the guilt we feel for nothing we did, but simply because we got here. It's a form of survivor's guilt for having won the cosmic lottery.

Apparently, Jesus was trying to talk to people about this more than two thousand years ago.

But then we receive the second half in the one-two punch of the human condition: just as we come face to face with the wonder of our existence, with the enormous responsibility this honor seems to demand of us and the terror that we'll likely do nothing to prove ourselves deserving of it, we start to sense an end point lurking.

○

I arrive at the church at noon expecting to go through the stations alone because the minister mentioned that they'll be numbered and easy to traverse. I don't really know what to expect. I picture a Halloween haunted house with little vignettes—some frightening, some merely creepy—set up around a series of darkened rooms. Here is a ghost that pops out at you; here is a bowl of spaghetti that feels like human brains. Are you sufficiently terrified? Why, yes, I am, thank you.

When I walk into the sanctuary, a small group is assembled near the altar, three older women and a man plus the minister. I recognize one of the women; she sat next to me at the Sunday service. I told her I liked the enormous fans above us, and she explained they were the kind used in dairy barns. She also explained that the concrete floors had recently been exposed and polished so the sanctuary would look "more modern."

She spots me and waves me over. Her short white hair surrounds the adorable face of a Cabbage Patch Kid doll grown old. "We're just getting started," she says, putting her arm around me and giving a squeeze. As soon as my shoulder presses against hers, I realize how relieved I am to have companionship on this strange little journey. I wrap my arm around her.

The stations are not crosses or carvings like the pictures I saw online. These are computer printouts, with simple designs and mostly words, laminated and taped on the walls at intervals. The course starts on one side of the altar and takes us around the perimeter of the sanctuary until we end up on the other side of the altar. When I join the group, they are standing at the first station: Jesus prays in the Garden of Gethsemane. The minister reads a short paragraph about this brief respite that Jesus and three of his disciples take as they walk into Jerusalem. Jesus knows he's going to die soon, and he's suddenly overcome with grief; until this moment, he had seemed stoic about his fate. He tells his companions, "My soul is exceeding sorrowful unto death: tarry ye here, and watch." He asks them to stay with him while he prays for one hour. When he looks up, his friends have fallen asleep, and for the first time Jesus is upset. In this personal moment, he expresses his disappoint to his friends. He says, "Sleepest thou? couldest not thou watch one hour?" The minister finishes reading, and our little group stands quietly, letting it sink in.

How would I feel knowing it was the eve of my own death? I remember being thirteen when the idea of death first wrapped its long, ugly fingers around my neck and squeezed—it went from an abstract notion that happened to other, mostly old, people to being something that would happen to me eventually. It was nighttime, and I was lying in bed when this thought entered my mind: someday I will be gone. I felt so permanent; how could it be? I found the thought preposterous and, then, horrifying. I imagined all the years that would go by after me and how I wouldn't know what was happening because I would be one of those people in a graveyard, just someone who lived long ago. I gathered fistfuls of bedding and kicked wildly at the air. I was throwing a tantrum directed at . . . what? God? When the notion strikes just right I still get a flash of disbelief followed by a wave of suffocating panic. I was terrified by death then, and not much has changed.

I ponder the complexities in this simple event: Jesus wanting companionship as he struggles to accept mortality, while his friends, despite all good intentions, encounter their own human frailties. Jesus is momentarily disappointed, but he doesn't dwell on it. Not long after, he tells his friends his two hopes, which seem to be all of Christianity in a nutshell: "That my joy might remain in you, that your joy might be full" and "That ye love one another as I have loved you."

Over the next several stations Jesus is arrested, judged, and condemned. It occurs to me as we're going through these steps that the real crime here—the reason Jesus faced such a harsh consequence—comes from the beliefs others had about him. Anyone can say he is divine and simply be dismissed as a lunatic. What set Jesus apart, what made him a true threat in the eyes of the leaders of his day, were not the claims he may or may not have made but what existed in the hearts and minds of those whose lives he touched.

My little group is now facing the grim downhill slope. I offer my friend a wan smile. If I were alone, I would race through these last stations and make a beeline for the exit, but I slow my pace to that of the group's. I recall a statement made by the rector at an Episcopal service I attended a couple weeks earlier. She said, "If you're willing to look directly at the grim death of Jesus, you'll find it creates spaciousness in your heart." What a strange and mysterious thing to say, I thought at the time. What did she mean by it?

Then, like a motley crew on a turbulent sea, we forge ahead: Jesus is scourged, crowned with thorns, forced to carry his own cross, and, finally, crucified. Jesus says, "Be not afraid." It is the same simple instruction he has offered on many occasions over the course of his ministry, but it takes on new significance as he now offers it from the other side of death.

The last station is a life-size wood cross that has been set temporarily in the middle of the altar. Now Jesus is in his tomb, and the cross is draped in black cloth. I stand directly in front of this crucifix. It is taller than me, about the size of a doorway. Jesus said, "I am the door." I close my eyes and imagine this big cross as something I can open. What's on the other side? Can it be as expansive as the Episcopalian priest suggested? I see my hand on the knob as I twist and push.

o

I decide to skip the churchgoing on Easter Sunday. I know in a way I am cheating myself. I endured the gloomy crucifixion only to miss the celebratory conquering of death. Part of the reason I decide to take the day off is I'm not quite sure what to think of the supernatural aspects of the Jesus story: making blind people see, feeding a crowd of thousands with a few fish, and, the biggest of all, rising from the dead. I've read that some modern theologians insist these events have been fabricated or embellished; the stories about Jesus were told by word of mouth over many years until they developed these fantastical elements. I haven't sorted out what I believe—or if it even matters that I form an opinion on the subject. But, to be honest, that's more of an excuse. Here's the truth: a group of my pals is meeting for brunch. After several months of reserving my Sundays for God, I'm feeling homesick for my old ways. For Nones, Sundays are for getting up late, lazing around at home, and if we do go out before noon, we are most likely to be up to one thing: having brunch with friends.

I wonder, as I am downing a couple of mimosas, if we aren't more Christian than we realize—even those of us who might balk at the suggestion. We may not be overtly religious, but in ways we might not even recognize, Christianity shapes our day-to-day lives. Our very concept of historical time: we organize our calendar years into "before" and "after" Jesus. Even the word "holiday" comes from "holy day." I accept Jesus's main teachings on an instinctual level, as do the people with whom I'm close. From a very young age, I understood that others are no different from me and that anything I do or say is experienced by them in the same way I might experience it. I also understand that every person is a significant and equally valuable being. So integral is this to my way of thinking that it's difficult to imagine a time in human history when this reasoning wasn't the norm, when certain people were considered no better than lion bait, existing for the sole purpose of being ripped from limb to limb for entertainment. I can imagine that Jesus's Golden Rule must have seemed like a novel idea back then. But have we evolved past this? Could it be that the spiritual exploration and evolution of our ancestors has accumulated in our DNA or "collective consciousness" so that what were once alien teachings are now fundamental to who we are?

I read about a recent spate of billboards an atheist group paid to have erected in a few key cities. They show smiling individuals with the quote, "I can be good without God." I have no doubt this is true, that the people pictured are kindhearted and well-meaning, though I might argue that technically the "without God" is a bit misleading as they are likely leaning on the spiritual work of previous generations. So while these individuals may personally be taking a break from thinking about God, their great-grandmothers and great-great-grandmothers probably spent quite a bit of time honoring the divine and whatever wisdom they gathered they passed down to their children who passed it down to their children and so on.

But this billboard raises an excellent question for me personally: isn't religion about a lot more than being good? I hope so because I'm not looking for motivation to be good—like the atheists on those posters, I don't think of myself as particularly in need of help in that area.

I am shooting for something more along the lines of inner peace.

I want to learn what, if anything, Christianity offers to soothe deeper and more personal afflictions. Already it's forcing me to examine obvious causes of suffering, like the idea of death. But another source had never occurred to me: having been born. So much anguish is tied to these twin realizations—existence, granted and revoked. Each of us will tussle with them again and again throughout a lifetime, giving rise to bouts of guilt and fear, two sides of the coin of life. Perhaps the idea is to familiarize ourselves so intimately with these truths or understand them in such a way that someday we can move beyond this struggle.

o

Several months after moving with Phil to our new town, I started to notice the churches. Almost like one of those digital-patterned images in which a prominent shape emerges if you gaze with eyes relaxed, the churches in my neighborhood began to stand out. I counted six within a mile radius of my house—three if I went one direction and three if I went the other. The older neighborhood that surrounds the college campus boasted even more churches—historic brick and stone buildings nestled on almost every block. They also popped up in unexpected locations, between retail businesses in strip malls or amid doctor's offices in a medical complex.

I would stare as I drove past, wondering what was going on inside. I'd see their crowded lots on Sundays, the parked cars spilling into the residential streets. I'd also see churches whose lots were half empty, and I'd wonder about those too. It struck me as extraordinary: in every neighborhood in every town in this country sit command posts of attempted transcendence. What exactly did they do in there? Why was I not with them? Church has been the stepping-stone for newcomers since this country was founded—first when European settlers arrived and then as pioneers made their way west. Whatever new place has been arrived at, church has helped people plant their roots and establish relationships—with God and with each other. Those happened to be two types of relationships I was interested in cultivating, so why should I disregard this tried and tested means of adjusting to, and perhaps even thriving in, a new place?

But where does one begin when no beginning has been mapped? How was I, a second-generation None, meant to make sense of this sea of choices without benefit of having been handed an affiliation by birth, marriage, or some other unique circumstance? The extent of my knowledge in this arena involved that old childhood game of putting my hands together, digits intertwined, index fingers up and reciting the lines, "Here is the church. Here is the steeple." Then "opening the doors" and crying, "And here's all the people!"

I plucked the Worship Directory out of my local paper. I usually swept right past it, but suddenly there it was: an entire page dedicated to listing the places of worship in my community. I studied it carefully. I found names I recognized but knew almost nothing about, then the denominations splintered into groupings that were foreign to me. In alphabetical order, the list read: Assembly of God, Baptist, Bible, Catholic, Christian Science, Church of Christ, Church of Jesus Christ of Latter-Day Saints, Church of God, Disciples of Christ, Episcopal, Evangelical, Foursquare, Full-Gospel, Lutheran, Methodist, Nazarene, Non-Denominational, Presbyterian, Quaker, Reformed, Seventh-Day Adventist, Unitarian Universalist, and United Church of Christ. (I also noted a listing for a mosque and a "Jewish community" that doesn't have a synagogue but gathers for worship and fellowship.) Most headings boasted more than one church to choose from.

Overwhelmed, I thought I could satisfy my curiosity and avoid the churchgoing issue by taking a page from the life of a poet I admire: Kathleen Norris. She writes about moving back, in her thirties, to her ancestral farming town in South Dakota after living in New York City. I was drawn to her story because it seemed like an extreme version of my own—her urban experience more urban, her small-town experience more rural. Her relocation was accompanied by a spiritual shift as well. Raised with regular church attendance, she had come, for a time, to consider herself an atheist. Her pull toward home was more than an attraction to her family homestead; it was also a return to her religious roots. She rejoined her grandmother's Presbyterian Church. In addition, she takes sojourns to a Benedictine monastery, staying with contemplative monks who practice Catholicism.

I decided to copy Norris. Preferring my destination to be within a day's drive of my house, I went online and searched "Benedictine Monastery Washington State." This little "spiritual vacation" wasn't meant to be the beginning of anything; it was supposed to be the entire journey. I imagined it as a divine car wash: in one end I would go with the jangled nerves and disconnectedness of modern life; out the other I would appear with the serene smile and beaming aura of the Virgin Mary. What were the events that I thought would transpire in between? I had no idea. But I was pretty sure angels would sing.

Immediately I hit upon the website of a monastery that fit the bill; it seemed almost too easy, as if it had been founded in the 1970s for the sole purpose of one day being at the receiving end of my Internet search. Unlike the one Norris visited, this was a 300-acre farm and the "monks" were all nuns. It was as far away from my new town as possible while still being part of the same state; though, technically, it wasn't even touching the state—it was several miles offshore, on a small island. Online photos showed habited ladies atop tractors and lippy llamas smiling for the camera. I read that visitors are welcome, especially when they help with chores. I loved the idea of working on a farm, especially if what the website said was true—that it was a "form of prayer." To arrange a weeklong visit was simple enough: click to e-mail a nun.

I drove my car onto the ferry. As we pulled away from the dock, I felt like I was entering a dreamscape where seals might pop up from the murky depths to lead the way. I imagined I would be a sort of "temporary nun," one of the gals making my way down the monastery halls to the light of a flickering candle. I would eat my meals sitting elbow to elbow with the sisters; we would work in the garden side by side, fast friends giggling at the absurdities of the world. The nun atop a tractor in the picture from the website? I'd be sitting right next to her, her field-plowing copilot. All the while, they would take me under their billowy sleeves and teach me the divine lessons they had gathered over a lifetime.

Once we hit land, reality whooshed back.

The monastery itself—where the nuns lived—was behind a high wall. The guest accommodations were located down the road in the original house built when the property was a secular farm. My companions for the week were not nuns at all but other visitors staying at the guesthouse: two young women interested in organic farming, a middle-aged woman deciding whether to become a nun, and a teenager from Seattle trying to kick a drug habit.

Between the nuns' quarters and the guesthouse was a little chapel, the interior made entirely of wood harvested from the nearby forest. Big windows overlooked the sheep pasture. I only saw the nuns at the two daily worship sessions I was invited to observe—morning mass and evening vespers. (Occasionally, I spied a nun as she drove by in a pickup truck.) After mass I waited at the door of the chapel to receive my daily assignment. Our days were very structured: two hours of morning chores and two in the afternoon, time for silent contemplation (a walk was encouraged), and meals to be shared communally among visitors. (The nuns ate the same food together in the monastery.)

During my stay I sifted compost, planted hundreds of tulip bulbs, and pulled bushels of mustard greens. I enjoyed the work and the reassuringly rigid timetable of our days that enforced quiet retreat. I savored the periods each day that I sat in the simple chapel. The nuns would sing and pray while the candles coaxed a golden glow from the wood surfaces, and I would get faint glimpses of the transcendence of faith, but these were as ephemeral as one of those delicate paper lanterns that float into the sky on the heat of a single flame and then burn up and disappear. I returned home with a sense that religion offered something substantial, enough to sustain those women on that remote island, but I had not grasped what it was.

o

Back home, the Worship Directory still sat on my desk, growing crispy from the sun. As I read through it again, I realized some options were missing; a church just down the street wasn't listed. I consulted the phone book to fill in gaps. The religious landscape was even more confusing than I initially realized. I counted about fifty options within a short drive of my house.

Did my new town have more than its fair share of churches? In 2001 the Pacific Northwest earned the nickname "the None Zone" after the American Religious Identification Survey found a disproportionate percentage of Nones residing in the region—63 percent compared to the national average of 41 percent. More recent studies show that Vermont and parts of New England have since surpassed the Pacific Northwest in percentage of Nones. Still, even within these "None Zones," exist pockets of religious zeal. My community is home to two public universities, which fill these waters with proverbial fish, and I have seen old letters between church officials agreeing that outposts should be established here if they are to keep a "hook in the sea." So my sense that this community hosts an inordinate number and variety of churches may not be far off.

I would visit them all, I decided. The wisdom of this solution was twofold: I could quench my thirst for spirituality and address the religious ignorance I had felt so acutely in the wake of 9/11.

Before going forward, I needed to tell Phil what I was doing. I couldn't just wake up Sunday mornings and leave the house with my husband wondering where I was headed. When I told him that, at least for a while, I would be gone for a portion of every Sunday he furrowed his brow and muttered, "That sucks." He grew more supportive over time when he saw my determination. By the time Sundays turned to Saturdays and, eventually, to Fridays, he was cheering me on.

I told my grandmother, my dad's mom and my only living grandparent, over the phone. Grandma is the most religious of my remaining family, although her association with the Greek Orthodox Church in Dallas has become mostly cultural: christenings, weddings, funerals. I explained that I was going to stay in a monastery for a week, and she cried, "They'll rape you!" Her hearing is not so good, though it turns out she heard me just fine. I eased her into the idea over several conversations, but she remained skeptical.

My parents were the ones I was most worried about. When I was growing up, we had a family friend who became a "born-again" Christian and it was with a mixture of pity and sorrow that we spoke of her. She may have been reborn someplace else, but she had died on our side. They took the news of my project stoically, though with a bit of confusion at first. It helped when I couched it as "research" and explained I was going to many places of worship and exploring several religions. How would they feel if I selected a religion with which to identify and became a member at a single place of worship? I had a feeling that would be much harder news to break.

A Man Who Changed the World

Phil plunked his beloved *History of the World* into my lap. "Read," he said, pointing to the open page. "The Protestant Reformation," announced the heading. Over several paragraphs I learned the condensed version of the story: the devoted monk in medieval Germany whose dissatisfaction with the Catholic leaders of his day led him to challenge their interpretation of Christianity. His bold gesture of posting an outline of complaints to his local cathedral door is credited with starting a wave of religious rebellion throughout Europe. Had I been taught the broad strokes of these events in high school? It rang a faint bell.

I went online to order a book about him. I selected one entitled *Martin Luther: A Man Who Changed the World*. It was a little on the pricey side, but I decided to go for it. I pictured a weighty tome like Phil's *History of the World*. I would keep it on my bookshelf and, years from now, reflect that my journey into religion had been shaped by this dense and dusty volume. I would heft its bulk into my lap and relive my beginnings as a self-made religious scholar.

Several weeks later a package arrived. Too wide to fit in the mailbox, our mailman propped it against the garage door. It was about the shape of a record in its cardboard jacket, perhaps a hair or two thicker.

I ripped it open.

It took me several seconds to understand. It was my book, *Martin Luther: A Man Who Changed the World* . . . but it was for kids. I had accidentally ordered an illustrated children's book.

The cover, realistically rendered in gloomy colors, showed an unsmiling young monk pressing an old scroll against a wood door. I didn't know what was more frightening—his intense watery eyes or his bald dome ringed in bangs.

I would learn later that Luther said, "God likes to perform miracles in order to mock and trick me and the world." He was referring specifically to his unexpected marriage, at age forty-two, to a former nun, Katherine Von Bora. Who would have thought they would deviate so drastically from their monastic vows? Yet they embraced their new lives and celebrated them as a divine gift. By all accounts they were extremely happy together and had six children.

At first I was annoyed about the book mix-up: I needed to repackage and send it back, hassle with customer service. Then I paused. Something clicked, some spark of recognition, and I promised to take note of all the goofy and insignificant things that happened along the way—even if they were ridiculous or seemed to take me backward instead of forward. I was bound to learn as much about the divine from these "failures" as I was from what I might consider the successes.

I opted to keep the book and prop it up where I could see it every day. Over time I found the whole thing funny. Could this be one of God's little tricks? If so, God is hilarious.

I also decided to obtain the rest of my reading material from the local college library.

o

As I pull into the parking lot of the Lutheran church, the first stop on my journey (second if you count the monastery), I am sweating. I feel like a poorly trained FBI informant on an undercover mission, a bulge of wires strapped to my chest, a lumpy dead giveaway that I am not to be trusted.

As I approach the church doors, I have comedian Dana Carvey's "Church Lady," in my head. In an interview I read recently, he explained that he based that character on the women in the Lutheran church he grew up attending. Prim and judgmental, I can picture her interrogating me. "You've decided to attend church after all these years? And you're how old? Well, isn't that *special*?"

The first person I see greeting people at the door is a middle-aged man who looks vaguely familiar. Perhaps I've seen him at the grocery store or post office. His droopy eyes and full mustache give him the appearance of a walrus; he even has the soft, seemingly boneless physique. He is perhaps the least intimidating person imaginable, and I can feel the tension in my shoulders release.

"Are you a student?" he asks me. It's the second-to-last weekend in August, and the fall semester has just begun. On a table are red lunch bags, rows and rows of them, each with its own little sticker: "Welcome, Students," they announce.

I shake my head apologetically. "Community member."

He looks disappointed.

I feel like telling him I've been a student for most of my days on earth. In fact, this is the first time in my life I'm not a student—officially, that is.

A pained expression comes over his face, as if he's struggling with a moral dilemma. "Well, we made these bags for students, but I guess you can have one? Since you're a visitor."

"No, I couldn't," I say. I wave away his offering. I imagine busloads of students will walk through the doors any minute. "Save those for the students."

Now that the pressure is off, he seems eager to give it to me. He opens the mouth of the bag to let me look inside. Among the photocopied leaflets, I spy a plastic baggie of homemade cookies.

"Well, now that you've shown me those cookies," I say, taking the bag.

I'm so focused on making my way into the sanctuary that I don't notice the ladies passing out stacks of paper. I'm a few feet inside, standing at a basin that looks like an empty wishing well and surveying the room. Here's what I'm preoccupied with: the chapel is a giant circle. There's no "altar," just a small raised area in the center, and no traditional pews, just rows of identical chairs like you might see in a hotel conference room. They are set up so that short aisles radiate out from the central platform.

I'm captivated by this configuration because it bears little resemblance to the image I had concocted in my mind of churchgoing in Luther's time. To understand his dissatisfaction with worship in his day, I created an imaginary scenario. In my daydream I am a regular lady of the town of Wittenberg (in current-day Germany), a hausfrau going about her daily chores when the church bells toll, indicating to everyone within earshot that services will begin imminently. I corral my wayward pig and tighten the strings on my bodice and begin the ten-minute walk to church. By the time I get there, it's packed. I find a seat in the last pew. In the front, at the altar, the priests and other church officials have begun the ceremonial rituals: the movements and prayers that look familiar to me, as I have seen them performed my entire life. Even so, I have no idea what they mean as the words are in Latin, a language only the educated study (basically just the "men of the cloth"). So I sit quietly, enjoying the intonation of their voices. I inhale the woody smoke of incense, and appreciate the smell even as it further obscures my already poor view of the holy stuff happening up front.

Of course, my hausfrau alter ego has never actually read the Bible, as it has yet to be translated into common languages from Greek and Latin. However, I have been told about God, the ruler of the universe, and it is my understanding that I can do specific things to please Him. This is the only hope I have for my animating essence—my soul—to live on after my body dies. Furthermore, I have options to improve the quality of my eternal life. For example, I can give money to one of the traveling religious officials collecting donations to take back to headquarters in Rome and, depending on how much I give, the number of days that I have to wait to gain admittance into heaven after I die will be reduced, which seems like money well spent if you ask me, as I will have an official certificate of this purgatory-reducing transaction.

But the most important reason I'm here is to participate in the holiest of the holy: communion. This is when the priests turn bread and wine into the real flesh and blood of Jesus and, by eating it, a person ingests God—this merging with the divine is where an individual is meant to feel closest to the Supreme Being. Not that I get to eat the bread and wine myself, mind you. No one in the congregation gets to do that, as the elements are too precious to be handled by regular people. What if the wine were to spill? That would be Jesus's blood! The good men in robes grow close to Him on our behalf.

A tap on the shoulder snaps me from my medieval revelry. "You forgot this," says a bright-eyed woman. I look at her offering. "Today's program," she says. Ah, the Xerox machine: just one of the many ways the churchgoing experience has become more accessible since Luther's time.

A quick glance at the program indicates how different today will be on account of Luther's ideas. It was Luther's own struggles with depression that forced him to reconceptualize the churchgoing experience and, most importantly, his relationship with God. He admitted he hated the God the church was presenting because it seemed as if nothing was enough to satisfy Him. He thought becoming a monk would alleviate his anxiety—at last he would feel as if God were pleased with him—but even in his devout monastic life, he felt rotten.

My children's book does an excellent job of conveying Luther's torment; in fact, I probably wouldn't have understood how bad it was without the realistic illustrations. For the first half, in every picture, the guy looks absolutely traumatized. He's on his knees in a thunderstorm, woefully gazing at the heavens. Turn the page and he's on his knees again, this time furiously scrubbing the monastery floor. The accompanying text reads: "Brother Martin was surprised and saddened that the harder he tried to keep God's commandments perfectly, the more he felt like a failure."

Then, in a quiet moment while reading the Bible, everything changes—such a simple and private act that it doesn't warrant an illustration in my picture book. Luther suddenly understands that God's love is free for all who wish to receive it. It dawns on him that nowhere in the Bible does it say donations of money are required or that priests are necessary go-betweens.

He experienced elation at this realization. Of this moment, he later recalled, "I felt as if I was entirely born again and had entered paradise itself through gates that had been flung open." (Legend has it that this "Aha!" moment actually occurred while he was on the toilet, which is perhaps the best argument I've encountered for reading in the bathroom.)

Luther wanted to share his revelation and remove fear from people's motivation for attending church. He wanted them to show up to be loved. Given that the natural human default setting seems to be unworthiness, this small difference was extraordinary. Perhaps it alone put the "revolutionary" in the Protestant Reformation. He hoped others would go directly to the source and make this joyful discovery, so he personally translated the Bible into German and, luckily, the invention of the printing press helped him get the word out. Luther wished to empower people to do their own spiritual work and for churchgoers to form what he called a "priesthood of believers."

I take a seat in the last row, but it's still only a few rows back from the center. Already I feel an inclusiveness the monastery chapel lacked. My time there gave me a sense of what it must have been like to be a churchgoer during Luther's day. The area where the nuns sat and conducted the services was separated from the pews by a wood lattice, more of a symbolic divide, as I am almost certain I could have ripped it from its ceiling hinges. It was a reminder to them and to me that we occupied different worlds. The nuns sing-songed all the prayers, the words to which were provided in a little booklet, but they were in Latin; even as I tried to follow along, I didn't understand it. For me the daily services were a show, a lovely show for sure, but nothing more than something to be passively gazed on. As a non-Catholic, I was asked not to partake in communion. So I watched during mass every morning as each nun stuck out her tongue to receive her wafer, followed by the nun-in-training and then the two organic farming volunteers, both apparently Catholic, and I felt like the kid not invited to the party, just a tiny bit like they were sticking out their tongues at me.

The more-level playing field Luther wanted is apparent today in the minister's central location, his simple white linen robe, and his casual demeanor. He seems more a master of ceremonies than a special conduit of God. No need for him to hear our sins and forgive us on behalf of God; he instructs us to take a moment to confess silently and then leads us in reading a prayer of forgiveness printed in the program. He hands the microphone to a young woman from the congregation who reads a passage from the Old Testament and then to an older man who reads from the New Testament. He cues us when it's time to sing hymns.

At today's service the program clearly states that everyone is invited to participate in communion, but I decide to abstain. Luther may have argued with many practices of the Catholic Church, but he never contradicted the meaning of the Lord's Supper: that in consuming the bread and wine, one is consuming Jesus's flesh and blood. He made only one small amendment. Whereas the Catholic Church claimed that the bread and wine transformed completely into the body and blood of Christ under the authority of the priests, Luther argued that both body and blood were united with the bread and wine; they coexist in the communion elements. From an outsider's perspective, it is a slim difference: Jesus *is* the bread and wine or is *in* the bread and wine.

I can see why the nuns at the monastery forbid outsiders from taking communion. I'm not sure how I feel about eating Jesus or why it's necessary. Is it because he "conquered death"? I suppose I'd be lucky to have even the tiniest bit of whatever made that possible reside in me. Will it make me stronger? Or just more accepting of my weaknesses? Maybe it's the kind of thing where it's impossible to imagine the benefits until you do it.

As I exit the sanctuary after my first church service, I'm feeling proud of myself for having overcome my fear and entered those mysterious church doors. Now for my reward: an ice cream social in the church lobby. Someone has set out tubs of vanilla and chocolate with little bowls of toppings and squeeze bottles of caramel and fudge. I marvel at how many enticements have been added to the churchgoing experience, yet fewer people seem to be showing up. The chapel was about two-thirds full, and out in the lobby more than half the welcome baggies for students remain in neat rows. Five hundred years ago, regular folks weren't allowed to participate in the Lord's Supper. Now we can wash Jesus down with a free sundae.

o

For individuals who are supposedly spiritually complacent, my None friends sure are hungry for religious information. They know I've set out on this quest, and now every time we see each other they want to shake me down like some giant tree of knowledge. But I'm not even a sapling yet.

"Where are you now?" Kelsie asks when I see her at a party.

"Pentecostal," I tell her, raising my eyebrows up and down real fast like this is some sexy info I'm letting her in on. "Speaking in tongues?" she wants to know. I shrug. "We'll find out Sunday."

They requested every detail after I visited one particular church in our community whose pastor is a controversial figure. He is something of a local celebrity, though infamous among my peers for having gone on record several years ago suggesting that American slavery may not have been such a bad thing because it exposed Africans to Christianity. (Never mind that many abolitionists were Christians.) Of all the churches in my local Worship Directory, this one had me the most wary.

"Yuck," Emily mutters. "That guy." She's the only one I know who claims to have seen the actual video footage where he made this remark.

"You went *there*?" Sueann asks incredulously, though I'm not sure what surprises her more: that I got in or that I was able to get out.

To prepare myself, I visited the church's website where I spotted an advertisement for its upcoming conference. Using a medieval-looking typeset (where "u" looks "v"), the title read, *The Institute of Awesome: Keeping Calvinism Sassy for the Next 500 Years*. I chuckled: a bit of Protestant reformer humor, and I've come far enough to get the joke.

Going to the library to find books about John Calvin, I scratch my head at how many there are and how broad the titles: *The Calvinistic Concept of Culture*; *Calvin and the Foundations of Modern Politics*; *Calvinist Roots of the Modern Era*; *Calvinism and the Capitalist Spirit* . . . several shelves that include Calvin but then expand into social concepts much bigger than any single individual.

I had no idea Calvin was credited with developing the foundational structures we in the United States hold dear—you know, little things like our version of democratic representation—and how closely these are tied to the history of Christianity. If such basic activities as voting and accumulating wealth can be considered derivative of Jesus, can any of us really claim to be a None?

Calvin, who was just a few years younger than Luther, entered the picture just as many Europeans were expressing a growing disenchantment with the Catholic Church's current leadership: its bishops and pope. In a classic instance of "right time, right place," the detail-oriented Calvin decided it was up to him to develop a new governing structure for the churches. He would create a system that could take the place of Rome and allow the gist of Luther's ideas to be practiced on a wide scale sustained over many years.

His idea was for each region to have a church guided by a group of elders ("presbyters" in Greek—which is why churches modeled in this vein are often called "Presbyterian") selected by the congregation; a few chosen elders from each church would meet in a larger body to discuss issues on a regional scale. A leader would be selected from these chosen elders to head the whole operation. It was a bottom-up structure versus the old top-down—an embodiment of Luther's "priesthood of believers." Basically, he developed the blueprint colonists used when they formed the U.S. Congress—a wee fact you'd think I would have learned as a political science major who was employed for several years by the federal government.

While the church with the pastor my friends find distasteful shares theological roots with Presbyterianism, it goes by the more generic Calvin-inspired label of "Reformed." This word suggests devotion to Calvin's theology but permits a dodge from the overarching governing structure he developed. Instead, this church belongs to a looser affiliation of like-minded churches that seems to better suit its maverick leader.

He established his church in the 1970s, then slowly expanded its network to include local private-education options from elementary school all the way through college. The college, which enrolls about two hundred students a year, offers a "classical education in light of scripture" and is located just a few blocks from the state university, in a building on Main Street—though I had no idea it was there until someone pointed it out. It occurs to me that kids born in this congregation whose parents are inclined to send them to its series of private schools could grow up having almost no meaningful contact with the outside community.

In addition to the education system, several local businesses are affiliated with the church, some more forthrightly than others. The most well-known is a café (named, I realize now, for an obscure Protestant reformer) just down the street from the college, where cappuccino is served in honor of the Lord. The latest is a bustling clothing shop. This business savvy is a realization of Calvin's belief that every aspect of society, including the economy, could pay tribute to God. My None pals give those establishments a wide berth if they can help it.

o

I muffle a gasp as I enter the gymnasium a few minutes before the service starts. If fewer people in general are going to church these days, here's one congregation that's bucking the trend, although it's possible they aren't attracting converts so much as giving birth to them. There are so many young children that I feel like I've been teleported to the part of Disneyland where the rides are for preschoolers. Every woman seems to be pushing a baby stroller or holding an infant on her hip.

All around, dads are pouncing on little escape artists. Chains of hand-holding siblings make their way gingerly through the crowd. There have been some children in every church service I've attended so far, but I could have counted them easily. I wouldn't even know where to begin the tally here.

The congregation long ago outgrew the regular church building they once occupied, and while they plan construction of a megachurch on the outskirts of town, Sunday worship is held in their private school's gymnasium. Row after row of folding chairs have been set up, everywhere more folding chairs, except in the few aisles I'm sure the fire marshal has declared are necessary for possible escape. In a daze I take the first available chair at the end of an empty row near the front. A woman with a halo of blond curls asks if the seats next to me are taken. When I tell her no, she nods to a man who comes over with a newborn sleeping in a carrier and four small children trailing him like fuzzy ducklings. They file in to the chairs next to me, which is how I end up sitting elbow to elbow with a very well-behaved five-year-old boy whose honey-colored crew cut sparkles under the fluorescent lights.

As I look around the gym, I'm realizing the accuracy of a theory my None friends have about this church. They suspect its congregants of being alarmingly . . . stylish. Aside from the few who look like they've stepped out of *Little House on the Prairie*, the women sport short skirts with leggings and cool chunky boots or shiny high heels, colorful scarves, and fun haircuts. The men have more of a lanky lumberjack look: close-cropped hair, broad shoulders, plaid. I get the impression they chop firewood and build things—and look handsome doing so. The couples are "hip" in an urban kind of way; if I saw them in a different context I would totally peg them for Nones. But they're actually anti-Nones. These are exceptionally fruitful multipliers who most likely believe in "double predestination," which is Calvin's idea that all individuals fall into one of two groups: "saved" or "damned." Calvin's little twist on Christianity had huge consequences.

Unlike Luther, who thought anyone who chose to receive God's love could be saved, Calvin alleged that people had no say in the matter. Some (the "elect") had been earmarked in advance. These people had done nothing in particular to deserve their special status and could do nothing to mess it up, just as no amount of good behavior or faith would help the damned. For those on the right side of this equation, I can see how this could be a reassuring concept. While mainstream

Presbyterians have officially given this idea the boot, here it lives on. I feel everyone is looking at me wondering where I'm headed when I kick the bucket because they've got heavenly eternal life in the bag.

A man approaches the lectern and the congregation stands. So this is the infamous pastor. Oh, the one-sided debate I've carried on with this guy. (In my fantasy I shout, "What happened to 'Do unto others'?!" as he cowers.) In person he is not so beastly: middle-aged, sporting a well-groomed beard, dressed in a suit. I hate to admit it, but a certain kindness radiates from his eyes. Is it only for the people in this gymnasium?

The first order of business is announcements, and the first announcement is of the engagement of a couple who met in church. Everyone applauds. A robed choir I hadn't noticed because it's on the far side of the room springs to life, accompanied by a keyboard. They sing "Hallelujah Praise the Lord," a traditional hymn dating back to 1562—though I don't know the words because I don't have a hymnal; they aren't tucked into the backs of the pews because there are no pews.

Then it's time for confession. The congregation falls silent; for several minutes, the underlying symphony of baby babble surfaces.

Today's sermon topic is from the Old Testament, Psalm 54. To accompany the talk, everyone has received an ordinary sheet of paper printed single-spaced on both sides. The psalm is six lines; the pastor's "summary of the text" is three times that length. The psalm is a quote of David talking to God after he's been informed that he will be turned over to the tyrant Saul. The minister dissects the text, looks at it this way and that. He carefully examines its thorny minutiae, unswayed by antsy children or squawking babies to skip parts or cut to the chase. His talk spins off into elaborate discussions of atheism and judgment. The pastor brings up the "troublesome issue of works." This is the old Calvinist catch-22: why bother doing good things when God has already made up his mind about who's saved? The pastor explains that rewards and punishments will be distributed among the saved based on "how we live our lives."

After forty-five minutes of sermon, two shorter Bible passages read by one of the congregation's elders, and several more hymns, we get to communion. I decide this is a good day to begin my communion taking. Much to Luther's chagrin, Calvin argued that the bread and wine do not actually become Jesus; Christ's presence is purely symbolic but pours a "life-giving power" into those who partake. In addition, I learned that participating in communion isn't just about one's relationship to the divine; it's also about being a part of a community. It comes from the Latin word for mutual participation. I don't know that I can consider myself as having properly shared in worship if I refrain from this central act.

A group of about ten men in suits make their way to the front of the gym; the pastor introduces them as church elders. They stand shoulder to shoulder like a band of kindly gangsters. As they pass a basket of bread, each takes a piece. Together they eat it. Next, the thimbles of wine pass, and those go down the hatch. Then, in a well-choreographed routine, each of the elders takes a basket of bread and a section of audience and oversees the distribution. The mounds shrink as they glide down each row, handed quickly from one person to the next, and soon everyone has a hunk. I hold on to mine, thinking we might kneel to eat together, but then I realize the kid next to me has already eaten his so I pop mine in my mouth.

I close my eyes briefly to focus on how this first communion feels. I'm not getting a read on the divine. What stands out is that I've just shared bread with this gymnasium full of people I have always dismissed as lunatics and all I feel is a calm connection. Perhaps this unlikely coming-together is related to the divine?

I open my eyes and watch the kid for clues. The tray of wine passes us, and I follow his lead as he quickly drinks his. Surely his was grape juice, though I didn't notice any mention made of gluten-free and nonalcoholic substitutes like at the Lutheran services. Perhaps these folks have stronger digestive tracts and less-thorny pasts. I can feel that tiny sip like a measure of warmth traveling down the center of my body. The kid has noticed me checking him out, and his actions have become very pronounced, followed by a pause and a glance to see that I've mimicked him; he is the scientist and I'm Koko the gorilla. A few moments after communion, he sends his arms into the air and turns to face me. I consult my program. We're at something called "Commissioning," where "God blesses and sends his people." In very tiny print it says, "The congregation may raise hands." I put my hands up, the classic pose of surrender, and the kid looks pleased. Along with everyone else, we hold them there like caught criminals as the choir and the rest of the congregation sing a song.

At the end of the service, there's no open invitation to hang out and socialize, no table with cookies and coffee. I have a feeling that groups will break off and gather in private homes. I suppose that makes it easier to ensure that the other souls with which you mingle are also saved. I wonder if when Calvin advocated for all civic institutions to honor the Lord he meant for a shadow society to operate on a parallel track to everything else.

I wander toward the exit slowly, tonguing the remnants of bread stuck in my teeth. Having shared spiritual nourishment from the same source, I am reluctant to leave so abruptly. I feel as if I showed up on their doorstep hungry, and they fed me. Perhaps theirs was a house about which I had heard ugly rumors, and I was a person they weren't sure they could trust; somehow we had moved past this to see each other's common humanity. I wonder if consuming elements that represent Jesus helps a person embody some of his characteristics. It's not until I get home and look again at my program that I see the fine print: all communion takers are to be baptized and current on church membership.

My heart sinks. Our beautiful moment of mutual acceptance was illusion. I had breached their bubble of safety.

The King and I

I arrive at a cozy-English-cottage version of a church. A red door leads directly from the street into the chapel; no grand foyer eases the transition from the regular world. The scale of the building is intimate, with exposed wood beams running the length of the chapel's ceiling and stained glass windows at eye level. I can almost smell the lush pastures dotted by sheep. The images on the stained glass are unmistakable in their realism: wise men, Jesus, angels.

I take a seat halfway down, on the left side of the aisle. The bus from the old folks' home must have arrived early. The congregants are bent in half by age or reverence or a little of both. Hair is teased, leisure suits are brightened by colorful scarves, walkers are placed discreetly out of the aisle. A wave of latecomers hacks a good twenty years from the median age, helped by a sprinkling of teens at my back.

For a moment I'm overcome by the fascinating history of push and pull encapsulated in this simple place: the "Episcopalian" title of the denomination harks back to the colonists' demand for independence after the American Revolution, when they changed the moniker from "Anglican" to dissociate with the monarchy. Yet everywhere are loving nods to Great Britain. Colonists may have rejected the king as divine head of the church, but they embraced this version Christianity, outlined during Henry VIII's reign, as a middle ground between Catholicism and Protestantism.

Like a daughter who balks at the rules under her parents' roof only to re-create their orderly world in her own home, the Episcopalian colonists wrote a Book of Common Prayer almost identical to the one in the motherland. Henry VIII installed himself as "pope" of the Church of England to marry and divorce as he pleased. His motivation was to secure a male heir to the throne. The irony is that his efforts created one of British history's most powerful queens and a church with progressive gender roles. Unlike Catholic and even some mainline Protestant denominations, women are allowed in leadership positions in the Episcopal system. The first female Episcopalian bishop was appointed in 1989. Today's service is dominated by female leaders. The priest or "rector" (as the role is called here) is a woman, as are most of her ministerial helpers. The most traditional house on the block is surprisingly progressive.

The choir begins to process down the aisle toward the altar. They wear emerald green robes with bright yellow hoods. A majority of the congregants stand, though there is a little disclaimer in the program that reads "please assume postures comfortable for you," explaining, "Our first Book of Common Prayer noted in 1549" that positions can vary "as every man's devotion serveth, without blame," a nod simultaneously to English roots and physical differences. A handful of the elderly remain seated, and I might have too if I'd realized what was in store. Today we perform something called "the Great Litany," a series of forty-three calls and responses; after each one the choir takes a baby step toward the altar. It starts with the rector saying, "O God the Father, Creator of heaven and earth," and then the people and choir intone, "Have mercy upon us." Over the next six pages of the program, the rector asks God to spare us from sin and everlasting damnation and earthquake and fire and flood and plague and to bless and keep all people, to increase our grace, to make wars cease, to inspire us, to comfort those in danger, in childbirth, and all who suffer. The responses the congregants provide change every few lines, so in turn we beg: "Spare us, good Lord"; "Good Lord, deliver us"; "We beseech thee to hear us, good Lord"; "O Christ, hear us"; and "Christ, have mercy upon us." It all seems a bit overdramatic; you would think we were in a pit of hungry lions instead of a pretty little church. Finally, fifteen minutes after they started at the top of the short aisle, the choir takes seats at the altar and I fall into my own, worn out.

Then it's time for what is called in the pamphlet our "feast"; when I read that, I think I've hit the jackpot. I've come on a day when the congregation has gone all out. I'm picturing fat slices of ham, scones piled with jam. I'm wondering if they'll use the good china and whether the OJ will be fresh squeezed. I scan a little farther down and realize with great disappointment that "feast" is just another word being used here for the nub of bread and sip of wine received during the Lord's Supper. I suddenly recognize this as an instance when the power of piety transforms one thing into another. Normally I find the idea of this spiritual alchemy beautiful. Today, my stomach growls its disappointment.

The intricate movements of the rector and her assistants kick into overdrive. One of the helpers approaches the altar with a mound of bread on a silver tray. Another comes forward with a glass canister of clear liquid—holy water?—and a second canister of wine. A chalice appears; liquids are poured, mixed, tasted. Such are the movements of the individuals at the altar that if a different color ribbon were tied to each of their robes, I can imagine I beautiful braid forming as they weave in and out and around one another. There is much bowing, pressing of foreheads against the surface where the bread and wine sit, lips moving in silent prayer.

The peace is shattered by a loud crackle from the speakers, and the serious moment is split open by a trucker's voice. The interstate runs out of town only a few blocks from here; the church's PA system must share a frequency with the CBs. "Rain . . . road . . . ?" I can't help but smile, thinking what a funny moment this is: could there be anything further from "high church" than an eighteen-wheeler hauling goods across the American West? I look around to gauge reactions, but no one flinches. The rector bows her head; she lets the trucker's voice fade.

The rows are invited to the altar one by one. I realize we are back to eating the actual flesh and blood of Jesus, but I join in anyway. We kneel on beautifully hand-embroidered pillows designed to fit perfectly on a little ledge below a railing that lines the altar. Mine has an image of an old scroll and some sort of harp. We wait for the bread lady to come around. I watch her work her way down the row toward me, whispering something to each person as she hands them their bread and they whisper something back. "This is Christ's body given for you," she says solemnly as she stands before me. "Thank you?" I reply, taking the bread and popping it in my mouth. I'm relieved when she smiles. Then it's the wine guy's turn. The one man in today's ceremony is keeper of the chalice. I watch the transaction between him and the first person on my side: she hands her lump of bread back to him and he dunks it into the wine and drops it into her mouth. He does the same thing with everyone down the row until he's standing in front of me. I show my empty hands. "I ate mine," I whisper. He shrugs and moves on.

At the end of the communion, which marks the conclusion of the service, something happens that I haven't seen before. In an extension of the ceremony, the rector packs all the elements of the sacrament—the remaining bread and wine—into a small red cooler. She explains that these will be taken to the homebound. She carries the communion-to-go kit down the aisle and hands it to a woman who stands and accepts it with a slight nod. I think how nice it must be for the recipients of this small token. Even if Jesus is just the excuse, even if some people are more eager to see the person than the goodies she brings, it's such a beautiful gesture to sit and spend a few minutes with someone who is not well.

Healthy and sick, individual and community, the ordinary and the unexpected—communion inspires worlds to collide. Perhaps its power resides in the unity of two seemingly unrelated entities: bread with flesh, human with divine, vulnerability with strength. In our search to find meaning in our lives and our deaths, here is an indication that some answers lie beyond our understanding, beyond our perceptions. I picture an eighteen-wheeler rumbling down the freeway, its cargo nothing but bread and wine. On the side is written, "Good for the Soul!" Then I see the trucker's face: it's Jesus, his long hair blowing through the open window. He winks and pulls the horn for me.

Holiness Hill

What would it feel like to be so overcome with religious enthusiasm that I find myself howling like a dog in front of strangers? For the last few days, I've had my nose in a book about the firsthand accounts of early religious revivals in frontier America. It's had me in stitches, everyone spilling the beans on the wackiest things they witnessed. It reminds me of when I used to go to nightclubs, and for days afterward I felt compelled to share the crazy highlights. "I saw Siamese twins doing the moonwalk!" I'd say to anyone who would listen.

Here's a scenario that plays in my mind: It is two hundred years ago—the early 1800s—and I'm a young woman living on the frontier in what is roughly modern-day Ohio. I'm attending my first "camp meeting," which is an open-air church revival presided over by traveling preachers. These are not priests that have been formally educated and ordained by a bishop; they are men with regular jobs, like blacksmiths and farmers, who exhibit extreme dedication to the Lord by adding preaching to their list of responsibilities. They are far from the fancy-robed men my frontier father has told me about. They call themselves "Methodists." The gathering takes place in a big field not far from my house.

In a daydream, a preacher tells us that God isn't just something you open a book and read about: God is here right now. He's inside each of us, and if we feel Him working in us, we shouldn't be shy—we should shout or do whatever else the Lord instructs because these expressions demonstrate our love for God and His love for us. As he speaks the preacher paces back and forth and his face turns red; he looks like a man possessed. He begs God to make his presence known, and when he falls to his knees and puts his hands in the air, it's as if the Holy Spirit rips through the crowd. People shout, shake, and cry. There's moaning, babbling, fainting—and, yes, some even howl and bark like dogs, all physical proof of being saved.

Two centuries and two thousand miles farther along, I'm making my way to the Sunday worship services of a group of Quakers. The Quakers earned their nickname from their reputation for trembling with emotion during their services. I'm eager to take the pulse of these early purveyors of religious passion.

o

When I walk in, I'm a few minutes late, having struggled to find the right building. About ten people sit on overstuffed couches and chairs arranged in a circle. The median age is mid-seventies at the youngest. It could easily be a group therapy session at an old folks' home—except nobody is talking and their eyes are closed. I spot a cylindrical device out of the corner of my eye and think "oxygen tank!" Turns out it's just a fire extinguisher. I join the circle and get comfortable. My heart is racing from climbing a hill outside.

After fifteen minutes of silence, I open my eyes and take a closer look at each person around the circle. I wonder who is in charge. If I had to guess, I'd say it's one of the two bearded guys who look like ZZ Top's less-kempt cousins, or maybe it's the old lady smiling like a beatific Ma Kettle. For a group whose name is based on shaking, they are surprisingly still.

This must be the "open worship" portion of the service I've read about where each person is engaged in her own private communications with God. If that's what this is, I need to try to do it right. I close my eyes again. I imagine my scalp retracting like the roof on an observatory: now receptive to messages from God. I see patterns dancing against my eyelids but no giant thunderbolts of insight. At thirty minutes, I open my eyes and look around the room again. Will there be a sermon? If so, who will give it? George Fox, the founder of Quakerism, said each person is illuminated with the "divine light of Christ," so any of these people may be the leader. I close my eyes and try opening the roof again. After forty-five minutes, my eyes pop open. Is this even the Quaker group? Who are these corpses? I'm not going to put up with this for much longer! At the hour mark, I feel a rush of relief when Ma Kettle opens her eyes and says peacefully, "Does anyone have anything to add?"

Over tea and Fig Newtons, I chat with Ma Kettle. She has a wide smile, rosy cheeks, and several prominent whiskers. She explains that some "Friends," as Quakers sometimes call themselves, incorporate more traditional elements into their services like sermons and hymns, but that at the core of all Quaker gatherings is the open worship in which each person becomes a conduit for divine wisdom. If an individual feels moved to speak at the end of worship, he or she is invited to do so. Some may interpret a fellow worshipper's words as messages from God.

After Fox's death in 1691, the idea that worship could be a stirring experience must have stayed buzzing in the ether because soon John Wesley, who is considered the father of Methodism, was weaving it into his own thinking. As a student at Oxford, Wesley developed a systematic approach to living a religious life. He created guidelines based on his own schedule of daily Bible reading, prayer, and communion with fellow Christians. At the heart of his format was the "Holiness Club," a small group whose members encouraged one another's study, spiritual questioning, and regular attendance at Church of England services. After years of developing and preaching this methodical approach, he sensed a gaping shortcoming: it was devoid of passionate devotion. Not long after, he was imploring listeners to embrace faith with an unparalleled vitality—and insisting that this fervor can even be proof of God's continuing work in a person.

From an outsider's perspective, I can see how the combining of these two styles of worship—one orderly and the other spontaneous—made for an odd marriage. As Methodism spread like wildfire throughout the United States, in large part through the efforts of itinerant preachers, and then became more established, and some might say "staid," those who gravitated to the expressive side began to feel dissatisfied. Thus, the "holiness movement" was born and the splintering off of Pentecostal denominations whose members wanted to engage in the demonstrative displays they say arise when the Holy Spirit moves a person. These are not just flights of fancy, they believe, but an essential part of the ongoing process of becoming a more evolved Christian. The centerpiece for many who practice this style of worship is the act of "speaking in tongues."

If this project were a board game such as Candy Land, this next series of churches might be a strange little offshoot of the main course—something that might bear the marker "Holiness Hill." Is it dark and scary? Or enchanted? I'm not sure, but it's a safe bet that the trees will talk.

I have mixed emotions about treading this particular path. As a newbie to Christianity, I'm worried about witnessing fervent displays of faith. I feel it's akin to sitting in on a stranger's therapy session or watching from the gallery of an operating room—you're witnessing an intensely private moment. Except in this case the subject not only knows there will be spectators but welcomes them. Part of the point is to demonstrate to others the work of the Holy Spirit. All of which is perhaps okay except . . . what if the spectacle becomes particularly freaky? What if the patient struggles with multiple personalities or the surgery is gory open-heart? What if people are jabbering uncontrollably up and down the church aisles? Is it too much for an innocent bystander? Or, more frightening still, what if the Holy Spirit grabs hold of me?

Already I've discovered that one of the best friends I've made since moving to my new town was, until recently, one of them: a Pentecostal. When she told me, I was knocked off-balance for several seconds. I knew she had been a committed churchgoer until about five years ago when her devout then-husband ran off with another woman, I just didn't realize it had been *that* kind of church. Today she's a card-carrying None. A few years ago she was speaking in tongues. Is it really such a fine line?

So I start off gently, with a Church of the Nazarene, which is a type of holiness church that doesn't do speaking in tongues. I imagine putting my finger to the patient's wrist. Unlike others that had a stable rate, this one calms and quickens, calms and quickens. It begins slowly with announcements and hymns. Then the preacher says we are entering prayer time, and a handful of people approach the altar to kneel, their arms wrapped around each. Others raise their palms into the air. When the preacher says, "God put you here to lift you up," the rate spikes. A man cries, "Yes!" and several others shout, "Amen!" Several weeks earlier, a similar thing happened in the middle of an Episcopal service, but with a much more awkward result. A woman blurted "Amen!" from the back row and everyone turned to look at her and smile. Here, the exclamations rise up unacknowledged, par for the course. The pace slows for a Bible reading and then the preacher says, "God hates luke-warm—he likes his church hot!" Shouts of "amen" ripple through the congregation like audible exclamation points at the end of his statement, and I can almost feel the temperature in the sanctuary rise.

Then it's a Pentecostal service. Churches in this category might go by the names Assemblies of God, Church of God, Full Gospel, or Foursquare. One service I join is held in what appears to be a double-wide trailer. It's located just out of town on the side of the freeway in the shadow of a grain silo. Inside, where fewer than twenty people are gathered, I sense the casual vibe of familiarity. A sullen and stud-adorned teenager drapes herself across an entire row. It's hard to imagine these laid-back congregants wound up with spirit.

At the front are two women: a keyboard player and a singer with a microphone. Does she need amplification in such a small space? My guess is no, but she holds it earnestly, speaks into it with such sincerity that I sense to her it is no less than the ear of God. She leads us in a series of hymns, and at the end of each there's a fluttering of voices, each person saying, "Thank you, Jesus" or "Praise the Lord." They repeat the same phrase over and over, each time with such feeling that it's like a brand-new thought, like they've never said it before. I'm starting to get the hang of this, these waves of exuber-ance washing over us. Here are the "Holy Rollers" I've heard about. I once imagined that nickname referred to writhing on the floor, but maybe it has more to do with the way the energy in the room climbs and dips like a roller coaster.

The preacher is a neatly coiffed older woman wearing chunky turquoise jewelry. I would never in a million years peg her for a Pentecostal preacher—more like a painter in Santa Fe or an art teacher in Berkeley. She is talking about feelings now, how they start as thoughts and end in actions. We are climbing. She says that while all those things matter, they are not the primary focus. She shouts, "God looks at the heart!" I brace myself. Any second, someone will yell in an incomprehensible language I've heard described as sounding like gibberish or Hebrew. It is the perfect crescendo, the logical conclusion. Instead the repetition of each person's pet phrase of praise or gratitude winds down into something softer, more guttural, though I can't make out if it is words. If I closed my eyes, I might think it was a stream running over rocks.

My ex-Pentecostal None friend insists it doesn't always happen like that—sometimes people really will shout stuff in what is considered a foreign tongue. Others, she explains, might follow up by calling out the English version of those first shouters' words. So what sounded like babble might be interpreted as "God hates money!" Different individuals have the propensity toward one or the other—some have "the gift" of tongues, some the ability to understand those utterings. But what I really want to know is how my friend feels about her own history of speaking in tongues. I expect her to claim it was all hogwash. It would certainly be an easier sell among her new crowd to dismiss this past behavior as an aberration—but she doesn't. She can remember doing it twice, and both times it felt like a genuine response coming from the depths of her own being. She says she made the same sound over and over again. She tells me, "Maybe I was saying, 'red' in Hebrew or 'squash' in Korean, but it felt like I was saying, 'God, you're cool!'"

I leave the Pentecostal service more upbeat than I've been in weeks. The exuberance has rubbed off on me. With all the energy I've spent over the last several months thinking about Jesus's death and how his example can help me and others, this feels like a respite. Put away the thinking for a moment, this worship style seems to demand, and let emotion take center stage. It revels in our shared vulnerability, perhaps even exploits it. Shed the stoic demeanor: clap, shout. Howl away the pain; weep with gratitude; limbo down the aisle. Grappling with the one-two punch of the human condition—the dying, the being born—can take a multitude of forms. Here, one is asked to grieve and to celebrate.

In the parking lot I'm giddy, like I've popped a dozen Prozac. Whatever this feeling is, if revisited regularly, might help a person through a multitude of hard times. I get in my car and peek at myself in the rearview mirror. Did I just get a hit of the opium of the masses? It reminds me of the part of *The Wizard of Oz* when Dorothy is in the dark forest and unexpectedly one of the big trees starts to talk. I remember when I saw it the first time, I thought nothing could be more frightening—how the trunk shifted to reveal facial features, how the bark formed a mouth. I wanted to scream. I wanted to run from the room. But I waited, frozen. I looked out from squinted eyes as the tree says a few things, and then Dorothy says a few things back. Then I laughed at my initial reaction: what's so scary about a talking tree? Even if it has a face, it's still just a tree. It can't chase you. Maybe it's even kind of cool. It doesn't even compare to the flying monkeys.

What Jesus Wants

"This is the church Jesus would have established," the woman tells me. We are sitting next to each other with about thirty other people in the living room of an old house that is now a church. Four rows of chairs face a wall that is adorned by a single map of the Middle East with territory lines that don't appear to be modern-day countries. Is it supposed to be from Jesus's time? The woman is in her sixties, but the big upside-down glasses and floral-print dress put her worlds away from my own hip mom, whose usual Sunday attire is yoga pants. She elaborates, "Say you came to earth and you didn't know anything, and you found a Bible and you read the New Testament. This is the church you would create based on what it says in there."

"Oh, good," I respond, nodding as if this makes perfect sense.

I've entered what some people might call the "fundamental" phase of this experience. This comprises churches whose congregants insist that the Bible is the "inerrant" world of God and, from what I can tell, that means they think every word is absolutely true, including the part about how the earth was made in seven days. These are the folks who call theories of evolution "false science." I was sort of hoping they were mythical creatures I would never encounter. But here they are in surprising abundance, in my own community, home to two major research universities.

This strain of literalism began over five hundred years ago, before Luther came on the scene. Some people who read the Bible noticed a key discrepancy between the Catholic Church's practice of baptism and how it was described in the book itself. The church sprinkled babies with water, but in scripture Jesus is fully submerged as a grown man. The people who called the church out on this inconsistency gained the name "Anabaptists," meaning "to baptize again." They argued that the Bible version of baptism, what some called "believer's baptism," was far more meaningful because an older person had the wherewithal to understand and choose Christianity. A powerful argument, I must say, and church leaders felt threatened enough to have many of these outspoken opponents put to death. Luther did not support their criticism of infant baptism, but I wouldn't be surprised if their instinct to turn directly to scripture had an enormous influence on him. Though Baptists evolved from these early would-be reformers, today they may fall anywhere along a wide spectrum from fundamental to more liberal. The official heirs of the Anabaptists include the Amish and Mennonites.

I had started on this path the previous Sunday when I attended services in a one-room Baptist church. It was an adorable building, whitewashed wood with a perfect little steeple, just the sort of church you might find at a hobby shop for the town of a train set. But when I walked in the front door, I was automatically standing in the chapel. The congregation of about twenty adults was assembled early for a bit of Bible study; I had entered in the middle of this activity, and everyone in attendance turned at once to see who had come in. They were all in couples, and suddenly I felt like the Jezebel come to snatch husbands. I have never been more thankful for my default angel status. The Bible says, "Forget not to show love unto strangers: for thereby some have entertained angels." I forced my friendliest smile, and they had to smile back because it says so in Hebrews.

o

Churches in this vein might bear the name Church of Christ, Christian Church, or Disciples of Christ. Some might call themselves Bible Church. Their participants believe about mainstream Protestant denominations what the original Protestants felt about Catholicism: the church itself, its institutions and structure, has muddied the true message of the Bible. Their stated desire is to unite all Christians under a purer version of the faith. Protestants thought they were returning to the basics, but this new crop craves something even more essential. For them, the Bible is not just a collection of stories and wisdom gathered over the ages but also a guidebook.

Founders of these churches do not want to be a part of any denomination or established church structure. The names they give their congregations are simple labels to identify them as followers of Christ—the same words that could have been used for this purpose two thousand years earlier. Here are Christian icemen perfectly preserved in a just-thawed glacier.

Today when I walk into a Church of Christ, everyone is a little more subtle about checking me out, so I am relieved. A man gets up and makes a few announcements, and then several of the men in the congregation chime in. From their various seats in the chapel, they chat while the women sit quietly. Just like the week before, the ladies utter not a single word. It says in Corinthians, "Let your women keep silence in the churches: for it is not permitted unto them to speak."

As the men blather on—one has gained the floor and is outlining his recent battle with congestion—I find myself looking around the room, a silent scream—"Who are you people?!"—echoing between my ears. The man who leads us in singing has all the vocal subtlety of a foghorn. Why he would be selected for this particular job is beyond me. There's no musical accompaniment to temper the ear assault because apparently instruments in worship service are not biblical, so the parishioners have no choice but to lend their voices in an effort to drown out his. We sing "Jesus, I Come," a hymn based on Psalm 130, which reads, "Out of the depths I cry to Thee, O Lord," and then we sing "Master, the Tempest Is Raging," based on a story in Mark. With so few people and no instruments, I feel a greater sense of responsibility for my vocal contribution. I may be guarded, but my voice is all in.

They say Jesus is the head of this church, and his message its only doctrine, so I would think there'd be some mention of loving one another and being joyful. Instead, like last week, the theme of today's sermon is sin. The minister is pale around his eyes where sunglasses go. I imagine him on a speedboat with blue-glitter racing stripes. He tells us the story of David seeing Bathsheba on a roof and, even though she's married, he's determined to have sex with her, and this sin unleashes a world of pain. The preacher says this shows us we must always, always say "no" to temptation. He says, "You can say 'no' a thousand times and just one 'yes' undoes it. It's like a child with a cookie!"

The message is almost identical to the Baptist minister's the week before. That preacher told me after the service that he was once a cop who received a communication from God that he must "roar" the word of Jesus Christ. Luckily, God's instructions coincided with his retirement. Now he enforced Jesus's law. He warned the congregation to turn away from worldly things, to stay away from those activities like drinking alcohol that many of us engaged in before being saved because that is how you "open the door wide to Satan." He shouted, "My job is not to be tolerant! My job is to explain what Jesus Christ wants!"

o

Like the week before, at the end of the sermon, my temples throb and I feel confused.

I can't accept that not sinning is really as black and white as steering clear of booze and illicit sex or anything "bad," really. What's wrong with a kid eating a cookie? If I went just on what these two preachers said, I would walk away thinking the goal was to stay away from "demonic" influences and "unclean" people—but what does that even mean? Jesus laid his hands on lepers and hung out with prostitutes. At every turn, Jesus entreats us to throw assumptions out the window: people we think are holy may not be, just as the seemingly wicked could be righteous. At a Methodist church several weeks earlier, the female minister even told us that if we wanted to be true evangelists, we should "go to where the people are, go into the night clubs, and in those places be example of Christ's acceptance." I remember this very clearly because it conjured a mental image of me sitting at a bar trying to beam rays of unconditional love onto the dance floor. Would I need to order ginger ale? She didn't specify.

After the service at the Church of Christ, I am perusing the literature table when the preacher approaches me. Up close, I can see dark splotches of sun damage across his forehead and cheeks. I tell him his sermon was impressive, because for every statement he made, he directed us to a line in the Bible. We flipped pages like maniacs. "Well, I know a thing or two about sin," he says. "There was a time when I smoked a lot of marijuana." I appreciate his honesty, but that seems paltry qualification.

Before I leave, he hands me a workbook on being a better Christian. "This has a lot of good info on sin," he says.

At home I open the workbook. The introduction reads, "No subject or principle bears upon the Christian's life more than sin." It provides a laundry list of biblical references to sin and Satan with bits of interpretation thrown in. Sin is a "deceitful force" (Hebrews 3:13) that "kills the sense of shame" (Philippians 3:19) and "pays wages" (Romans 6:23). Satan is a "coward" (James 4:7) and "father of lies" (John 8:44) who "does not appear as he really is" (2 Corinthians 11:14). I go through the pages several times until I'm too tired to think straight.

In the middle of the night, when I wake up and can't get back to sleep, my thoughts turn to the Bible. The primary message of the Gospels is so much simpler than I would have thought; Jesus says the goal is to love ourselves and one another and be joyful. The next morning when I'm going over my sin treatise, this pops out: those in the world are of the devil until they obey the gospel. Is it possible that the devil isn't some boogeyman hiding in an alley but the force inside ourselves that says we aren't good enough, that we don't deserve this life we've been given, that we have no right to experience joy? And how can we love anyone else when we can't love ourselves? A voice deep inside me shouts, "Yes, that's it!"

With fresh eyes, I go back over the references, which are all over the place—obviously, people have been struggling with this idea for a long time. But it says the meaning of sin most commonly used in the Bible is "to miss the mark." This clicks. Sin is the voice inside my head that prevents me from hitting the bull's-eye of love and joy. The booze or the sex or the drugs—those aren't the sins. Those are just the tools a person might use to perpetuate the missing of the mark, the addictions we might put in place of the struggle to achieve the love and joy. They could just as easily be television or video games or food. Anything we use to anesthetize ourselves, that we think will stop the throbbing pain of unworthiness when, really, the only true solution is to find the bravery to accept and love ourselves so that we offer that love to others.

So maybe this interpretation of "sin" is right, or maybe it's wrong. That's the thing about the Bible; you can think you've hit on just the right meaning of some significant phrase or concept, but no one knows for sure. There's always going to be an element of mystery to it. What bothers me is when someone claims they know the exact truth, like what God said or meant is absolutely clear. Doesn't it seem arrogant to dismiss two thousand years of church history, to brush away years of people debating, all those stages of understanding, the reexamining of old ideas, to announce you know better than everyone?

The Baptist minister said he wanted to clarify something about "judgment day." He said some people think that when Jesus comes back, he will judge every soul that ever walked the earth to decide who is saved. This is incorrect, the minister insists. Rather, those who have already secured eternal salvation will be listed in the "Book of Life." Jesus will only judge those whose names do not appear in the "Book of Life." Everyone in the congregation just sort of nodded and accepted this, but I felt like standing up and shouting, "Hey, minister, here's another idea: what if everyone who's ever lived will be listed in that ol' Book of Life? What if that's the whole point Jesus was trying to make? That each of us is inherently valuable by virtue of having lived? I mean, if your intention is to be exactly literal, it is called the Book of *Life*. Maybe it means no one is getting judged. Maybe Jesus wants us to stop obsessing about living forever and focus on living with joy and love right now." Then I would sit back down and say sweetly, "Just another possibility."

I try to enter each church with an open mind, but sometimes I struggle. Among the fundamentalists I'm wary. But along the way, I notice something interesting: I will wander into a church whose name seems to indicate it belongs in this group, only to find it sits on the opposite side of the spectrum. I was greeted at a United Church of Christ by a female minister along with announcements for yoga classes and an LGBT support group. With a little digging, I find the cause of my confusion. As the country urbanized, the leaders of some independent churches wanted to form alliances with one another. It was similar to what happened over a hundred years earlier, when two thousand independent Congregational churches established by the earliest settlers decided to trade their autonomy and name for the Presbyterian structure and title. As is often the case, such unity forces compromise and inclusivity. Even an iceman must adapt once he thaws out and rejoins the human race.

After many Sundays, I'm eager to move on. The last stop is listed as "Baptist / Disciples of Christ." Double whammy, I think. On my drive there, I sense my defenses forming. As I park, I feel them going up. How ridiculous is it to think you have found an ancient rule book that, if interpreted and followed with 100 percent accuracy, will relieve your suffering? Bypass all the messy vulnerability. Instead, busy yourself watching for missteps and then double down on those efforts. It's one way to deal with anxiety. But not a very effective one based on results because it often turns outward into anger and finger-pointing at all the perceived rule breakers. I suppose when I interpret this behavior as a smokescreen to avoid thinking about what's really going on inside—the fear, the guilt, the terror—I can muster a bit of compassion.

I approach the door to the pretty brick church, and mentally prepare: judge not, I tell myself. I take a deep breath and walk in. I'm greeted by a female preacher and pews filled with old hippies and academics. Like the United Church of Christ, here's a place that also considers itself true to the essential teachings of Jesus, only its fundamentals are love, joy, and acceptance. I feel my shoulders relax, and I can't help but smile. Just when I think I have it figured out, it's time to throw my assumptions out the window.

Holy Bible App

A few weeks into my churchgoing experiment, I was pawing my new smartphone. It was about four a.m. and I was awake enough to have grabbed the phone off the bedside table, but dream images were still fresh in my mind. Since getting the phone a month earlier, I'd been carrying it everywhere and toying with it constantly. I was awed by its capacity. It seemed like a magic window onto the world, equipped with hundreds of possible applications (or "apps") to aid in various aspects of life, such as strengthening my memory with puzzles or encouraging exercise by counting all my steps.

I'm sitting there staring into it when a note pops up: download your Bible app! I hadn't touched anything to prompt this message; I didn't know a Bible app existed. This version promised to be "easier and more powerful" with "performance enhancements" and "faster help." I had this bleary moment where I thought my phone was a portal through which to interface with God. I had miraculously received this message, hadn't I? It was just the sort of immediate personal connection for which each new incarnation of Christianity seems to strive.

Then the fog lifted, and I hit the download button. What did I have to lose? It was free.

This app has the full texts of about twenty translations of the Bible—and that's just the English versions. It's also got the Bible in every language imaginable, including Arabic and something called Malagasy, which Wikipedia explains is the national language of Madagascar. The best part is the word-search feature. You go to the translation you want and type in a word or a phrase and it scans the entire Bible and then presents a list of every section where this word or phrase appears plus the actual text highlighted for quick reference.

It starts innocently enough: I pick an English translation at random and type in the words "mustard seed." I'd first heard reference to the mustard seed at the monastery in a gospel reading in which Jesus is explaining what the kingdom of heaven is like and he says, "It is like a mustard seed that has been planted and develops into a bush." He's not talking about the seed alone, which contains all the information the plant will ever need; he's talking about the realization of the seed's dormant potential with the proper care and nourishment. I find it such a simple and powerful idea. He's saying the kingdom of heaven is life, the actual process of living and growing. From my Holy Bible app, I learn that Jesus uses this analogy six times throughout the Gospels.

Then things take a darker turn: I word-search "hell." I do this because I've been mulling a theory. Jesus is supposed to be the "door" Christians use to access an understanding of the divine, but I think the point of entry for a lot of people is hell—the idea of hell. Of all the Christian concepts, it's the most shocking. You ask what it is and the next question becomes: how do I avoid it? It was the first thing that got my attention as a kid, and if I'd had access to church back then, I would have worn out my knees praying not to go there.

I had an impression that the Bible was littered with references to hell, especially the Old Testament. God of the Old Testament is a bit of a wild card. He may love humanity, but he doesn't hesitate to wipe thousands of people from the face of the earth. He wasn't uncaring, he obviously cared very much, but that intense love could turn on a dime to fury. I can see why Jesus was so helpful in clarifying God's loves for us. He basically says, I love you and God loves me; therefore, God loves you. It's like a mathematical proof. If you believe Jesus, there's no room for doubt as far as God's love goes.

The search feature scans the text of the American Standard Version and presents a list. The first few references aren't to "hell" but to a word I've never seen before: "Sheol." I go through every item, and here's what I find: not one instance of "hell" in this translation of the Old Testament. For each entry the search engine has pulled up "Sheol" instead. So I look up this mysterious word. It's Hebrew and means "the grave" or, more generally, "death." It's a far more benign concept than hell; it's an afterlife destination for everyone regardless of the choices they have made. To be sure, there are references to unpleasant places in the Old Testament, "lakes of fire" and such where there is much weeping and gnashing of teeth, just no terrible underworld for the dead. In the King James versions, "Sheol" has been translated as "hell." Suddenly it hits me: we humans are so terrified of death that our own demise *is* hell. It's not until the New Testament that the idea of hell, or Hades, officially enters the picture; its counterpoint—salvation—is referred to as "eternal life." Having been given the gift of life, we obsess about holding on to it forever. All the while, insecurities about our worthiness have us preoccupied with hell—we are unable to deserve this life, much less eternal life. It's fallout from the one-two punch of the human condition.

The people of Jesus's time suffered from that one-two punch just like we do, and Jesus did everything he could to help. He explains to them over and over again that they don't have to do anything more to feel worthy of life than to love one another and be joyful. He says, "Rejoice, and be exceeding glad"; "Ye are the light of the world"; "Take no thought for the morrow." He wants them to know that it's all good, that everything is fine. "Ask, and it shall be given you, seek, and ye shall find." But that message seems to fly over most of their heads.

In the first three Gospels, the same little scene plays out: Jesus is with a group of people, doling out advice and healing, when a man steps forward. The man asks, "What good things can I do to ensure eternal life?" I can picture Jesus muttering "Oh, Brother" under his breath, but he humors the guy. He tells him, "Keep the commandments." The guy pushes it further: "Which ones?" So Jesus lists them: don't murder, no stealing, love your neighbor, etc. The man says, "I've done all that since I was a kid." At this point, the man probably should have shut his trap. He could have walked away having done everything Jesus told him. Eternal life was his! Instead, he asks, "What do I lack?" He was carrying around the burden a lot of us lug: we aren't good enough. I think Jesus can see that this guy is dead set on finding some way in which he falls short, so he answers, "Oh, well, if you want to be perfect then give everything you own to the poor and come with me." The guy goes, "I can't do that!" and walks away feeling terrible about his chances for salvation. It seems to me that he found the only answer that made perfect sense to him.

Jesus says several times, "God is not the God of the dead, but of the living." But the people are still afraid, still hung up on dying. So he does the most radical thing imaginable: he demonstrates the bravery one can have in the face of death by allowing them to watch him die.

Dying is such an intimate process that most of us, until we experience it ourselves, will only personally witness it if we have loved ones who are willing to share their passing with us. Yet Jesus shares his death with everyone. Thousands of years later, it is still the central component of the Christian faith, relived again and again.

Since I started this project, I keep hearing people say that Jesus "conquered death." I'm not sure what they mean by this—if they're talking about the part of the story where Jesus dies fearlessly or the part where he rises from the dead. Maybe it's a little of both. He faced death, but some version of him went on. Either way, I don't think Jesus would have us get too hung up on it. He demonstrates how to face our mortality and move past it. His willingness, his courage—here is the physical embodiment of his maxim "be not afraid."

Even if death is what piques our interest in existential issues, even if we arrive via the hell door, I think Jesus means for this to be no more than a screen door or a storm door or, at most, an outer door that leads to a vestibule before you get to the real door. We're meant to keep going. We're meant to find our way to joy and love, to the profoundest appreciation for living. Now that I understand this, all the theological debates that split hairs over salvation—whether it's something that can be earned through good works or by faith alone, or whether it's a gift one is born with—seem utterly beside the point.

Time of Trouble

I try to imagine what it must have been like to be an American in the early and mid-1800s, when what seems to me a particularly desperate time gave rise to a brand of Christianity that includes the Seventh-Day Adventists, Christian Scientists, and Jehovah's Witnesses. Textbooks teach the broad social changes: urbanization, industrialization, rapid population growth. But what did this mean to individuals? In a nutshell: filthy living conditions. Most of those piling into the cities did not have refrigeration and indoor plumbing. The "Gilded Age"—steel, lights, science!—had not brought much innovation in the way of medicine or sanitation. Being sick or dying was practically a national pastime. The two basic things you needed—food and hydration—were also effective transportation for those other colonists not detectable to the human eye. Bacteria were winning. In the 1832 cholera epidemic, thousands were felled by drinking water.

How would I have held up under those conditions? I am highly susceptible to suggestion. In junior high, I contracted AIDS after an assembly about the epidemic. For weeks I went around listless and vacant-eyed, jotting out my last wishes. I had not so much as swapped spit with another human being. I can only imagine my condition if I'd actually been exposed to the disease and all my associates were either sick, recovering, or trying to avoid getting sick. From what I can tell, women in the mid-1800s were particularly vulnerable to illness not just because of sensitive imaginations but because their floor-length dresses dragged through feces-soaked streets. Left and right, people came down with the weirdest-sounding stuff: yellow fever, chronic dyspepsia, dropsy. I have no idea what any of those are, but I'm certain I would have suffered them all.

In this context, some people became convinced that current conditions were so terrible it must be the End Times that Jesus alludes to in the New Testament, a time of trouble and tribulation heralding the return of the messiah. America wasn't just some far-flung new land, it was the epicenter of biblical prophecy. The present wasn't a random chapter in human history but a vital piece of the story, the point at which the circle comes round: the grand finale. Previous generations had fought for a closer relationship to the divine; now, through Jesus, believers would be reunited with God. The Bible was filled with clues of how our last days would play out. After careful consideration, William Miller, a farmer in New York, came to believe that the thousand years of peace prophesied in the New Testament would come only after Christ returned—not before, as typically assumed. He scientifically decoded the Bible's messages and began to spread the good news: Jesus was coming back in 1843.

o

The Seventh-Day Adventists do not promise me everlasting life, but they do offer an extra decade. When I enter the church doors for the Saturday morning service, I'm handed a flyer for their "10 Years More Series: Happier, Healthier, Longer," a set of special presentations about the importance of weight control and proper sleep. Before now, what I knew of this denomination came from the media attention given to a Seventh-Day Adventist community in southern California for having an average lifespan many years longer than the national average. They promote a plant-based diet. They are basically messianic vegans, which apparently is not as oxymoronic as I would have thought. Their inter-est in sustainability and growing food is part of an effort to return the planet to a Garden of Eden–like state in anticipation of, and perhaps even to accelerate, Jesus's return to earth.

Seventh-Day Adventists hold their services according to the lunar Jewish tradition of Sabbath, from sundown on Friday to sundown on Saturday. The Bible suggests that Jesus won't return until the "Sabbath is restored," and early founders of this group interpreted this literally to mean that the holy day must be celebrated on Saturday instead of Sunday as popularized by most Christians. The service program I was given on the way in announces the time of today's sunset so I'll know when Sabbath ends, as well as the sunset for the following Friday evening to keep in mind when the next Sabbath begins.

Ellen White, the woman credited with founding this denomination, was devastated when Miller's prediction of Jesus's return in 1843 turned out to be wrong. When Jesus did not return at his appointed time, Miller revised his prediction. He decided his miscalculation was the result of an oversight; he failed to take into account a "tarrying time" referred to in the Bible. He announced the corrected date: October 22, 1844.

The faithful waited all day and then stayed up that night hoping for Christ to appear. I stumbled on an account of a farmer who described the anticipation. He stood in a field with other believers, their eyes trained to the sky. Were they hoping for some bright light or benevolent fireball and then the figure of Jesus to appear and stretch out his arms to them? Perhaps a golden staircase would materialize for the faithful to climb so they could sit with Jesus as he ruled over the earth for the anticipated thousand years, banishing evil and restoring the tranquil conditions of Eden. According to the farmer's story, when the sun rose on October 23 he and his companions were devastated. The failure of Jesus to return on that date has gone down in the history books as "the Great Disappointment."

Not long after the Great Disappointment, Ellen White began to have visions. She would fall into trancelike states in which celestial messengers would communicate with her. Though I haven't found anything that explicitly says so, I can only imagine that these visualizations and the Disappointment are related, as they happened the same year within a few weeks of each other. Maybe something about Miller, a seeming authority figure, making such a massive mistake emboldened this otherwise ordinary young woman to trust her own ability to channel divine messages. In these episodes, White would apparently grow limp and unresponsive on the outside, but on the inside, angels and other benevolent creatures were guiding her on epic journeys. She learns from them that Christ's failure to appear was all part of God's plan. Jesus hadn't come to earth, but he had taken up residence in a "heavenly sanctuary" that, from what I understand, is sort of an intermediary space a little closer to earth than wherever he was before. From this new location, the angels tell her, Jesus is conducting "investigative judgment" of the planet's inhabitants. In the meantime, true believers must get ready for the moment when Christ's invisible presence becomes visible. Today's Seventh-Day Adventists are still in this preparatory phase.

Of all my church visits so far, I have not yet had anyone readily admit to personal interactions with celestial beings. Today is a first. Several minutes before the program is to begin, I slip into a chair next to a woman who is dressed to the nines. She and I appear to be close in age, though I am a dull stone next to her sparkle. She is wearing a bright yellow dress with a full skirt and matching heels. The color is electric against her black skin. The vibrant, ladylike attire simultaneously fights and flatters her tall, athletic physique. If life were a fashion spread, hers would be part social commentary, part satire: a fresh interpretation of a 1950s housewife. Her smoothed-back hair highlights a perfect heart-shaped face.

In a charming patois, she explains that she is from the Dominican Republic and has just moved here for a graduate program. Growing up, she wasn't religious, but she would watch from her window as a school acquaintance waited every Saturday morning for the bus that took her to church. Then in high school, she explains matter-of-factly, she received several visits from Jesus. Night after night he came to her in dreams, very vivid and real. Not long after, she asked the acquaintance if she could take the bus too.

My new friend is hoping to meet Jesus again, this time in the flesh.

After two introductory hymns, it's time for "Sabbath School," the part of the service in which the congregation breaks down according to age groups. My new friend will be leading the young adults, and she invites me to sit in even though I don't quite make the cutoff. The program announces that the scripture reading for discussion is from the Gospel of John: "But the hour cometh, and now is, when the true believers shall worship the Father in spirit and in truth: for the Father seeketh such to worship him." About ten college-age congregants join us in a little room adjacent to a kitchen; several more arrive late and expand the circle. "What does this quotation mean to you?" my friend asks them. They rub sleep from their eyes and stare into their smartphones. I scan their faces trying to imagine being in their shoes. I don't recall knowing anyone who attended church during college. They must have existed, as my university was surrounded by places to worship, just as this one is. Do they come out of a sense of duty or something deeper and more personal? My friend narrows the focus, "What does that mean: to worship in spirit and truth?" After a few more minutes of silence, one girl gives it a shot. "Not just your thoughts?" she says quietly, "But also your actions?" The group manages to squeeze out a few more replies, but I can't decide what's more painful: the awkward pauses between remarks or the forced comments themselves. I'm reminded of how hard it was for me to talk in front of people when I was that age, much less attempt to articulate notions about God—which, frankly, never gets much easier.

Men and women from the congregation take turns leading the worship service. Back in the main sanctuary, today's leader is the spitting image of my uncle, a retired geologist whose full beard and lanky frame belies a more conservative interior. His two loves: earth's strata and Reaganomics. This doppelgänger has left his right pant leg cinched from biking. He begins his talk with a slide show from a recent hike he took. He clicks through shots of mountains and boulders and lakes. When he stops on a screen with Psalms 27:8, "Seek ye my face," I notice that he's weeping. He tells us, "Mrs. White wrote that the natural world offers us a front-row seat on the face of God." Over the course of her life, White was a prolific author, turning the lessons from her many visions into such volumes as *Steps to Christ*, *The Desire of Ages*, and *The Great Controversy*, much of which focuses on the epic struggle between Satan and God. The slides continue: a particularly remarkable tree, sunlight reflected in ripples of water. He wipes his eyes, "To quote White: 'God is love' is written upon every opening bud, upon every spire of springing grass." He turns to take in his own photo and says, "Look how beautiful it is," with such pained sincerity that I feel a lump form in my throat.

The service culminates in a big feast, or what the program calls a "fellowship meal." Unlike other communions, this is will be actual lunch. We file into the kitchen area to enjoy a vegetarian smorgasbord. Like much in this denomination, the end result is progressive; though I'm not sure the same can be said of the logic used to get there. White encouraged women to wear pantaloons—not for equality's sake but to avoid long dresses with their street-scraping hems. She urged followers to give up tobacco and alcohol because they "stirred up animal passions." She said meat carried "disease-producing humors" (later discovered to be germs). In the name of Jesus, she addressed many ills of her day. Today's equivalent would be saying we should abolish capitalism and rely exclusively on barter and sustainable energy to ready the world for the messiah. In the modern partisan landscape, Jesus is often associated with a conservative agenda, but his ideals actually lend themselves to a radical revision of our political and economic system.

Never in my life have I seen so many variations of zucchini in one place. I fill my plate and take a seat with everyone else at a long table, family style. I can almost imagine that beyond this room the earth has been destroyed but we faithful have survived and are eating the yummy produce from our after-the-rapture gardens. Through the eyes of these self-sufficient congregants, the End Times are nigh. Soon they will have a chance to lavish Mother Nature with the respect she's due, and in return, she will bless them with her bounty.

o

What if these are real-life zombies?

This thought flashes into mind as I'm standing in the entrance to the Kingdom Hall with people milling around me. Maybe what the Jehovah's Witnesses say is true, and here are some of the multitudes whom Jesus has made rise from their graves. Their happy expressions and business-casual attire carry the whiff of inauthenticity. It's as if they're trying too hard to seem alive. The atmosphere in the building can only be described as funereal: fake plants, floral carpet, mauve wainscoting. No windows; the only light emanates from fluorescent tubes. Decor best appreciated by the dead. I keep expecting someone to turn and have an eyeball dangling from a socket.

Some denominations focus on Jesus coming back but don't worry too much beyond this event. Others, like the Jehovah's Witnesses, have invested more energy into planning for the aftermath of Christ's return. One of the key elements to the story of Jesus returning is that the dead are expected to rise from their graves. My only frame of reference for this phenomenon comes from popular culture: zombies.

Secular society is obsessed with dead people who reanimate, usually in mass. Movies, books, and television shows—we are hungry for stories about the "Zombie Apocalypse." Is this another example of a Christian idea so thoroughly integrated into our collective imagination that we hardly remember where it came from? Obviously the theme has been embellished for entertainment value. Zombies come for us with their arms outstretched. They make strange guttural noises and eat human brains. That part isn't from the Bible—or at least I don't think it is.

Since I moved to my new town, representatives from my local Jehovah's Witness Kingdom Hall have been to my house at least a dozen times offering me copies of various publications including the *Watchtower*, their semimonthly magazine. Most recently they handed me a pamphlet entitled "Life in a Peaceful New World." The cover illustration shows an idyllic scene of meadows and snow-peaked mountains. It's half pastoral England and half Swiss Alps. The foreground is decorated with people of all races smiling, gathering fruits and vegetables. An Asian toddler feeds blueberries to a grizzly bear. The inside text reads, "The whole earth will eventually be brought to a gardenlike paradise state . . . no longer will people be crammed into huge apartment buildings."

Even though representatives from the Kingdom Hall have been to my house, I was hesitant to go to theirs. I called earlier in the week to make sure it was okay. They aren't listed in my newspaper's Worship Directory. It goes along with their distrust of all things civic: they don't vote, hold office, salute the flag, serve in the military, or volunteer their information to the newspaper authorities. It is part of their commitment to avoid the world where evil lurks. Theirs is a safer parallel world that intersects with the evil world at countless doorsteps.

It turns out there's one civic instrument they are powerless to avoid: the phone book.

On the phone I talk to a woman named Sadu, and she tells me I am welcome on Sunday. She speaks with a strong accent that I imagine is from some place in India or maybe Africa. I picture her as exotic and statuesque, like one of the dark women from the *Watchtower* illustrations. She of the colorful headscarf and flowing robes. Sadu asks me to look for her when I visit.

At the Kingdom Hall entrance, a man in a suit smiles broadly. He has big white teeth and sandy blond hair shellacked into place. If he's not a dentist, he could play one on TV. "I'm looking for Sadu," I tell him.

He frowns and turns to a woman, "Have you seen Sadu?" The first woman asks a second. The second tries a third. Sadu? Sadu? On down the line. A young woman approaches. "Sadu isn't here today." She is apologetic. "You can sit with me if you'd like." She is white and short and ordinary, but I accept her invitation.

I take a padded seat near a polyester plant while she fetches me a small songbook called *Sing to Jehovah*. I recognize the style of the illustration on the cover, the hordes of happy people of all colors and ages. Here they cradle hymnals and float in a golden light. The tinkling of piano keys begins, and we stand to sing hymn number 19, "God's Promise of Paradise." We warble the first verse:

A paradise our God has promised,
By means of Christ's Millennial Reign,
When he'll blot out all sin and error,
Removing death and tears and pain.

In this interpretation of Christianity, followers appear to deal with the difficulty of being human by focusing on an imaginary world where the difficulties don't exist. The pace of the piano is painfully slow, and everyone is trying to match it; each person draws out different words and in different ways. "Where's the piano?" I whisper to my companion. She points up. Suddenly it makes sense. It's prerecorded and piped in through speakers in the ceiling. It's unable to respond to what's actually going on in the room. I guess the same could be said of any prepackaged solution: the degree to which it may or may not be appropriate is impossible to foresee.

The founder of the Witnesses, Charles Taze Russell, believed Miller's theory that all signs pointed to Jesus's imminent return. Like White, he accepted that after the Great Disappointment the messiah took up residence in a heavenly sanctuary and will soon make it the rest of the way down. When he does, the dead will rise and everyone who ever lived will be sorted into either believers or nonbelievers. Nonbelievers will be obliterated; no hell, just poof and gone. Believers will occupy earth forever with perfect bodies that never get old.

Unlike the Witnesses, the Seventh-Day Adventists don't appear to split hairs over the details. The apocalypse thing felt more implied until the end of the service when the microphone was passed around to members of the congregation. It landed in the hands of an older Asian woman. She looked aristocratic, with her hair in a chignon and streaks of grey at her temples. She said, "I'm just so thankful the lord will be returning soon." I thought that was a funny thing to say, as she seemed so confident. But everyone just nodded, and then it was time for lunch.

Until this part of my explorations, I haven't thought too much about Christ's actual return to earth, although it is a fundamental belief shared by all Christians. They agree on two main points: first, Christ will return, and, second, his return will either usher in—or cap off—a thousand years of peace. As for the specifics, most mainstream denominations stay mum, which is just as well. People tend to freak out when they think of End Times, and details in the Bible don't help. The Book of Revelation appears to state that only 144,000 faithful will escape obliteration. This must have seemed a sufficiently huge figure two thousand years ago, but now it's not even a fifth of Albuquerque. So uncomfortable is the general public with talk of apocalypse that the media has a field day anytime some oddball announces a new date for the end of the world. Journalists clamor for interviews, media outlets pick up the story, and those of us who don't believe have a good chuckle and then quietly hide our relief when the date passes.

In the sanctuary of the Kingdom Hall, I'm seated directly behind a young woman with Down syndrome. She could be as old as twenty. She's holding a tablet of paper with extra-big spaces between lines. Someone has written in big, fluid script, "I will not listen to Satan" three times down the sheet leaving room for her to copy the words underneath. Throughout the morning, she works diligently, painstakingly forming each letter and then holding the page close to her face to inspect her work.

The Jehovah's Witnesses have solved the whole 144,000 dilemma, and they aren't about to keep it hush-hush. It's kind of the whole point. That relatively small number only refers to a special group—what they call the "small flock"—that will help Jesus run the new earthly paradise. It includes the original apostles and all the faithful who ever lived, so you'd have to be exceptional to make it in—though past and present leaders in the Jehovah's Witnesses organization are shoo-ins.

You can still be an inhabitant of the new earth without being a member of the small flock, which I think sounds like the better deal because it means you get to live in paradise without taking on any managerial duties. According to some old *Watchtower* articles, members of the "great flock" won't just feed blueberries to grizzlies all day—they'll have tasks too. For example, they will be on post-apocalypse cleanup duty. The article mentions that they will be assigned the rather unpleasant job of gathering the bleached bones of the annihilated. You'd have to dream awfully big to be included in the small flock, but the only requirement for becoming a member of the great flock is to be an obedient Witness.

For all the shades of grey that exist in Christianity, here is a denomination that lays it out in black and white. When the new world arrives, the Jehovah's Witnesses organization will become what it was destined to become: a global governing structure. Kingdom Halls are ready and waiting in communities all over the world. These will be the new Kingdom's headquarters, and the remaining people will be a single race speaking one language. What language? According to an old *Watchtower*, it will be like ancient Hebrew—except the letters will look more like our current style of alphabet instead of that weird blocky text. How will you learn it? The *Watchtower* assures its readership that the Kingdom will employ plenty of good language instructors. How reassuring to surrender fear about the unknown to a wise authority and to have it all presented with such specificity.

If you're the kind of person who wants answers, here they are in spades. In fact, you don't even have to think of the questions—those are provided as well. The day's "sermon" is a question-and-answer session lifted directly from the most recent copy of the *Watchtower*. Every Kingdom Hall all over the world is reviewing the same article this weekend. The governing board of the organization keeps a tight grip on the curriculum. Everyone is asked to read the article in advance. Now an elder stands at the podium as we open our copies of the *Watchtower* to the correct page. Today's lesson is about "Entering into God's Rest." Examples from Genesis and Hebrews reveal people being punished for not being obedient to God. The guy at the podium asks the questions printed at the bottom of each column and then calls on people by name. "Why is obedience essential if we are to enter into God's rest?" A few people raise their hands and provide an appropriate snippet from the article. "How does one enter into God's rest today? Brother James?"

"By being obedient," says Brother James.

For those who want a bottom line, a "pull quote" is printed at the top of the page: "We can enter into Jehovah's rest today by obediently working in harmony with his advancing purpose as it is revealed to us through his organization."

So many spoon-fed answers, but I'm left scratching my head.

I wrote my name and address down. I thought for sure their persistence would increase. All these months the Witnesses have been showing up at my door every few weeks, and now I come into their Kingdom Hall and write my name and address on a piece of paper. That is like throwing bloody chum into a shark tank, right? As I am leaving, I can see a group gathering around a flip chart. This is the meeting where they go over their personal ministries, which is what they call their doorstep proselytizing. They are dividing up the neighborhoods, making sure every door gets knocked on. For the first time, I want them to come because I actually have questions. I've skipped ahead to the next week's lesson; it is about family members who leave the faith and how they must be shunned. The attached photo shows a young man walking out the door with his suitcase, his weeping mother watching. I want to ask about family and friends who would never in a million years join the faith. Can an eternal paradise really be that great if no one I love will be there?

I also need clarification on the things I am supposed to avoid. I can live without celebrating Christmas and birthdays and other holidays. I can steer clear of smoking and gambling and pornography. But there seems to be a massive grey area. During the service, one of the leaders from another Kingdom Hall gave a brief talk about immorality and he singled out Web-based social networking as an example of one of the ways "wicked men will be progressing from bad to worse." Will I need to delete my Facebook profile? All this attention is surely giving the forces of evil more power, not less. I can't shake the image of the young woman diligently copying her sentence about avoiding Satan. I keep waiting for my doorbell to ring unexpectedly. It does once, and I run only to find kids selling cookies. Then weeks turn into months and still I'm waiting.

o

This story circles death like a vulture. People gather to indulge in identities that will continue without end, to claim eternal life or salvation. Pleasant post-apocalyptic scenarios soothe myriad anxieties, I imagine, taking the focus off more personal sources of suffering. Nothing takes the sting out of the idea of death quite like believing you'll live forever.

We think up solutions to death and disease, giving ourselves perfect bodies endlessly, which, in a sense, is to acquire the characteristics of God. Because what is God if not flawless and eternal? It seems most believers, regardless of what shape their almighty takes, can agree on at least those two characteristics. However, stating plainly this underlying desire for humans to achieve godlike qualities seems to be frowned on, making the clarity with which it is expressed in Mormon theology almost a relief. Joseph Smith, founder of Latter-Day Saints, made no bones about it: man is on an epic quest to become a god. He was equally clear about the flip side of this equation: God, the Heavenly Father of this world, was once an ordinary man.

I've been admiring and rubbing shoulders with Mormons for most of my life. It began when I would sit in front of the television, enthralled by the *Donnie & Marie* show. Since then, I've had Mormon landlords, coworkers, and acquaintances. I've watched the Mormon Tabernacle Choir perform Christmas carols on television. I've visited Salt Lake City and walked around the temple complex, their most sacred collection of buildings. I've marveled at the basic story of these pioneering people who trekked across the country, got kicked out of a lot of places, and finally settled in Utah. But until now I had almost zero knowledge about their belief system. Harold Bloom, the brilliant cultural critic, sees Mormonism as the final expression of "American religion," those offshoots of Protestantism invented solely on these soils that include Seventh-Day Adventists, Jehovah's Witnesses, and Christian Scientists but culminate with Joseph Smith and his Latter-Day Saints. It wasn't until near the end of my journey through Christianity that I even dared pick up a copy of Bloom's book *The American Religion*.

According to Bloom, this period in history was particularly ripe for religious innovation not only because of broad social changes like rapid urbanization but also because the notion of God as punishing and judgmental had permeated every nook and cranny of the national subconscious. The first waves of settlers had been heavily influenced by Calvin, who taught that everyone was either saved or damned from birth. This idea may have worked for a self-confident theologian whose cushy existence seemed to confirm a privileged status, but it was too much for most Americans whose difficult lives offered no proof of salvation. These years seem to be unique in the degree to which physical illness preceded religious innovation. Ellen White was bedridden for much of the first half of her life. But perhaps no one suffered more than Mary Baker Eddy, who "discovered" Christian Science.

Phineas Parkhurst Quimby flat-out blamed Calvin. Quimby was the clockmaker-turned-healer who treated Eddy when her condition failed to improve under the care of traditional doctors. He claimed his mission in life was to free people from Calvin's "iron grip," which he believed was making Americans sick. For many, Calvin's interpretation of Christianity was doing the opposite of what one hopes religion will do for people, which is to make the mortal experience less problematic. Instead, Calvinism seemed to ratchet up the anxiety associated with the most terrifying aspect of the human condition: death. As Quimby surmised, "The fear of death is the cause of nine-tenths of all disease."

Quimby was all for Christianity, but he advocated for a return to the healing aspects of Jesus's work. It's hard to imagine today because so much progress has been made in the fields of medicine and psycho-analysis, but fewer than two hundred years ago it was not unusual for doctors to give up on patients whose indeterminate sources of suffering did not respond to the usual remedies. This is where Quimby came in. He treated scores of people, some of whom traveled great distances to his office in Maine for help. What was Quimby's remarkably effec-tive medicine? Empathy. He noted that if traditional doctors couldn't categorize the malady, the patient would be labeled "nervous, spleeny or hypochondriacal and receive no sympathy from anyone." His treat-ment included holding hands with his patients and listening intently.

I can only imagine how it must have felt back then to be trapped in a prolonged state of physical suffering. I'm ill, and no one but my closest family members will come near me for fear of contagion. Not understanding the source of my disease, it would feel like punishment for whatever unworthiness resides in me. Suddenly a stranger that everyone admires and thinks is special, this sort of celebrity, approaches me and puts his hands on my head and looks me in the eyes. Perhaps he says "God loves you" with such sincerity that I have no choice but to believe it. How much better would I feel from that small act of kind-ness? I might still have leprosy or a lame leg, but the degree to which I believe this limits or isolates me almost certainly would be diminished. This makes me wonder if some of Jesus's miracles weren't actually rooted in a very human phenomenon, the simple yet powerful gesture of connection, which in my mind makes them no less extraordinary. Quimby recognized this aspect of Jesus's talent and tried to replicate the technique. He employed compassion to break through the alienation that plagues the human condition.

Misery is constant, but the names we have for it change. Accord-ing to Quimby, the day's standard diagnosis of "neuralgia" was giving way to a "new invention called spine disease." Mary Baker Eddy suffered all of the most popular ailments, including neuralgia of the stomach, nervous inflammation of the spine, and the mysterious-sounding "renal calculi." She was nearly an invalid when she sought out Quimby, and under his care her health improved, though the year he died, 1866, Eddy relapsed dramatically after a slip on an icy sidewalk. The attending physician predicted she would die; instead, she discovered Christian Science. Quimby had taught that physical ailments could be manifestations of our anxieties; Eddy saw further that disease and death were not real at all, but inventions of our mortal minds.

o

I drive past the church several times without seeing it, which I find hilarious once I start to grasp the tenets of Christian Science. I don't know if it's because I'm expecting the exterior of the building to be white, which I've read is the color favored by Christian Scientists to represent the "divine light of truth." The third time past it seems to materialize: an ordinary little brown-shingled building, not particularly churchlike, more reminiscent of a small medical office, but obviously my destination. I pull into the parking lot a few minutes late and run inside.

I've seen the rare news story about a sick kid who died because his faithful parents chose not to seek medical attention. While Jehovah's Witnesses are known to refuse blood transfusions due to references in the Bible prohibiting the ingestion of blood, many devout Christian Scientists never see doctors. This choice is not tied to any specific citations; rather, it stems from a general understanding of reality and illness as illusion.

When I enter the main sanctuary, the proceedings have begun, and I slip into an empty row. The room feels more like a small court than an ordinary chapel. The pews face a raised podium that stretches almost wall to wall. Three women sit behind the podium; they're visible only from the shoulders up, but I imagine they wear ethereal judge's robes. Aside from two men, the congregation is all women. I feel as if I've stepped into a parallel society, some tribunal in a feminist alternative to *The Handmaid's Tale*. The wall behind the podium sports two quotes. On one side is Jesus: "Ye shall know the truth and the truth shall make you free." The other side is Eddy: "Divine Love always has met and always will meet every human need." I notice that each has been

CHRISTIANITY 063

given exactly twelve words, but somehow I feel Lady Justice's scales tip ever so slightly toward Eddy.

Calvin, like other Protestants, saw man as a thing apart from God. Eddy understood differently: God is all that exists, so man can't be a thing apart. Calvin believed that to achieve holiness, man must battle his creaturely nature. Eddy understood that man, having no identity separate from God, can be nothing but eternal and perfect. The challenge is to overcome all beliefs to the contrary.

Just when I grasp a tenet of Eddy's Christian Science, I try tracing its meaning to a logical conclusion only to find that it seems to vanish, as elusive as a broken filament in an abandoned spider's web. Yet I can sense that she's onto something profoundly true. She says all suffering is caused by the false belief in a selfhood apart from God. Illness is illusion. Individual identity is imaginary. Matter is unreal. This discovery, writes Eddy, "rolls back the clouds of error with the light of Truth, and lifts the curtain on man as never born and as never dying."

As we sing a hymn penned by Margaret Matters, head of the Mother Church in the mid-1900s—"O Science, God sent message! Today Christ's precious Science thy healing power makes plain!"—I think about Eddy's detractors. The common refrain: "What she discovered is neither Christian nor science." Perhaps they're being too literal. Hers was something above and beyond human science, a new way of understanding all that we see and experience. She just as easily could have called it God's Truth. She collected her insights in a volume she named *Science and Health with Key to the Scriptures*, which along with the Bible is the primary text used during Christian Science services.

I can't help but be awed by Eddy's life story. Even Mark Twain, who wrote hilariously scathing opinions about this "discoverer of truth," seems to have respected Eddy as one of the most influential and fascinating women of his day. No doubt she was a groundbreaking person, especially for Victorian times. A divorcee who gave up her only biological child, she lived the first half of her life sick and weak and dependent. But the second half was all vitality and authority. If ever there was a role model for what can be accomplished after age forty, here it is. Churches built, devotees wooed, servants employed. She was almost ninety when she founded the award-wining newspaper the *Christian Science Monitor*.

Even if her unconventional thinking was helped along by episodes of morphine addiction, as some historians speculate, I don't think it changes the bravery of her vision. She offers the most original reason to forgo suffering from the human condition: it's not real. You were never born, so there's no need to twist in the wind over your level of gratitude for that particular event. Furthermore, what's the point of fearing death when it will never take place? Eddy tackles the anguish associated with the one-two punch of the human condition by dismissing its most traumatic notions.

Yet Eddy had to stretch the limits of her insight when her followers asked tricky questions like why they continued to perceive the birth and death of people. Mistakes in thinking, she answered. But what if more than one person perceives the mistake? A collective error, she surmised. As her explanations dance toward the edge of reason, I can see why some people draw parallels between the development of Christian Science and the dawning of the New Age movement. Both embrace reality beyond perception and champion the power of thought to shape experience.

But Eddy's amazing interpretation of reality is almost too removed from my perception to help me with my ordinary struggles. What to make of how real the human experience feels? My own little mind screams, "I exist!" My body, this chair, the room . . . they seem so true and solid. At the same time, the notion that God is all that exists and that I'm nothing more than some expression or fantasy of this enormous force of love is a beautiful idea to entertain. Just thinking it seems to ease my anxiety, even if temporarily.

At least some of Eddy's followers were shocked when their prophetess appeared to die. They must have felt a sense of guilt knowing their erroneous thinking was to blame. In the small chapel in which I sit today, all the way across the country from the denomination's headquarters in Boston, I do not perceive Mary Baker Eddy as being physically present. I've seen pictures of her—she was exceptionally pretty with fine, high cheekbones—but none of these faces match hers. Still, she lives on in the sequence of the service and all the words, including little notes explaining elements of the service, which are read just as she instructed over one hundred years ago. There is no traditional sermon, no new thoughts sprouting from the minds of these church leaders. The three women behind the podium give voice to Eddy's sentences as outlined in a slick pamphlet produced quarterly by the Mother Church so that all her little church goslings are perfectly in step. Even the various readings from the Bible are followed by Eddy's interpretations; up against Jesus, Eddy gets the last word. The service ends, as it always does, with the reading of what Eddy called "the Scientific Statement of Being, and the correlative scripture according to I John 3:1–3" from page 468 of *Science and Health*. It might as well be Eddy's voice as the reader intones, "There is no life, truth, intelligence, nor substance in matter. All is infinite Mind and its infinite manifestation, for God is All-in-all."

American Grace

The woman beelines for me. I've been standing in the crowded chapel for fewer than five seconds when her eyes lock on me from across the room; she turns in my direction with the single-minded intensity of a cougar stalking a chipmunk. I force a smile that says, "Please no."

I am surprised at how quickly she recognizes me as an outsider. For the first time ever, I actually looked up, and then followed, the dressing suggestions. It says ladies generally wear skirts or dresses. I had worn the same pair of nice black pants to every service so far, so I dug deep into the back of my closet. I even dusted off a pair of old tights. Maybe I'm a bit on the jumpy side because of my preconceived notion that Mormons form a somewhat closed society.

"I saw the commercials," I say defensively when the young woman asks what brought me to church today. I had been planning to worship with the Latter-Day Saints all along, but I was feeling reluctant. Then I began to see the commercials on television.

I don't know if it's a national marketing campaign, but the commercials are in heavy rotation where I live. Each one has a similar format. The camera focuses on a face and flashes different scenes of the person going about his or her day like a mini-documentary about an ordinary, yet somewhat interesting, individual, and just when you're wondering what the heck this ad is for, they spring it on you: the person says, "I'm a Mormon." It tells you to get more information at Mormon.org.

The ones I've seen feature a young Chicano dressed in a shirt buttoned at the collar and baggy pants and sunglasses. In Los Angeles he is what one might call a "homeboy." The camera follows him riding his tricked-out bicycle with the handlebars way up. Then it shows him giggling with his mother, and the voiceover goes, "My name is Valentin, and I'm a Mormon." The first time I saw it, I was like, "No way. Valentin? A Mormon?" The other one that's caught my eye highlights a big dude with a bald head and full mustache who looks like he runs with the Hell's Angels. But, no, Allan is a Mormon.

It's an effective marketing strategy because it increased my confidence about attending services. I mean, if Allan and Valentin are welcome, then I shouldn't be a problem, right? At the very least, it signaled to me that Mormons are looking to change perceptions regarding their inclusivity.

"That's great!" she says. She invites me to sit with her, and I trail her to her pew. Up close, she is surprisingly young. I was fooled by how mature she looked from afar. That's the thing about Mormons: they look and behave like grownups very early. They seem to avoid the angsty pitfalls so many of us experience in our twenties and thirties. We Nones are lucky to approach middle age having developed the emotional capacity and patience to share our personal space with a pet and perhaps another human being. By then, Mormons have a bundle of children and marriages going on twenty years.

Technically, the building in which I'm standing in is not called a "church." Mormons refer to their places of worship as "meetinghouses." In many larger metropolitan areas, Mormons also have "temples." These are usually fancy buildings on a hill with smooth stone surfaces and tall otherworldly spires. Sometimes they're lit at night so that you can see them from faraway, like the headquarters for some fantastical land. If you look closely, you might see a figure at the tip-top of the tallest spire. This is the angel Moroni, who visited Joseph Smith Jr. and led him to the golden tablets from which he translated the Book of Mormon. A lot of times the statue is gold and holds a bugle.

The temples are the sites of special ceremonies and baptisms, not ordinary Sunday services. Every region has access to a temple even if you have to go a ways. The closest one to me is about an hour's drive. But regular weekly services take place in the meetinghouses, which often look like typical churches. One day I drove past a newly constructed Mormon meetinghouse about eight miles from my house. It seemed to have sprung up overnight behind an Office Depot. I was curious, so I pulled into the expansive parking lot and got close enough to read the simple stone plaque: The Church of Jesus Christ of the Latter-Day Saints. Then and there, I made up my mind: this is where I wanted to attend Mormon services. It was so pretty and new. The only task was to determine what time services began on Sunday.

I discovered Mormonism doesn't work like that, however. Unlike other denominations where you can decide where you worship based on a whim such as a pretty building or attractive congregants, where and when you attend Mormon services is tied strictly to the location of your home. On the official LDS website, I typed in my street address and zip code and up popped the identity of my small geographical zone, or "ward." From this, I found which meetinghouse to attend and at what time. The bad news: I was not assigned to the new building behind Office Depot but to a much older place closer to my house. The good news: my meeting time wasn't until one o'clock. I could sleep in!

Maybe I can have my brunch and be a Mormon too.

o

The year of the "Great Disappointment," when Jesus didn't return in 1844, Joseph Smith was gunned down by an angry mob in Missouri; apparently they didn't much appreciate his ideas about plural marriage in part because some of his would-be wives were already married to other men, and he was, by all accounts, an exceptionally magnetic and good-looking guy, so it was sort of like if Brad Pitt came to town and put out a shingle that said "wives needed." Smith was killed in June of that year, just a few months before Jesus missed his October cutoff date. How abreast Smith was of the prevalent messiah deadlines is unclear, but it's a safe assumption that he was at least in tune with the popular anticipation and died believing Christ's return was imminent because much of his church's theology hinges on this point.

Harold Bloom calls Joseph Smith Jr. "the most gifted and authentic of all American prophets." Bloom explains that Smith didn't just passively read the Bible but "drowned in the Bible and came up with an almost near identification with the ancient Hebrews." Smith believed he was a vital piece of the biblical story, as was his country and his time. In Smith's world view, the Bible's Garden of Eden was actually located in western Missouri and Noah built his ark to survive the swelling of the Mississippi River. Smith taught that after Jesus was crucified and rose from his tomb, he roamed the American continent to preach directly to its inhabitants before ascending to heaven. All this and more, said Smith, he learned from a collection of "golden tablets" created by Native Americans, who were actually descendants of one of the lost tribes of Israel. They committed these secrets to precious metal slabs, which he had found on a hillside in upstate New York. Smith claims he was led to them by an angel named Moroni and that he translated their message by looking through a set of "seer stones." Many non-Mormons have had a good chuckle over some of the more outlandish aspects of the faith. I've even heard late-night comedians poke fun at the Mormon practice of wearing "magic underwear." Smith's story has been set to show tunes and dance numbers in a tongue-in-cheek Tony-award-winning musical called *The Book of Mormon*.

But can we possibly understand Christianity, especially as practiced in the United States, without taking Mormons seriously? According to some sources, theirs is the fastest-growing Christian denomination in the world, thanks in no small part to the two-year "missions" every Mormon teen is encouraged to take, proselytizing in the United States and abroad. And what does it say about how useful a tool Christianity can be that this group of people used it as motivation and guiding principal as they traipsed across the continent, pushing forward the frontier of the American West? But what I find most fascinating is that an otherwise ordinary New York farmboy took a centuries-old faith and made it so utterly his own, inserting himself into the story and claiming complete ownership. If that doesn't scream "American ingenuity," I don't know what does. The Book of Mormon and Smith's other writings are like a bridge connecting biblical times to the here and now. Together with the Old and New Testaments, they are the Mormon holy books, bound into one tome that is striking in its girth. Stand on it and you're at least a foot closer to God. The fact that Mormons carry it as one giant book is as telling as their church's official name. Jesus's time and today are not separate entities but one continuous era in which we are now in the latter days.

If every religious innovator adds his or her own twist, Smith went all out with a component so cosmic that I struggle to wrap my mind around it. His vision includes a heaven filled with billions of spirit children "begotten" by "Heavenly Father" and "Heavenly Mother" in a celestial world near Kolob, the name Smith gave a theoretical star in the universe. The human forms we experience now are but a mere step, a brief incarnation, on an epic journey toward perfecting our spirit existence. The scope of this drama dwarfs anything that plays out on this planet.

For all the specificity of Smith's vision, at its core it speaks to the same sources of suffering that Christianity has addressed since the beginning—though with an added twist. For those of us grappling with worthiness, Smith taught that being born as a human on earth is a reward for proving ourselves faithful to God in the spirit world. Though we may not remember it, each of us on this planet has demonstrated our value and is currently enjoying the prize. What a lovely solution to the guilt we might feel even subconsciously that we'll never do anything good enough to deserve our lives: we've already done it. Smith also taught that death is nothing but a return to our true nature as eternal, cosmos-dwelling spirits. If anything, death is an event to welcome because greater things lay beyond it. Our earthbound incarnation is simply an opportunity to demonstrate our ability and desire to be fathers and mothers of our own celestial kingdoms. Smith considered polygamy a necessary tool for repopulation.

Given this premise, I was apprehensive the service would contain elements I would find a tad "out there." Instead what I got was a room full of clean-cut people conducting the most conventional of affairs. I scanned fruitlessly for even one homeboy or pseudo biker. No, this was just a big room full of my best but most boring neighbors—the ones who keep their lawns meticulous and who never park their cars on the street. I had inadvertently stumbled on the faithful foot soldiers of the garage-proud army, the ones who "accidentally" leave their automatic garage doors gaping to show how meticulously organized and spotless they've made these spaces that are so vulnerable to filth and chaos. As if tidiness is a reflection of the purity of one's soul, the final frontier in getting right with God. One of the early Mormon settlements before Salt Lake City was called "Orderville," which I thought was a terrible name; now I realize it is a term of endearment given by these experts at organizing people and places. I understand why new converts might have been inclined to join these individuals so skilled at taming the wildness of each new frontier.

The day's proceedings are decidedly earthbound. The program doesn't include an official sermon, just regular congregants who have signed up to give brief talks; it seems everyone is encouraged to commit to one of these from time to time. Today, two teenage girls share the podium, each dedicating a few minutes to the topic of volunteer work. Next, a young man elaborates on the theme of righteous living. None of the speakers demonstrates particularly stellar oratory skill; they are as awkward and stumbling as I might be. Most of the remaining time is dedicated to an administrative matter: this ward is splitting in two. I can't believe my luck to witness the reproductive process this organism of a denomination has used to grow so mighty over the last hundred years.

Apparently the population of Mormons in the vicinity of my house has climbed steadily for a decade, and now the congregants who show up at this time slot are too numerous. The pews are not enough, and the addition of several rows of folding chairs is no longer sufficient; latecomers often have standing room only at the back of the chapel. The assistant bishop, whose domain includes several wards, takes the podium to say a few words regarding this matter. Starting the following week, he explains, one portion of this ward will show up for the one o'clock service and the other will begin at the new three o'clock slot. Like everything else, the division is determined by the location of each family's home. He acknowledges how difficult this transition is, especially because the group has been worshipping together for many years and close ties may tempt some to choose one time over the other based on friendships rather than street addresses. He stresses the importance of abiding by the rules. He assures us that over time we will grow not only comfortable with but even to love our new ward mates, and he hints that soon what began as this one ward may require a brand new meetinghouse. I sense chests welling with pride, and the seeds of determination silently sprouting. Slowly, taking cues from nature, one ward split at a time, the Mormon Church will expand.

It's all so rudimentary. Here is a congregation channeling existential anxiety into epic to-do lists. Anyone who has ever participated in a campaign or community organizing effort will recognize the basics of this discussion. For the first time ever, I actually know the hymns. We sing "O Come All Ye Faithful" and "Joy to the World," even though it is over a month until Christmas. Despite the inclusion of verses I have never heard, the familiarity is comforting. The only hint of something exotic occurs during the blessing of a newborn. In a frilly bonnet and ruffled dress, she looks as lifeless as a doll. Her father carries her to the altar and a group of men gathers, each putting a hand to the baby. Together, they wish only good things for this precious life, but something about the sight of a fortress of men surrounding a tiny floppy girl sends a tingle up my spine. I'm reminded that Mormons consider only men priests; every adult male qualifies. For a second, it's like the diaphanous curtain flutters open and I get a quick glimpse of the quirky ceremonies that supposedly take place in the hidden chambers and back rooms of Mormon temples everywhere. From what I surmise, believers act out momentous occasions; they might pantomime death, make believe meeting God, and pretend to travel through the afterlife. These rituals are the elaborate secret handshakes in a cosmic clubhouse. I can only imagine that to participate helps pacify whatever existential fears one might have.

After the service my Mormon mentor explains that the congregation will now break into smaller groups for further discussion. The men/priests will stay in the main chapel for their meeting, some of the women will gather to go over charitable duties, and the rest of us are invited to join study groups. She suggests a beginner's class for me and leads me down a long hall to a back room with rows of plastic school chairs and a pregnant teacher who is so far along with twins that she has a hard time getting close enough to the chalkboard to write. I have to admire her determination.

The students each have a copy of a thin book called *Gospel Principles*, comprising forty-seven short chapters designed to introduce the faith to newcomers. Flipping through, I notice photos of regular people doing boring, everyday stuff peppered with cheesy illustrations of Jesus and intergalactic cloud bursts. The artwork perfectly captures this religion's dualism: earthbound responsibilities side by side with celestial fantasies.

As we go over the details of a chapter called "Signs of the Second Coming"—which are pretty much the usual wickedness, war, and turmoil, as told to Smith by Jesus—I have to wonder about polygamy. Today's mainstream Mormon leaders denounce the practice, but it was essential to Smith's vision. I also keep thinking of the baby who got blessed. I can't shake the feeling that this belief system is like an iceberg: for every inch you see, below the surface lie a thousand you don't.

o

The history of Christianity, especially on these soils, is an endless series of modifications to create practices more meaningful or palatable to contemporary tastes. Over and over, people have taken the parts that work for them and discarded those that don't. With this in mind, I make my way to my first Catholic services. If I think I've come a long way on this journey, it doesn't compare to the distance the Catholic Church has traveled.

When I was much greener, with my Martin Luther picture book in hand, I had imagined the experience of worshipping in a Catholic church as a beautiful, remote spectacle. I have stepped foot in countless Catholic churches as a tourist both here and in Europe, admiring their opulent interiors that even when not in use are alive with statuary and reflective surfaces. Which makes the plain and intimate chapel I walk into all the more surprising. The walls are stark white, the wood furniture simple; the one bit of sparkle comes from the flames of two candles atop the modest altar. If I didn't know better, I'd think this was a Protestant church. As I walk down the aisle and take a seat in a pew, I have an image of a pampered and perfumed lady making her way across the American plains in a covered wagon. Each stage of the journey, she sheds another facet of her fancy facade. She's forced to trade her jewelry for medicine; her silk scarf blows away in a sudden gust; her porcelain skin darkens. Finally she arrives at her destination indistinguishable from the other pioneering women who've made the same journey: weathered, weary, and wiser.

The only hint that something's different here is a fat book tucked next to the hymnals, which I pull out and flip through. In this volume, every mass of the entire year is spelled out. The "lectionary cycle" ensures the Bible is completed on a regular schedule, mandating when to read which parts. The format matches Catholic services all over the world: a first reading from the Old Testament or, at specific times of the year, certain books of the New Testament; a responsorial psalm that is, ideally, sung; a second reading from one of the New Testament letters (only on Sundays); and finally a gospel reading. Throw in a few hymns and communion and bada bing: you've got a service. Even the communion wafers are centrally mandated; the priest hands each person an identical disk from some Lord's Supper supplier. No random chunks of misshapen loaves like in most other churches (and no crumbs!). Consistency is key, as are the codes and canons. It's a reminder that this denomination has a figure who speaks on behalf of God, and while each church is a finger or toe of this single body, decisions are made by the head. It's in part what Luther was reacting to. He wasn't so much opposed to the centralized power as to what it spelled: mandates or traditions that could not be altered without agreement from the top.

Yet in the five hundred or so years since Luther, the Catholic Church has made significant changes, some of which the famous reformer was calling for in his day. Congregants are no longer relegated to the role of passive observer. They are welcome to take communion and, at every mass, the priest is assisted by a small group of helpers who have signed up in advance. On this church's website you can print out the guidelines for each role. One person carries the Book of Gospels and does the first reading and the responsorial psalm. Another is responsible for the second reading and the Prayers of the Faithful.

Altar servers carry the cross and candles. The priest and his helpers walk down the aisle in a processional sequence explained on several printable pages on the website—when to bow at the altar, what side the cross is placed, where to put the candles. Perhaps on some days the priest will say a few words of his own. Today he sticks to the script, every word and movement fixed by higher authority.

My thoughts rise like a helium balloon, freed by the spectacle of ceremony that feels otherworldly. I imagine myself as one of a huge brigade of soul soldiers stepping in unison. The congregants here know that millions of others across the globe are reading the same Bible selections, contemplating the same issues, experiencing the same basic service. It's like the menu at a McDonald's or Starbucks. I see the appeal of an item that arrives exactly as you expect. But this is more than Big Macs and mochas. It's a connection to the infinite, to a higher power. The choices made here are at the crux of all religious innovation: does one accept a product as-is, and the backing that comes with it? Or opt for something new and risk standing alone?

For those familiar with this tradition, the sounds and the incense and the rhythm of the service must open a portal to some other dimension, a mysterious "soul space." Even for someone as inexperienced as I am, it seems to flip a switch that allows my thoughts to meander. Being in the Catholic church keeps hurling me back in time because the connection, I see, is not just to others living around the world today but to previous generations; it offers a continuity with the past that newer denominations must wait centuries to achieve. I picture the face of my great-grandmother Aphrodite, who, by the time I met her, was toothless and whiskered and blind. I rein in my musings only to have them float off again. I'm on to a day I haven't thought of in years. My grandmother and I are on an errand to drop off her homemade cookies for the upcoming Greek Festival. In my memory, the outside of the Orthodox church in downtown Dallas is pure white—smooth stucco with a big mound in the middle like an overgrown igloo, its ancient ways preserved on ice by the long-ago split with the Catholic Church.

Tables are being set up in the courtyard and in the hallways. Grandma lets go of my hand. The door of the chapel is ajar, and I can see a sliver of bright red so incongruous with the pearly exterior that I feel drawn to it. Opening that slit and stepping through was like performing an autopsy, peeling away the smooth skin to reveal a beating heart. Crimson carpeting lined the aisles leading to the altar like arteries carrying me along. The ceiling was painted with faces motioning for to me to look up. The light reflected off the abundant gold in the murals creating a warm glow; a smoky sweetness lingered in the air. So otherworldly did this seem—so unlike the corridor outside where kids were running around and boxes of baklava were being dropped off—that I felt like one of the characters in *The Lion, the Witch, and the Wardrobe*, my favorite book, who had stepped across a threshold into a different dimension—only this was a world that existed on the inside of a person. My grandmother, her grandmother, and all our mothers before that, we each had our individual heart that beat in our chest, the one that pumped blood and kept us alive, but here was the heart we shared—one that might never die.

Walking with Jesus

Some of today's Protestant denominations are taking cues from the Catholic Church in an effort to feel more in sync with one another. Many have compiled their own lectionaries based on the Roman Catholic mass lectionary; as they read through the Bible during services, they are literally on the same page as other Protestants. Traditional elements—more frequent communion, celebrating Lent, or setting up stations of the cross—strengthen their ties to other Christians around the world.

Protestants may be reaching back for inspiration, but they're reaching forward too. It's not until the end, when I'm standing in the parking lot after worship services at one of the last stops on my Christian journey, that I see clearly the ways some mainstream denominations are embracing new trends. Out here, denominational distinctions have faded, church names have gotten creative, the music has grown a steady beat, and worship is stripped of ceremony. I've just left a rented event center packed to the brim, mostly with young, good-looking college students. The band members were five guys, each more adorable than the last. The title of this church does not tie it to any kind of Christianity that came before. It's named for a sound and news too good not to share. I'll call it "the Buzz." The cavernous auditorium was filled with studs and jocks and even handsome hipsters. So many clear complexions, so much silky hair. A sprinkling of stylish middle agers and mature high schoolers rounded out the crowd. These were the kind of worshippers who don't believe in wearing business casual to honor the Lord so much as the right wash on their denim. The lighting during the services was dim and moody; I felt like Jesus might appear on stage with a big digitally remastered halo around his head.

From this vantage I see it clear as day: how youth culture, particularly trends in popular music, which developed at the periphery, worked their way into the more established branches of Christianity. I was confused when I first encountered the evidence. Several months earlier, at a Presbyterian church, I was asked the question: "Are you here for the contemporary or traditional service?" It had been posed to me by a young man at the chapel door.

"What's the difference?" I asked. This was the first I was hearing of two services.

"The music mostly. I think. I don't know." He looked around self-consciously. "I always go to the contemporary one. I'll get Pastor Eric. He can explain."

He returned being tailed by a baby-faced man in an enormous blazer. Either Pastor Eric had recently lost a hundred pounds or he just appreciates a loose fit. The big coat made him appear even younger than he already seemed, like a kid wearing his father's suit.

"You're visiting us today!" He had oodles of confidence and a booming voice. He was handsome in a clean-cut way. I pictured him at Christian camp as a teenager, all the girls chastely fawning over him in the mess hall. "Right on!" he said enthusiastically, using a phrase I associate with surfers.

He explained that the contemporary service showcases newer "rock" songs and guitar, whereas the other features older hymns and a choir. Besides this, they're the same: identical message and readings and sermon. "The newer music rubs some of the older folks the wrong way," he said.

I took the service starting immediately—the contemporary one.

In the main sanctuary, Pastor Eric said a few words of welcome and then disappeared into the corner. Suddenly, a loud guitar riff filled the chapel. I scanned the room and spotted what I had previously overlooked, off to the side of the altar: a full rock band including drums, bass, keyboards, and two backup singers sandwiched between big, black concert speakers. The pastor spun to face us, an electric guitar strapped to his chest. As the music reached full throttle, he approached a microphone and began to sing the first song, "Glory to God Forever."

It was Pearl Jam meets Jesus. I looked around to see if I could catch smiles on anyone's faces. This is unusual, right? The father of

Presbyterians, Calvin, was famously opposed to displays of flamboyance and mirth. He considered dancing at weddings a vulgarity, as was serving too many dishes at dinner. But the congregants were extremely earnest. I joined them as they stood. I was holding the lyrics on a photocopied sheet, but I couldn't for the life of me catch the beat; others were trying, with varying degrees of success. It reminded me of when kids sing a song they sort of know, and they mumble along until they grasp a string of words and blurt them out, usually a beat or two late. I was the worst offender—so it was like an echo of an echo: my mangled version dangling from the audience's slightly less mangled version, itself a desperate mimic of the pastor's performance. Pastor Eric had an excellent voice and an authoritative stage presence. If I could have, I would have voted we all just shut up and listen.

It was loud and thumping. If this had been anywhere else, I would have been swaying. I find it almost impossible not to move at least one limb to any music with even the semblance of a beat. They were a bunch of redwood trees in a forest alive with exotic birds. It was the strangest sensation, all this vibrancy electrifying the air, and they were as unmoved as lightning rods. Actually, this is precisely what I had been expecting before I showed up that morning. The rock star pastor was a shock, but the congregants fit right in with my preconceived notions. I had found my puritans—it's not that they don't feel passion for God, just that they are more comfortable with the pastor expressing it on their behalf. My mind and body compromised on a little unobtrusive foot tapping.

After a medley of opening songs, we settled into traditional service elements that included a Time of Silent Confession, Assurance of Pardon, New and Old Testament readings, giving of tithes and offerings, and the recitation of the Lord's Prayer.

As I continued my churchgoing, I realized many mainline Protestant denominations offered two versions of their Sunday services, one with traditional hymns and the other with a drummer behind a Plexiglas partition. Sometimes I saw older people in the contemporary service or young people in the traditional, but in general the age divide was clear. I wasn't sure who was making concessions to whom—whether the elders were accommodating current tastes or if new leaders were hoping to not alienate their base of long-time congregants, and likely their best tithers. It left me wondering if music is worth it. Each time I had to decide between services, I couldn't help but note how meager the attendance usually was and how, if services were combined, twice as many people would be present. Because what seems to matter much more than the music is that any of us bothered showing up to sit elbow to elbow and at least try to join our voices to whatever songs played. Two services is like one generation saying to the other, "Music is more important than you." Which seems just the sort of gap worship is meant to close.

o

The protestors become the establishment and a new wave of rebels rise up; in the history of Christianity, it has happened over and over again. In the early seventies, before rock instruments had been integrated into many Protestant services, after the explosion of youth culture in America claimed its first and second wave of devotees, some young people began to feel disillusioned by the churches they grew up in. They did not favor dead Jesus or spirit Jesus or even God Jesus. They were drawn to the real man who walked the earth in dusty sandals. They wanted to emulate his humility and simple desire to love and help others. Some were in the hippie counterculture when they began to gravitate toward a Christian message; others were Christians drawn to the counterculture. They saw Jesus as the ultimate hippie, and they aspired to be like him. They got labeled "Jesus people" or "Jesus freaks."

One church in town links its founding directly to the seventies' Jesus movement, and I've been anticipating my visit there all year, wondering what it will be like to penetrate the invisible barrier that seems to separate its congregants from the rest of the community. Their building sits in stark contrast to what I know of the group's humble origins. The founders of this church started as a ragtag group of college students who met wherever they could, in living rooms and borrowed spaces, until finally, twenty years down the line, they built their own building.

The building watches over one of the busier intersections in town, the impression of its size magnified by its position at the top of a hill. The church is a modernist structure, all right angles and glass. Large beams protrude above the entrance, each bent in the middle, supporting a long thin cross: enormous arms holding a sword poised to stab passers-by. The hillside leading to the church is covered in hundreds of juniper bushes whose branches have grown into big points like oversized shards of green glass. No path leads to the church's door, the only entrance on to the property is a driveway for cars, ironic given Jesus's reputation for walking. But even after all these years and the unapproachable building, the emphasis is still on the man in sandals. Every member is encouraged to take the "foundation course," called the "Carpenter Series," to help students build lives more like Jesus "whether you have never heard much about Jesus . . . or have been walking with Him for years."

The denomination is listed in the Worship Directory as "Interdenominational Charismatic," which downplays denominational divisions while focusing on the extraordinary works—"charisma" means "gifts" in Greek—faith can bestow. Such gifts may include spontaneous healing and impulsive displays of joy. Perhaps that's the legacy the hippie culture left here. The name of the church alludes to the burning conviction in such works; it's called something like "Vibrant Belief."

I've always looked up at the hill and the building towering on it, so standing in front of the church looking out offers an entirely new perspective. From here the sky is wide, and I can see a big chunk of town, including the Arby's just down the road. The atrium of the building reminds me of an office building or hotel. I pick up the program and a brochure that shows a faint image of a guitar superimposed over a shot of the hills that surround town. A young man standing at the door sees me studying the brochure and explains that the church pays a fee for the rights to use an entire catalogue of Christian rock songs.

The sanctuary is enormous, designed to seat hundreds, though it's only half full. The stadium seating and my spot toward the back gives me an excellent view of the stage and all the rows in front of me. The band opens with a medley of Christian rock songs: "I Surrender to You" blends with "Count Me In" and "Take my Life." Some of the younger audience members rush to the stage and dance in the aisles. They sway and hop. One overweight fellow bounds and twists as his pants lose their hold on his ample backside. A row of sorority girls look on, exchanging glances, their eyes growing wider with his every leap, sucking the straws in their frappuccinos to keep from snickering.

A man's voice booms from the loud speakers, authoritative and deep. I look around to identify its source. It takes me a moment to realize it's meant to be the voice of God. We are his children, and he commands us to love one another. I created the cosmos and the earth, God bellows. Video screens display hundreds of points of light that fade in and out, like fireflies or stars being passed at high velocity. I start to feel a little nervous tingle in my toes, a panicky sensation caused by this unexpected reenactment of hurling through the cosmos.

The microphone is being passed through the congregation. It stops on a woman who says into it very seriously, "I sense someone is experiencing blurry vision." I squint to check one eye and then the other. An arm raises in the front and everyone around that person places a hand on or near her; the rest of the congregation reaches their hands in her direction. For a moment, the audience looks like a big sea anemone reaching for a floating morsel. The microphone moves again, and another lady says, "I have a feeling of a stiff neck." I pull my shoulders down and stretch my head in both directions as someone else claims the ailment and the tendrils stretch in that direction. Even though I wasn't the one healed, my eyesight feels crisper, my neck looser. When the healing session is over, I see an older gentleman with a mop of white hair leaving an audio booth to the side of the stage. "That must be God," I think to myself.

After his brief sermon, the minister introduces a video on the installation of a new digital display board. I noticed it at the street corner, a wide monitor on the top of a pole with freshly moved earth around its base. The video shows the sign going up in time lapse. Everyone applauds at the freeze-frame of the finished product. This morning it flashed a screen saying the time service started and another with the words "Everyone's invited!" The new sign draws focus to a sight more welcoming than the hard edges of the building and hillside—though something about it feels a bit like powdering the nose of an aging star who has lost the bloom of youth. Not that she isn't lovely or can't be great in the right role, but first she has to accept that time has marched on. Otherwise it's just uncomfortable watching her.

o

I find the website for "the Buzz" and send a message to the head minister, Jackson, asking if he'll meet me. I'm still thinking about the sermon he gave, which was not at all what I expected. With all those young people in expensive denim as his audience, I imagined he'd talk about something generically positive like the power of love or manifesting abundance. Instead he gave a detailed lecture about Nehemiah, a lesser-known character in the Old Testament. I knew nothing about this guy who rebuilt the destroyed walls of Jerusalem hundreds of years before the birth of Jesus. Nehemiah had never even been to Jerusalem or seen the destroyed walls before he sets out on his life's mission. He was an unlikely candidate for the job. He was working as one of the king's servants miles away when he asked permission to go. The Old Testament seriousness made a surprising juxtaposition with the rock hymns and hands raised in praise.

I also realize I have no idea what denomination the Buzz is, or if it even has one. No mention is made of it on the website or in any of the literature from my visit. I go back and scour the Worship Directory, but the church's name isn't listed. I search the phone book, where all the churches are arranged by denomination, but don't see it there either. It's managed to fly completely under the radar. Its prospective congregants must learn about it by word of mouth only. Come to think of it, that's how I first heard of it. A teenage daughter of a friend of mine said I should check it out.

Jackson agrees to meet me at a coffee shop a few weeks after the semester ends. The girls working behind the counter know him by name. Others in the café say hello. Suddenly I feel like I'm meeting a member of Jesus's entourage. Maybe Jackson will be the next superstar preacher like Joel Osteen. He certainly has the camera-ready looks: friendly blue eyes and a full head of sandy blond hair with just a touch of grey starting at the temples. Maybe he'll head up a popular megachurch like Saddleback in California, providing sermons to hundreds of thousands both in person and online. Or he'll write a Jesus-centric best-seller like Rick Warren's *The Purpose Driven Life*.

Jackson and I face each other in two cushiony chairs. We are roughly the same age, and his easygoing and open demeanor makes him feel familiar. Although I suspect that his interpretation of the Bible gives him much in common with many fundamentalists, he seems less inclined to make points of contention his focus. It's an approach I appreciate, though it worries me that I'm being lolled into a false sense of nonjudgment.

I have my notebook on my knees, ready to take notes, but Jackson asks me to speak first. I tell him a little about my background: that I'm a None who's been attending church for more than a year now.

"What stood out most about your visit to my church?" he asks.

"The young, good-looking crowd," I say. I realize that's probably not the answer he was looking for but it's the truth, and I'm relieved when he laughs. Apparently this has posed some challenges. Before starting his talk on Nehemiah, he mentioned his previous sermon series had addressed the topic of love and dating. He briefly reiterated that while romantic relationships are healthy and good, it shouldn't be the motivation for coming to church. Once he said that, I had to admit I was picking up a certain vibe I'd never considered: Jesus as sex symbol. All the boys want to be like him and the girls want to date him.

I continue, "Besides that, your literature is so . . ." I search for the best way to describe the difference between the fliers and leaflets at the Buzz versus those from other churches. I was struck by how artfully they are put together. It wasn't just that the church has its own logo, it was how the text and the graphics were presented in fresh fonts and interesting colors with just the right amount of white space to make it all pop. Other churches cram black words on a white page. In fact, it's the quality of their materials that made me think they must be backed by an organization with deep pockets. "Professional," I decide.

He explains that one staff member has a background in design. It seems almost a requirement these days if you want to start a church: minister and graphic designer. People who have grown up since the seventies have such a keen eye. Almost no aspect of our lives isn't tastefully presented, from websites to wine labels. Today's average Joe is a sharp-sighted consumer—of Christianity and anything else.

But it's more than just aesthetics. So much information is available to us, both visual and factual. We need it filtered and arranged, and we reward those who do this well. Because we want the main point, but we also want the option for more. We've grown accustomed to the way the Internet works: stay with the headline and synopsis or click to go deeper. We decide.

It's a new way of navigating in the world, one that can permeate even the smallest tasks. Like singing. At the Buzz, the band played one of the same Christian rock songs I'd heard elsewhere, "Your Love Never Fails," but in a slightly different way. They branched out to more complicated verses, which those who knew the words could sing, but they repeated the lines of the chorus—"Your Love never fails / Your love never changes / You stay the same through the ages"—so many times that everyone could sing along. The band kept returning to the simple chorus, all of us singing it over and over, in a seemingly endless, comforting loop.

I'm surprised when he tells me that officially the Buzz is Baptist. After seminary, he was struck by polls showing the abundance of Nones in the Pacific Northwest and, with the financial backing of a national

Baptist organization, relocated here. He worked as the youth minister at a local Baptist church before striking out on his own about five years ago. Today the ties to the national organization have loosened. It pays only a part of his salary, and each of the eighteen or so people on his staff is responsible for securing his or her own funding, which comes from multiple sources. In the church he created, I see the influences of many incarnations of Christianity that came before: a serving of Jesus movement, a dash of fundamentalism, a side of Pentecostal exuberance—all served on a bed of mainstream Protestantism.

o

Our conversation turns to the less material. "I'm trying to better understand spirituality," I tell him. I'm surprised to hear myself admit this out loud, much less to someone I hardly know. Before I started this endeavor, I thought of spirituality like I think of ghosts—a phenomenon somewhere between fun and frightening but of which I have no firsthand experience. When I imagined what it might be, I always pictured a Native American dream catcher swaying in the breeze.

"What does that mean to you?" he asks.

How to put it into words? I rarely have this kind of conversation. My None friends and I—we lack the language. When we attempt to talk about these issues we turn into frustrated apes; we thump our chests and open our hands to the sky.

I know the official Christian answer would go something like "accepting Jesus as my personal savior," but I'm not exactly sure what that means. I tell him, "I think it's being more like Jesus . . . like how he was day to day." I feel as wobbly as a fawn taking his first few steps. "Jesus was aware of ordinary life and responsibilities, but he always kept something bigger in mind . . . an awareness that he'd be gone someday too, and an okay-ness with it that made the everyday more precious. It's the awareness and the okay-ness . . ." I catch Jackson looking at me in a way that suggests I'm either saying something profound or profoundly incomprehensible. Spirituality is difficult to talk about because it's the part of life that lacks solid form. I think that's one of the benefits of Jesus—he brought an abstract God to flesh; he gave shape to these hard-to-articulate ideas.

I want to keep going because it feels good trying to put words to this stuff even if I'm not good at it. I need to say something about compassion because I know that's a big piece of the spirituality puzzle, and the okay-ness is key because if we can be okay with the being here and the leaving, then we might even be able to love—ourselves and whatever force gives rise to us and then snatches us away. Guilt and fear make us act horribly to ourselves and others. I think back to the atheist slogan about being good without God. I had thought I didn't need help with that because I interpreted the goodness they were referring to as not breaking laws or making the right choices morally and ethically. But maybe it refers to something much more subtle: learning to be good to ourselves and others, gentle and kind, accepting of our own and each other's foibles. The okay-ness is the root of this love, which we can only extend to others if we first possess it ourselves. I have all this and more on the tip of my tongue, but it dissolves into a sweet puddle like a clump of cotton candy.

We talk for almost two hours, sometimes like inhabitants of different planets meeting for the first time and then suddenly like old friends who've never been apart. He confides that he and the other leaders of the Buzz have agreed they don't want to own a building. He says, "You put all this money and energy into getting this building and then . . ." I nod, understanding exactly what he's getting at. The Buzz just moved to an auditorium across town that accommodates more people than the previous event center. They were able to up and go like a tumbleweed. But if they owned a building, they wouldn't be able to adapt so easily. They'd be the church at Second and Main or Fifth and Elm; they'd be the church with a cavernous space or a square space or a small space or a round space. People think the building is the church, but it's not. The church is the people inside. The relationships. The ideas. The voices combined in song.

As a former servant, Nehemiah may have been an unlikely person to oversee the rebuilding of the walls to a holy city, but he was engaged in an unlikely job. His efforts weren't focused on the most obvious target: the Temple, which had also been wrecked. His idea of sacred space was much broader. It encompassed the areas where everyday life took place. Today, it might include the grocery store, the post office, or Main Street. Perhaps, too, it is the cyberspaces we occupy: Facebook, websites, and blogs. Nehemiah seemed to understand how everything that surrounds and supports the inner life is also worthy of attention and protection.

The Temple may not have been the only thing worth salvaging, but for many it was still the most important. A physical location for worship or prayer—a designated place where people gather to commune with each other and acknowledge something greater—remains a powerful draw. It seems the effort to build and maintain these structures, as energy-depleting as it may be, continues to be worth it. Even if we are only on the outside, driving past on our way to the grocery store, they remind us of life's less-material aspects.

Those buildings have spoken to me my whole life. Not one in particular, but each whispering as I passed, "Why don't you come inside?"

"Is Christianity changing?" I ask Jackson.

"No, but we are," he says.

I nod. Almost everything has changed since the first Protestant settlers came here: our cities, our houses, our transportation. Our tastes in music and fashion. How we navigate in space, how we take in information. All these broad shifts that influence the way we think and act. Not to mention the countless incremental and personal changes that occur over each of our lifetimes. Just in these last several months, I've changed. Who would have thought I would have engaged in this epic churchgoing experiment? Not I, and certainly not anyone who knew me. The mention of God used to make me uneasy because I thought it had to be a very specific thing.

Critics may claim that a particular generation or population group is more spiritually complacent or less curious, but they don't know what's going on in our hearts and minds. Because despite all the changes, something fundamental stays the same. It's what makes our need for the tools religion offers as vital today as ever. Each of us struggling to come to grips with being here on earth, and with the knowledge that we will leave—as if these realizations are a fresh new thing just added to the human experience. Christianity reminds us that people have been grappling with them for hundreds of generations.

We can be told what the problem is and how to deal with it, but being told a thing takes us only so far. It's like the mustard seed: all that potential sits in us, but what matters is the process, the expansion, the opening. We have to engage in it, put in the effort to make sense of it for ourselves. That's the main point Luther was making. Each of us must wrestle with the fear and guilt ourselves, and reach beyond for joy. It isn't the kind of thing where you hand over the reins to another entity—whether a dynamic leader or an organization. To do so is to defeat the purpose.

No one church has changed me, no one sermon. But the act of going, of entering places of worship, is changing me. As I cross each threshold, I turn fear into the strength to take one more step. I feel my heart softening to people I had dismissed, opening to ideas I once ridiculed. When I show up and come elbow to elbow with others who have showed up, the chances are I'll have a moment, however brief or fleeting, where the truth strikes me as so incredibly real—and it won't feel overwhelming or like something I can't handle, but poignant and profound.

One point Jackson made in his sermon about Nehemiah stood out for me. In the first moments after learning about the destroyed walls, Nehemiah is overcome with grief and begins to weep. Jackson paused and asked everyone to think about that, how painfully raw Nehemiah's emotions were, suddenly. The ancient servant's wave of anguish rises up and recedes, and then he makes his plans. A flicker of understanding visited me. I saw that every fresh recognition of the sources of our suffering is the huff and puff of gaining elevation on a mountain climb. Because it's the facing it, the working through it, the accepting it, that gets us closer to the top where true compassion resides.

Judaism

It's six forty-five p.m. on a Wednesday in late September. Summer officially ended last week, and even with Daylight Saving Time still in effect, the day-to-night ratio is leaning toward darkness. Scant vestiges of sun remain as I park on the street, making the light from the Unitarian church seem extra bright. I can see the silhouettes of people entering the front door and moving through the sanctuary. This church was an early stop on my excursion through Christianity, and now it launches the journey's Judaism leg. Normally the individuals who gather to worship in a Unitarian Universalist church are well outside the Christian mainstream; they tend to be well educated, liberal, and skeptical of traditional theological principles such as Jesus's divinity, the Trinity, and any sort of exclusive salvation. I suppose theirs is a marriage of Christian hearts with questioning minds. Their ranks have included some of the most beloved Americans of all time, including Thomas Jefferson, Susan B. Anthony, and Mark Twain.

Tonight the people gathering are even farther outside the Christian mainstream; they are, in fact, Jews. With the closest synagogue over seventy miles away, the Unitarians are graciously lending their space to the members of the local Jewish community to kick off the "high holidays," which include Rosh Hashanah and—ten days later—Yom Kippur, the holiest day in the Jewish calendar. Many within the larger Christian community might argue that Unitarians are not technically Christian. Regardless, I think it's safe to assume that Unitarians hold Jesus and his teachings in the highest esteem—and this they share with Jews.

Rosh Hashanah marks the start of a new year. It commemorates the biblical "day" when God completed the creation of the world. Many synagogues conclude their annual reading of the Hebrew Bible, the Torah, at this time and then proceed to start over again at Genesis. It marks an end and a new beginning. Something about the timing of this calendar rings true. I have no problem accepting a spiritual starting point that coincides with the onset of fall. Emotionally, it feels natural to me.

Days of Awe

I'm carrying a Tupperware of sliced apples with a little tub of caramel dipping sauce. I read that eating something sugary on Rosh Hashanah invites the rest of the year to be sweet. It is customary to enjoy treats like apples and plums from an early fall harvest or goodies left from summer like figs and dates. Before the days of refined cane juice, these fruits would be drizzled with honey, if it was available. I think the idea is to push the palate toward pleasure in hopes that in the darkest months the heart will remember this joy—even as the taste buds forget.

Inside the church's foyer, a man directs me to the basement, where I can set down my treats before joining the others in the sanctuary. Not long ago I descended this same narrow staircase for the post-Sunday service fellowship. I drank coffee from a Styrofoam cup as I chatted with a couple of friendly retired academics. Back then I was still under the impression that Christianity and Judaism were polar extremes—as if religions could have opposites. I hadn't yet grasped how closely the two are related and the strange mix of resentment and dependence bred by this kinship.

Tonight, two long folding tables are set up in the middle of the room, forming a capital letter T. The Jews have pulled out the stops: tins of dried fruit, piles of homemade cookies, fancy boxes of chocolates, and jars of honey. My mouth waters as I add my apples and head upstairs for the official ceremony.

On my way into the sanctuary, I pick up a book from a stack along with a supplemental photocopied sheet. I was told in advance that tonight's Jewish service would be led by a community elder in lieu of an actual rabbi. Except for the yarmulkes on the heads of many of the congregants, the room looks just as it did the last time I was here. A yarmulke, or *kippah*, is the little round skullcap often worn by Jews as a sign of respect to God above. Across the room I spy one of the amply bearded gentlemen from the Quaker service I attended several months earlier; here he is paired with a woman and dons a tie-dyed yarmulke.

Traditionally, yarmulkes are worn by men. Today, a few women wear them too, and several of the designs are surprisingly playful. A few rows ahead of me, a woman has one that appears very elaborate. Each quadrant of her cap sports an intricately hand-painted Teletubby, the popular cartoon characters that resemble chubby baby aliens.

I open my prayer book to have a look inside only to realize it's upside down. Hebrew is printed right to left instead of the usual left to right, so Jewish books, even when written in English, generally open in the opposite direction from those I'm used to. I flip it over: *On Wings of Awe*, a prayer book for Rosh Hashanah and Yom Kippur. What is normally the last page is the first page, and I think briefly how this would make a good metaphor for Judaism vis-à-vis Christianity: everything's wrong side up and backward! Only the relationship between the two is far more nuanced than that, and the way books are used in Judaism is such an elementary fact that my finding it surprising speaks more to a very personal ignorance than to any universal truths. For someone married to a Jew, who came of age surrounded by Jews, it's astounding how little I know. I would probably be paralyzed with embarrassment if it weren't for the fact that my lack of knowledge has found fierce competition with Phil's.

Case in point: Phil and I inherited a menorah from his family. It's the kind where each of the wicks feeds into a common basin of oil. When we were first married, I made a special trip to the hardware store for the right lamp oil and tiny funnel to pour it into the menorah's small opening. I went online to read about the lighting of the Hanukkah candles, but I skimmed the entry thinking Phil would know the specifics. When he was growing up, his family celebrated both Christmas and Hanukkah.

A day or two into our first Hanukkah, I realized it was time to pull out the menorah. "How do we do it?" I asked Phil. I had a lighter at the ready.

"I have no idea," he said.

"You're joking," I insisted. I had always assumed Phil knew more than he was letting on, that he was feigning Judaism amnesia.

"My dad always lit it."

"You really have no clue?"

He was dead serious. "None."

We were both hovering over the menorah. Just because neither of us knew what we were doing didn't mean we weren't going to light the thing. I tried to recall the rules from my brief Internet search: was it right to left, or left to right, and how many days exactly into the holiday were we?

Phil was getting impatient. "Just do it."

"Fine," I said. I held my lighter to each wick, creating a little Hanukkah inferno. After several minutes the wicks sucked up all the fuel and the flames died out. "Happy Hanukkah!" we cried, batting at the smoke.

o

This brings up the excellent question of what exactly I am trying to grasp as I attempt to understand Judaism. Pick up a "how-to" guide on being Jewish and encounter a collection of very specific mandates. It seems, at first blush, less a religion and more a list of rules. There are exact words to utter upon rising from bed in the morning, the precise blessing to say depending on what foods a meal includes, and prayers to be spoken at various sites—including what to declare should one happen to lay eyes on a rainbow.

Almost no aspect of an observant Jew's day is free from guidelines. These are not just the broad strokes I encountered on my journey into Christianity, like the orders to refrain from adultery and murder. Even though the Christian Old Testament is basically the same book as the Jewish Torah, Jews approach their holy book differently. An observant Jew will try to adhere to all the instructions contained within its pages.

In addition to the Ten Commandments, the Torah spells out 613 dos and don'ts—and from these, Jewish sages have spun additional mandates to promote adherence to the original 613. These are included in two supplemental guides: the Talmud and its modern companion, the Midrash. Take, for example, the biblical instruction "You shall not boil a kid in its mother's milk" (Deuteronomy 14:21). This simple commandment about how not to prepare a young goat for consumption has spawned instructions about never letting any dairy product come into contact with meat of any kind—and not just during the cooking process. Meat and dairy are never to occupy the same space in a bowl, mouth, or belly. Even a basin that washes the utensils used to prepare a recipe with one should not be used to clean the utensils used for the other.

The guidelines are so detailed that they require Jews to wait between three and six hours after consuming meat before eating an item containing dairy. However, if the dairy product is eaten first, one may reduce this waiting time to a maximum of four hours because dairy-based items tend to be softer and more easily cleared from a person's system. Unless, of course, the dairy was a particularly hard cheese—a piece of which may have gotten lodged between the teeth. In that case, sages have determined one should wait the full six hours—just to be on the safe side. All told, it's quite a bit of instruction generated from a brief line in the Bible, a comment that some contemporary scholars suggest may have been meant as a metaphor for a larger point about the ethical treatment of animals—even those intended for food.

All of which makes lighting the Hanukkah candles seem like child's play.

For weeks I pored over books trying to take in every letter of Bible-based law. I was in a state of wonder at both the breadth and specificity. I could never comprehend all the instructions, much less abide by them.

Had I set myself an impossible task?

I would never absorb all the rules and know the meaning and timing of every Jewish prayer. How could I? Rabbinical students spend years hammering out this stuff, and these are usually kids who grew up in observant households. I realized that if I wanted to explore Judaism, I had no choice but to loosen my grip. I would need to let the Hebrew flow without my understanding every single word—or even any of the words. Maybe I could hum along, or utter a syllable or two of a phonetic translation, or skim the English version if one was provided.

As I got farther along in this portion of the journey, with more experience under my belt, I began to see that not understanding every word is the norm—especially for English-speaking Jews. Many have learned just enough Hebrew to say the necessary prayers; others have learned by ear and through repetition. The extent to which individual Jews are familiar with or follow "the rules" varies widely. Labels indicate how closely a particular group chooses to observe the stable of rules: the "ultra-orthodox" and "orthodox" stick as closely as possible to the law, while "conservative" and "reform" have eliminated many traditional requirements.

Still, even the most observant among them can't adhere perfectly. In fact, the sages and wise men have developed another set of guidelines for how to make things right when the inevitable mess-up occurs (such as how to "purify" a utensil intended for dairy that may have accidentally encountered meat).

When I began to grasp the meaning behind the rules and prayers, I had to laugh at my earlier notions. I thought the actions and words were like scientific formulas—conduct them perfectly and unlock the mystery of being Jewish. I wanted to say the exact words the observant utter every morning, afternoon, and evening. In Hebrew these lines sound so complicated, so unattainable; I thought if I didn't say them, Judaism would remain shrouded in mystery. Eventually I learned what the words meant and began to grasp the simple sentiments they convey. The prayer before eating bread? It translates as: "Blessed art Thou, Lord our God, King of the universe who brings forth bread from the earth." The prayer one says upon seeing a natural wonder such as a rainbow or waterfall? It goes: "Blessed art Thou, Lord our God, King of the universe who has such as these in His world." Specifically, the prayers may offer a brief thank you or a plea or an apology—but they never stray too far from a simple expression of gratitude. The intention of the rules and the words is to honor God by demonstrating an appreciation for life and all that sustains it. They encourage Jews to stop and take notice.

An observant Jew might tell you the point of all the ritual is to remind him or herself, again and again, of the wonder of creation. But even then, he or she will probably fail at times to muster feelings of thankfulness. Luckily, an observant Jew has many do-overs throughout the day. Because the goal is not so much the flawless performance of whatever act is required as the joyful appreciation it is meant to cultivate.

So even if Phil and I botched the lighting of the Hanukkah candles, what mattered most is that we recognized the flames as a sign of hope.

o

Perhaps no time of year gets closer to the true meaning of being a Jew than Rosh Hashanah and Yom Kippur; together, they are sometimes called "Days of Awe." Synagogues that seem to have a paltry number of congregants the rest of the year suddenly burst at the seams on these two days, when every member appears at once. One synagogue I visited rents a nearby auditorium for those days, with reserved seating available months in advance.

The two holy days are like bookends that prop up a time of intense soul-searching between them. The Torah calls Rosh Hashanah the "Day of Remembrance." Jews are required to carefully review their actions over the previous twelve months, searching their memories for instances in which they have wronged any person perhaps by being less than kind or unfairly judgmental.

It's like God is the great videographer who has every moment recorded and now you have to review the footage without pretense. There's no fooling God, no making excuses for your behavior, no dodging responsibility. These days of introspection culminate in Yom Kippur, or the "Day of Atonement," when God grants forgiveness to anyone who sincerely seeks it; however, no effort is considered sincere unless the person has also sought forgiveness from the people he or she may have wronged. According to rabbinic maxim, before man can make his peace with God, he must make his peace with his fellow man.

The first night of my first Rosh Hashanah at the Unitarian church felt mostly celebratory, but with a whisper of something more melancholy. Though I could understand only the English portion of prayers and readings thanking God and acknowledging the wonder of creation, I easily detected a somber note in the expressions of gratitude. I spied a wistfulness in the eyes of my fellow worshippers as we wished each other *shana tova*, or "good year," and sampled from the table of confections. The flavors dissolved in my mouth like memories that fade into a sweet nostalgia.

The following day, those of us who were able met again—this time at an interfaith house on campus. Twenty or so from the night before moved the chairs into a circle. A teenager opened a box and pulled out a squat twisted horn, a shofar, which is a ram's stubby antler. As tradition dictates, he blew into it over and over again, creating a noise like an agonized primal cry, something akin to the sound Edvard Munch's famous painting *The Scream* would make if the central figure were suddenly audible. Some say this is precisely the point of listening to shofar blasts on this day—they mimic the inarticulate shriek of our souls as we shine the spotlight of truth on them.

If I had been sticking strictly to custom, the afternoon of Rosh Hashanah, when the shofar blasts were fresh in my mind, I would have made my way to a natural body of water to perform the ritual of *tashlikh*. This is the symbolic casting away of one's sins from the previous year. Many Jews who live near the coast will go to the sea and toss bread crumbs or pebbles, items representing their misdeeds, into the waves. Whatever water you choose is supposed to have fish in it as little witnesses. It seems to me that once the tidbits hit the water, you would lose track of them quickly, and that knowing how rapidly they will be consumed by the vast ocean and the fish it contains somehow makes the sin-digging process more palatable and less overwhelming. Since I am hours from the coast, I thought about approximating this act in the nearest natural body of water to me, which is a creek that flows through the center of town. This being my first Rosh Hashanah, I had many more months to review for sins besides the previous twelve; I would need an entire loaf of bread, perhaps several.

I imagined hauling a satchel of croutons to the small bridge downtown. Theoretically, the sins dumped there would eventually run into the ocean, but I shuddered at the thought of that heap lingering; Rosh Hashanah comes at a dry time of year when the water is low and slow. I decided to hold off: I needed additional time to review my past, perhaps to narrow my catalogue of sins or to find a body of water where the sin-to-H_2O ratio would be more favorable.

As I left the interfaith house on Rosh Hashanah afternoon with the haunting sound of the shofar echoing in my mind, I recalled a comment I had read by Maimonides, the famous Torah scholar from the Middle Ages. He said the sound of the shofar tells us, "Awake, ye sleepers from your sleep . . . and ponder over your deeds."

o

During my months of Christian churchgoing, I came to think of a sin as something a person did, an act perpetrated despite the knowledge that every aspect of nature, including all of humanity and even one's self, is an integral part of a greater whole. I understood a sin to be a deed of destruction, something I do (knowingly or not) to chip away at my own—or anyone else's—ability to thrive. It wasn't until I experienced the Jewish New Year of Rosh Hashanah that I began to grasp how a sin may also be the opposite of this: a thing I've failed to do. It could be not reaching out to, or even noticing, a person in need. It might be as subtle as being too preoccupied to properly appreciate the natural beauty around me. While these two versions of sin seem different, they actually stem from the same source: a failure to grant an element of creation the care and honor it deserves.

At the Rosh Hashanah service at the Unitarian church, one of the prayers we recited together in English centered on the theme of listening. Written by contemporary rabbi Jack Reimer, it included the lines "we hear the voices of our friends—or our neighbors . . . our family . . . our children—but we do not appreciate their sounds of urgency: 'Notice me . . . help me . . . care about me.' We hear—but do we really listen?" As I mulled over these words, I felt my heart grow heavy. For days they followed me around like the ghosts of my past.

Before the sun set on Rosh Hashanah, I knew where my journey to make amends would take me: Los Angeles, the city I had arrived in after almost starving myself to death in Dallas. On the cusp of my teenage years, as my mom and I moved around Dallas, I turned all the negative feelings swirling inside my gut into a silent rage directed at myself. I stopped eating. I suppose it was my own version of religious fasting: I was honoring suffering by actively participating in it. At first it felt like a special project to work on and think about endlessly. I gradually reduced my food intake, making mental notes of each bite that passed my lips until my daily sustenance was down to a few mouthfuls, the majority of which I consumed at dinner to throw any detectives off my trail. The results were rapid and marvelous. Every night, I would lift my shirt and inspect my belly. Over the course of about six months it collapsed into a bowl. But the thrill of my achievement was replaced by lethargy and exhaustion. I was too hungry to sleep through the night. Soon I wasn't able to hide that I was a hot mess; my protruding bones and lifeless eyes spoke for me. My mom agreed that I needed a drastic change of scenery and that maybe living with my father in Los Angeles would do me good. My dad and I had since reestablished contact and had caught up over a series of visits. He agreed to have me and, like millions of migrants before me, I moved west.

I came to L.A. as a soul-sick preteen who rarely smiled, and by the time I left for college, I was mostly a different person, much stronger physically and emotionally. I sometimes wonder what would have happened to me if I hadn't made that move. I know everyone has at least one event in his or her life that divides time into "before" and "after." For me it was going to L.A., which I didn't experience so much as a physical move from one state to another but as a spiritual move from darkness to light.

Looking back, I credit my healing in no small part to Judaism. Not because I went to synagogue or even understood what Judaism was but because my new environment was steeped in it. For junior high and high school, I attended a small private school that was roughly 70 percent Jewish. A freethinking educator named Shirley had started the school in her living room. When I enrolled in the 1980s, it had just moved into a new building not far from my house. Of my four best friends at school—Nina, Deb, Becky, and Lisa—all but Becky were Jewish, though their families were not particularly observant. Still, I've come to understand the ways my friends and classmates were Jewish deep down, back countless generations, and how their way of being in the world rubbed off on me.

I began that school in seventh grade, just as my classmates were turning thirteen, and my weekends were filled with a series of bar and bat mitzvahs. The mood of these events was the antithesis of what was going on in my head. I had grown accustomed to feeling deep currents of shame—somewhere, beneath the surface, I was not convinced I deserved the life I had been granted and I was toying with destroying it. Yet here, under balloon arches and atop temporary dance floors, families were conducting joyous celebrations of the lives of my peers. Next to these events, regular birthday parties suddenly looked to me like half-hearted nods honoring the passage of time rather than a person's having come into being. This was of a different magnitude altogether, starting with the guest list that seemed to include every person who had ever known the celebrant, including God. The event itself would begin in the sanctuary of a synagogue with my classmate being asked to stand with the rabbi and read from fancy scrolls.

I remember always being impressed by seeing my friend in this new context, speaking a different language amid grown-ups. Until then I had known the person only as a regular kid like me, but this hint of a multilayered backstory revealed a more complex individual and my respect never failed to increase. From the sanctuary we would move to a second location, often another room in the synagogue or someone's house. Here, the seriousness gave way to sheer fun: burrito bars and sundae stations and everyone from oldest to youngest shuffling and twirling to Cyndi Lauper and Depeche Mode. Looking back, I marvel at how this one-time extravaganza seemed to come just as a young person might need it most, injecting a shot of pure joy into the life of not just the celebrant but everyone in his or her circle. Today I understand the symbolic significance of the bar and bat mitzvah as the official introduction of a young person as a mature Jew, but I also sense how in a modern context it might not herald an actual arrival into adulthood so much as offer sustenance for those last difficult years leading to it, creating a memory that shines like a light at the end of a tunnel.

This life-affirming rite of passage is born of the most basic notion in Judaism, the idea of being "chosen." To be a Jew is to understand that your life is a purposeful creation, that you have been selected by God to exist. The belief that one's being on the planet is intentional lends meaning to all aspects of the struggle; each day and experience, whether painful or joyous, is significant. From what I can tell, it's this notion—the belief in being "chosen"—more than any other that seems to rub non-Jews the wrong way. The problem, I think, is one of misunderstanding: "I am here on purpose" gets interpreted as "God favors me above you." Or maybe they understand perfectly well, but the willingness to embrace such an optimistic claim runs counter to every fiber in their beings. Some say Jews intended this belief to be embraced by all of humanity, which is why Genesis starts with one man and one woman, both intentionally brought forth, from which all people descend. It is so radical a notion, perhaps the boldest idea ever invented, and certainly the source of other positive ideas like love and gratitude.

The Jews I grew up with didn't go around talking about being "chosen." They never once made reference to it or acted like they were better than anyone else. Yet something subtle that I couldn't quite put my finger on was different about how they existed in the world. They didn't seem uncertain like I was about whether they deserved to be here. They may have had a host of other insecurities, but that most basic and foundational one didn't appear to be among them. They took up their little bit of space in this world with a confidence I hadn't realized was possible. During my teen years, I remained tentative, the chip on my shoulder firmly in place, but my proximity to an alternative was a powerful antidote, and it was just enough get me through.

For all the good my time in L.A. did me, and for how much I appreciated my school and my friends, once I left I rarely returned. My mom and the rest of my family lived in Texas and when I visited "home," I went there. My constant moving made staying in touch with anyone from my past challenging, and over the years the lines of communication between me and my L.A. gang slowly unraveled. I kept in sporadic contact with one friend, Lisa, who acted as a sort of a lifeline to the others. In the time since I had last seen them, they had endured the usual hardships twenty years in any life brings, including the death of parents. Of all my friends, Nina seemed to have had more than her fair share of pain—her would-be fiancé was killed in an auto accident not long after her mom's sudden passing. I had not offered a phone call or even an e-mail of condolence. What kind of friend was I? What kind of person? I had heard them calling out to me, but had I listened?

o

When you haven't eaten all day and you are dressed like a corpse, somehow it is easier to accept where you've gone wrong. Ten days after Rosh Hashanah is the "Day of Atonement," or Yom Kippur. On Yom Kippur the custom is to refrain from all food and drink for a period of twenty-five hours. If you really want to go all out, avoid bathing and dress in white to mimic traditional burial garb. It's also best not to wear shoes, though sages have defined shoes as any footwear made of leather; plastic flip-flops or rubber sandals are permitted. It's fascinating how all these elements work together to send your body a powerful message: you are not the boss. It's not that twenty-five hours is all that long to go without any one of these creature comforts, but in totality their denial gives your system a shock.

The sages created a list of forty-four sins called Al Chet, which observant Jews recite ten times over the course of Yom Kippur in an effort to seek forgiveness. They range from the old-timey sounding ("casting off the yoke") to others that never go out of style ("passing judgment"). Some Jews also create personalized lists. They say their lists out loud because publicly admitting one's sins is a key component of this ritual. The first public admission is supposed to occur before Yom Kippur even starts, just prior to the meal that will sustain you before fasting begins at sunset. The timing of this first confession is intentional: if you choke and keel over during the meal, at least you had a chance to confess. That evening I was thinking about my L.A. friends and the important events in their lives I had missed. Before Phil and I began eating, I announced, "I just want to say I feel terrible for not being there for my friends in Los Angeles. I have failed and I hope to be forgiven." I suppose this statement appeared apropos of nothing, and he looked at me like a ventriloquist's hand was shoved up my back.

Back at the Unitarian church for the service the next day, I repeated my confession quietly to myself. With my heavy heart and tired body, I did not feel like attempting polite conversation. I snuck in and sat at the back. The community elder who had led the previous service was once again in charge. He said, "This reminds me of my criminal procedure class. No one wants to sit in the front two rows." Everyone laughed, but I did not detect the celebratory mood of Rosh Hashanah. Now I understood it wasn't just me—today we were all wary, each of us a felon in need of forgiveness.

In English we read aloud an alternative, contemporary Al Chet provided on photocopy. We asked forgiveness for not doing enough "to help the poor," "to protect our earth, air, and water," and "to stop violence and war." We also admitted to "remaining silent or indifferent in the face of discrimination, mockery, and offensive humor." Of course I was guilty of these as well. Next to these ills, my sin seemed ridiculously small. Yet I could also see how they were related. They were based on the assumption that I didn't matter all that much—so what if I hardly spoke out or if I disappeared from the lives of people I loved?

The official name for what Jews practice at this time is *teshuvah*, which is Hebrew for "repentance." It's built on the word *shuvah*, or "return." They're two sides of the same coin. Even if you don't actually go anywhere, you have to review your past actions, you have to go back to the people you may have wronged. You can't make amends without returning—the proof is in the language.

At the first signs of spring, I packed my car. I would drive to California by myself and stay for about eight weeks. I had two goals: to see my old friends and to attend services at as many synagogues as possible. I kissed my None husband goodbye. Perhaps I would return with some elements of his native Judaism he might embrace. I had three days of driving to speculate about what experiences this trip might bring. Would my friends even want to see me after so many years? Could a non-Jew just saunter into synagogues—especially ultra-orthodox ones—unannounced? At the library I checked out an audio version of *Great Expectations*—on cassette tapes. My car has a tape deck, and I was able to get the librarian to give me an extension on the due date. It was enough hours of story to take up a majority of the trip there with some left for the way back. I hadn't thought about it when I picked it, but as chapter 1 began to play, I reflected on how appropriate the title. Judaism, like Christianity, is built on great expectations. Jews anticipate the arrival of a messiah just as Christians await the return of a messiah. Both religions help instill life with a sense of optimism, a belief that something good is just around the corner. Now I had great expectations of my own.

Temple in Time

We all keep a mental map of the places where we grew up. All these years, "my Los Angeles" has remained preserved by teenage memories. It consists of my old school, two malls, the bowling alley, and the ice-skating rink. Each of my friend's houses is on the map, as is the beach—not so much the sandy part filled with sun worshippers but the boardwalk that runs from Venice to the Santa Monica pier. The bookstore where I worked for three summers in a row is on the boardwalk—and, just a few blocks up, Main Street, with its shops and cafés. Everywhere else where another person might perceive a vibrant city, I saw outskirts and filler. Now and again I would accompany my dad and stepmom to some place downtown or in Hollywood and a new spot would be added to my map—though how it fit with the rest was vague. The house where I lived was the center of the map, like a tack holding everything down.

Now I hoped to superimpose another kind of map on that same space. I had a list of every synagogue within a ten-mile radius of my dad's house, which wasn't the house where I spent my teens. The year I graduated from college, they bought a place a few streets over from the rental, near enough that my teen's-eye view of the city remained unchanged. Several of the synagogues on my list I recognized—in particular, one on the Venice boardwalk and another on my beloved Main Street. I had walked past them hundreds of times, and if I gave them so much as a passing thought, it was to lament the injustice of so unexciting a building daring to interrupt my window shopping. Some synagogues on my list I didn't know existed, yet they were adjacent to landmarks on my map—one near the bowling alley, another a few blocks from the ice-skating rink. Others were located in the blur of city, and I resorted to a street map of West L.A. to put them in context. I realized this venture would most likely render my mental map obsolete by providing a new frame through which to see the city, a spiritual skeleton I hoped to flesh out.

When I left for college, my three-year-old brother Alex wasted no time in taking over my room; our house was two bedrooms, and he had been residing in the dining-room-turned-nursery all his life, so I suppose it was only fair. Now he was grown and out of the house, and

I took over his old bedroom. "Take that!" Some long-dormant aspect of my teen self snapped as I fell back on his bed.

I was staying so long that I actually unpacked.

My dad wandered in and suggested we drive the short distance to Santa Monica. He wanted to search for the concrete slab on which he claims to have helped me write my name back when I first moved to Los Angeles. I had no memory of this event. I couldn't decide what was more surprising: that we had engaged in this subversive bit of bonding or that my dad recalled it.

I knew the sidewalk my dad was referring to because it had tons of names and ran the length of an old apartment building a few doors down from where we had lived. When I first arrived in Los Angeles from Dallas, before we moved to our two-bedroom house in a generic West L.A. neighborhood, we lived for over a year together in a five-hundred-square-foot bungalow in Santa Monica. It was like an outhouse that had sprouted additional rooms as an afterthought. I slept on the sofa. The house was dwarfed on all sides by apartment buildings. We tumbled out the front door like a clown family from a too-small car. I would have felt more self-conscious, but this was a neighborhood of misfits: single moms, eccentric elders, late-night yellers. Perhaps none stranger to me than the family of Hasidic Jews that occupied the apartment complex on the corner, the front yard crammed with old playground equipment and quarantined by a low but sturdy fence. The sidewalk with the names on it ran the length of their complex, a stretch I had traipsed countless times.

Some of the Hasidic boys were my age. I had never seen anything like them. They had tassels on their hips and curls at their ears. In those months, I officially went "boy crazy," and even they were weighed as potential romantic partners. I would see them in the evenings walking in their uniform of tiny suits with the rest of their family: one dad and one mom and a string of siblings from big to small like stairs stepping down. They looked particularly fetching when they topped their outfits off with kid-sized fedoras like old-timey gangsters from a school play.

I jumped at my dad's idea. Of course I wanted to find my name, but I was also curious to see if the Hasidic family still lived there. I hadn't checked on them since high school.

My dad and I walked slowly back and forth in front of the apartment building searching the names and messages. I had one eye on the ground and the other on the building, which looked much the same except the front fence was higher. For all the time I had spent eyeing those kids, I never once spoke to them, nor they to me. Whatever made their world operate was alien from the particulars of mine; it was like we occupied dimensions so distant that any sound I might utter would dissipate before it reached their ears. I had the idea that they might be an optical illusion, a projected image on a screen; if I snuck up and looked behind it, I'd see only dust bunnies and boxes.

Dad and I came to the corner without finding my name and then doubled back again. Had my name been rendered unreadable, washed out by time? Had that slab been replaced? Had my father only imag-ined our rebellious act? At first I was disappointed, but then I decided maybe it wasn't there for a reason. According to Jewish tradition, on Rosh Hashanah the "Book of Judgment" is opened and those who have lived righteously will find their names inscribed in the "Book of Life" while those who have not will be written in the "Book of Death." It's a theme that Christians have galloped away with, often to horrifying effect. When I encountered it at a little Baptist church, the Book of Life was presented as set in stone—your name is either in there or it's not.

In Judaism I find a more flexible interpretation. Besides these two options, there's another place your name can be, and it's where most names are located. For those people who are not all bad or all good, but a mixture of the two, there is the "Book of the Doubtful." Technically the period of reflection and repentance between Rosh Hashanah and Yom Kippur provides the opportunity to have your name reassigned to the Book of Life; more realistically, it's a long-term goal: one hopes to do enough good during one's days on earth that the scales tip in favor of life.

I don't know whether that stretch of sidewalk is an extension of the Book of Life or the Book of Death, but I suspect we didn't find my name because it's located in the Book of the Doubtful. I still have so many amends to make. As my dad and I got back in the car, I spied a Hasidic man standing near the building. I determined then that I would visit the synagogue the residents of this building worship in—the rules about not driving on Sabbath meant it would mostly likely be within walking distance of this spot—and, at the very least, try to find out what happened to our old Hasidic neighbors. As long as I was righting wrongs, this seemed a good one to add to the mix. I hoped our two worlds could finally speak.

o

I was prepared for how this journey would change the way I saw the Los Angeles I knew from my old mental map. To experience the Venice Beach boardwalk from inside an orthodox synagogue that sits at the end of a long line of shops hawking pizza slices, t-shirts, and "medical" marijuana is to never see the boardwalk in quite the same way again. What I did not expect was how it would change my perception of time, and not the epic generational time of the Torah but regular, everyday time: the ordinary hours and days that make up our weeks, months, and years. The most obvious difference is the start of the new day at sunset instead of sunrise. It cuts in half what I previously perceived as a single block of time, a small shift with surprising consequence. Suddenly I have twice the opportunity to acknowledge a new day, two access points where before there was only one. It's the difference between a watermelon and a watermelon sliced open.

But the more meaningful difference is how every week builds toward the Sabbath. I had not realized the significance of the Sabbath, how it beats at the heart of Judaism. I had thought it was equivalent to the Christian Sunday, the day Jews attend worship services at synagogues. As I got further along, I realized there was more to it, though at first I saw only a list of things you aren't supposed to do from sundown on Friday until after sundown on Saturday. On Sabbath, observant Jews can't drive, turn on or off a computer or television or light, write with pen or pencil, buy anything, do laundry, cook, clean, garden, lift or move objects—nothing that is "work." It seemed like a collection of rules so extensive and complicated that it would be more effort adhering to them than whatever toil they were trying to save you from. I wasn't surprised to learn that even the most religious use a myriad of creative loopholes like lights on timers and slow cookers set on Friday morning. Some even have low-tech solutions. One man I met said that growing up as an orthodox Jew his favorite Sabbath activity was playing Scrabble with his siblings and, to keep score, they would dog ear a book. "It's not writing!" he said when I narrowed my gaze at him. I wasn't too shocked to find out he was a lawyer.

It took a while, but I was able to pull my attention away from the activities that are not allowed on Sabbath to those that are encouraged. What's a Jew to do? Say her prayers and go to synagogue—of course. Other than that: read for pleasure, tell stories, play games that don't involve writing, nap, eat food that's been prepared in advance, kick back in a hammock, daydream, take a walk around the neighborhood, eat some more, nap again, contemplate the beauty of creation, be grateful to have one day every week where she is required to set aside the busyness of normal life.

But only after I met Barbara, mother of four and lifetime orthodox Jew (if you don't count the few years in her twenties when she became a practicing Buddhist), did I begin to "get it." We were talking about how she and her family prepare during the week for the Sabbath, the nuts and bolts of chores and errands that must be done in advance to free this chunk of time from other responsibilities. She and her family have the normal weekday obligations—jobs and school—but on top of these, Monday through Thursday is also the time when they grocery shop and clean the house and make food to serve through Saturday night. Friday before sundown, the finishing touches are addressed: the slow cooker is filled with whatever they might want to serve warm, the lights they want on are turned on, and the table is set for the primary meal the family will share on Saturday afternoon when they return from the synagogue. I had heard preparations for Sabbath compared to those you might employ before an honored houseguest arrives. You want all the cooking and cleaning finished in advance so that you can give your visitor undivided attention. But, as Barbara was explaining, I began to see that it was also like preparing for a stay at a remote cabin in the woods. Everything you need during the retreat must be purchased and prepared in advance because once you arrive there's no electricity, no cell-phone reception, no leaving to fetch something you forgot.

My understanding of the significance of Sabbath opened slowly like a rosebud to reveal a more complicated and alluring beauty than I had imagined. We humans think we are in charge of our worlds. We organize, create, build, and sweep up as if we are running the show. Sabbath is about giving up this control, acknowledging we aren't the bosses by surrendering the drive to alter the world in any way. At the same time, it's a celebration of being. It speaks to the fundamental struggles of the Jews. For a people with a history of being enslaved, this day off is a powerful statement of freedom. Slaves can't decide when they'll work and when they won't. Sabbath is an exercise of free will. That Sabbath can be practiced anywhere is vital for a people who spent generations on the move. Unlike temples made of stone, temples built in time are yours no matter where you are. When Jews go to synagogue on Saturdays, it is the Sabbath itself they are celebrating.

The idea of a weekly block of time free from work is a notion that much of the world has embraced, religious and secular alike. The weekend has become so central to how we experience time that it's hard to imagine when it didn't exist. Yet the original intent has been turned inside out: we use our weekends to prepare for the workweek—not vice versa. Laundry, groceries, cleaning—Saturday and even Sunday are opportunities to get chores done so that come Monday we can focus on our jobs or school or whatever it is we really do. Even the most observant Christian family that goes to church regularly does not necessarily use Sundays to suspend the daily grind. Meals will be cooked, laundry will be washed and folded, errands run. Special "family time" may be carved out, but no radical existential statements underlie the day. The Sabbath may have been a potent gift to the world, but we've been running with it so long and so hard that not only have the contents dropped out along the way but we've all but forgotten what was ever in the box.

My second Friday in Los Angeles, before my understanding of Sabbath had unfurled its first petals, I was at a conservative synagogue for the intimate evening service that officially welcomes the Sabbath. In a small room adjacent to the main sanctuary, about fifteen chairs formed a circle around the perimeter. I was one of the first to arrive, and as I waited, I took out my day planner and set it in my lap. I held a pen. The rabbi approached. As he knelt in front of me, my mind began to race with the possible admonishments I was about to receive. I'm not a Jew! I'm dressed like a slut!

"We don't write on the Sabbath," he said, his eyes locked on mine.

I looked at my pen like it was a fork I hadn't realized was so filthy. I let it drop into the gaping mouth of my bag. "Thank you," I said, as if he had just saved me from contracting bubonic plague. I had been mulling over how to recognize the Sabbath given that I needed to drive myself to and from the synagogues I was visiting and, as a guest, I was not in perfect control of my surroundings. The rabbi's reprimand gave me my answer. I could do this: absolutely no writing. No notes, no computer, no writing utensils of any kind. If I wanted to record events or thoughts from Sabbath, I had to wait till after the sunset on Saturday night. It was a small thing, but it invited the spirit of the Sabbath into my life and, from there, I found it so much easier to embrace other aspects of the day.

Eventually I realized how vital it was for me to just relax when I got home from synagogue on Saturday afternoons. At least until sunset, my job was to loll around. One afternoon when I was engaged in this task, my stepmom came into my room. "What are you up to?" she asked. I opened my eyes, realizing I had nodded off while contemplating the row of trees outside my brother's window. "Very important research," I said, wiping the drool from my lips.

o

I remember the baby in a basket, floating down a river. The entire movie about Moses and the Jews leaving Egypt en masse and receiving the Ten Commandments, and all I remember is that tiny floating baby. I was about eight when it was set to air. I was staying the night with my mom's parents, and I felt a buzz of anticipation to have a date that evening with my grandparents in front of the television. They were excited about this movie. I was belly down on the carpet. Fresh martinis clinked from the sofa behind me. The show began! My excitement quickly drooped like the saggy robes worn by the characters on screen, kicked away like the dust from their sandaled feet. The entire thing looked so old-timey and weird. What was this stupid story? I soon lost interest and drifted out of the room. But for a few moments, before it all fell apart into nonsense, I was spellbound by the most fascinating beginning I could imagine. A woman is shown setting her baby-in-a-basket into the river and letting go. The pained expression on her face reveals this choice as difficult: the baby will most likely drown, but it is safer than it would have been staying with her. What kind of trouble made this the better choice? Several frames focus on the baby up close, chubby and oblivious. The baby doesn't have long; the basket is no better than a sieve. I still had high hopes for this movie. A woman standing at the bank downstream spots the basket. That this stranger is big-hearted enough to fish out the baby and raise him as her own is almost too good to be true. That she turns out to be royalty and raises the orphan in the palace is the most surprising in the series of unlikely incidents that saved the baby. Then the kid grows up in a montage of like two minutes, and the best part is over.

I'm not the only one who got hung up on the baby. I've since spoken to others who confess that when they were younger and first exposed to the Moses story, the floating-baby part captured their imaginations too. It makes me wonder if this aspect of the account resonates so profoundly because it speaks to our own survival stories: the chances of our individual conception and survival perhaps even slimmer than those of baby Moses being scooped from a river by a queen. We may not be able to grasp the improbability of our own lives—the chain of events is too complex to fathom—but in the Moses story, the miracle of survival is writ large.

When I arrive in L.A., the synagogues are roughly on the same page in their weekly readings of the Torah: midway through Exodus. At long last I get a second chance to discover what's so great about the grown-up Moses. He leads the people to freedom with the guidance of God, who weakens the resolve of the Egyptian pharaoh through a series of plagues and then parts the Red Sea for a speedy on-foot escape and sends the water back together on the Egyptian army. It's all the plot points covered in the movie, if I'd been mature enough to understand.

"This is a critical juncture in the history of Jewish identity," the rabbi says in his talk. I'm at a reform synagogue in Santa Monica housed in a plain, square building. In high school I used to drive past it regularly on my way to my friend Becky's house. Inside, the atmosphere is laid back. Only a handful of people have come to formally celebrate Sabbath.

The rabbi here does not look particularly rabbi-ish. He more closely resembles an executive—perhaps a movie producer, but of wholesome, family-oriented films. "The foundation of Judaism, monotheism, is tested," he explains. The most important idea that distinguishes Judaism from other faiths at the time is the belief in one God. Before the notion of one God was introduced, tribes had their own stable of gods, each overseeing a domain such as water or sun or fertility. If a person had a need in a particular area, he would appeal to the god in charge of that thing, channeling his anxiety about the crops being too dry, for example, into worship of the god responsible for rain. I think it's difficult for someone like me, a modern person who's never had anything besides the idea of a single God occupying the background of my thinking, to fully grasp the dramatic shift in consciousness the introduction of monotheism represented. Before, people were accountable only to those who shared their gods; it was considered a crime to steal from members of one's own tribe, while stealing from other tribes afforded you a hero's welcome. One God introduced the concept of a unified humanity, making everyone connected—the entire world as a single tribe of people derived from the same source. The best-known and most-oft-said prayer of Judaism, "Hear, O Israel: The Lord our God, the Lord is One," makes no request of God. It functions as a simple reminder of a unified and unifying God.

Today the Torah section we read begins at Exodus 32.

The people Moses has led to freedom are freaking out. Moses promised to be back in forty days, and those days have come and gone and there's no sign of him. The rabbi explains that more than likely Moses wasn't really late, that it was probably a misunderstanding—the people had started counting the days at sunrise when Moses was counting them according to sunsets, something like that. Either way, collectively, the people enter the throes of a classic panic attack, their anxiety like a runaway train. If they can't trust Moses, then maybe the God who helped them escape isn't reliable. Maybe they are completely alone in a hostile world. To stop from spiraling out of control, they revert back to what they know: worshipping something they can see and touch—an "idol." The invisible-one-God idea is too scary. They gather their jewelry, melt it down, and shape it into a gold calf. They focus their energy on it. Soothed by the certainty and solidity of the object, their anxiety subsides. At that exact moment, of course, Moses returns.

Moses is furious. It's not so much the idol itself as what it represents: as soon as you create a material object to focus your worshipping on, you've broken the one-God idea apart. It might seem a small fissure, but it challenges the very essence of monotheism. It threatens to shatter a unified humanity and, perhaps to make this exact point, Moses throws down the stone tablets with the commandments from God and they break to pieces.

The rabbi slows down. He's making an important point here about the human condition. He says when faced with uncertainty, we tend to default to anger, depression, and fear. The one-God idea comes strapped with a degree of doubt—there can be no proof, nothing concrete to touch—as illustrated a few sections further along in Exodus when Moses's request to see God's face is denied. So the very thing we hope will alleviate our anxiety inevitably leaves some intact. "This pain," the rabbi says, "is written into the human condition." If you learn to tolerate it, you can trade certainty for faith. If you learn to trust it, you can swap being a part of something small for being a part of something infinitely vast. Here is the key: to bypass quick fixes for the slow trudge toward a deeper, more powerful solution. The rabbi puts a finger in the air and offers a sly smile that suggests he's sharing the simplest and most profound of secrets. "The pain," he says, "is the opening for the divine."

o

Lisa tries to get the old gang to meet up after the sun sets on my first California Sabbath. She sends out a group e-mail and makes reservations at a restaurant on Main Street. Becky and Deb reply that they can't make it, but Nina RSVPs she'll be there. I'm surprised she's the one who says "yes," as ours was always the relationship with the most friction. At times we acted like we were in a battle for who could be the biggest jerk. Last we had gotten together, about fifteen years earlier, she had stormed out. That afternoon she had seemed to be milking some residual neediness from her mother's death, which irked me. Everything I said and did communicated that I would not indulge her emotional fragility. When she scooped up her car keys and fled, I was officially the victor in our little war. We hadn't spoken since—not even when her boyfriend was killed a few years later.

Nina is running late. Lisa and I arrive at the restaurant on Main Street that sits opposite one of the synagogues on my list. I take a seat at our table only to look up and realize I've inadvertently positioned myself so that I can see it though the giant windows. The last vestiges from the setting sun cause its white facade to glow. This is the synagogue where I would later be reprimanded for holding a pen as the sun set on Friday evening. Two days earlier, on the Wednesday night after I arrived in L.A., I had attended a Purim party there. I didn't know what Purim was or how it would be celebrated, but the synagogue's website said the festivities started at eight o'clock, so I rushed down at the last minute. As I approached the building looking for street parking, I became alarmed. A man in a turban was gesticulating wildly near the steps. I won't sugarcoat it: with his long black beard and robes, this man looked decidedly Taliban. I thought he was shouting or causing some sort of commotion; as I passed by, I realized he was laughing—likely the maniacal cackles of a madman, I thought.

I was still apprehensive as I parked and walked back toward the entrance. Now the turban guy was gone, and a side door leading to the synagogue's basement was propped open. "Hello?" I called from the top of the stairs. No response. I descended one flight and tried again. Still no response. I went all the way down and there, standing at the base, was the guy. My first instinct was to scream, but I bit my tongue. He smiled and stuck out his hand for me to shake. "I'm Mordecai," he said. That's when I noticed the elastic straps on his beard and the cheap polyester of his turban. This was a costume. He was dressed as a character from the bible.

The rest of the evening was nothing I could have imagined taking place, much less in a synagogue that falls under the label "conservative"—even though I realize that in this context this is not necessarily an indication of political affiliation. I knew only that Purim is a celebration of the biblical story of Queen Esther convincing her husband, King Haman, to abandon his plan to kill the Jews in his kingdom. Esther, who is secretly Jewish, is aided in her efforts of persuasion by a family member named Mordecai.

Aside from several members of the congregation dressed as key characters from this drama, everything started out on a somber note. The rabbi read aloud from the Book of Lamentations as we nibbled hamantaschen, triangle-shaped pastries named for the king. Then a bag of noisemakers was passed around. I selected one that looked like a rattle with little balls inside; in tiny letters it said, "Happy Purim!" The room grew raucous as everyone tried out their noisemakers, some of which were cardboard horns that punctuated the general racket with ear-splitting blasts. Every time King Haman's name was mentioned, we stomped and rattled and blew to drown it out.

The rabbi raised a bottle of beer as if to toast the cacophony. Thus began the "Hamy Awards," a spoof of the Academy Awards. The master of ceremonies was a rabbinical student with wheat stalks glued to his t-shirt. He announced the category for "Best Queen." He read, very seriously, "and the nominees are: Queen Elizabeth . . . Queen Latifah . . . the rock band Queen . . . Queen Esther for saving the Jews. And the winner is . . . ," he paused for dramatic effect, "Queen Esther!" The crowd went wild: noisemakers in the air, feet stomping the floor, the rabbi chugging beer. A beautiful young woman dressed in robes and a gold chain across her forehead made her way to the front of the room. She graciously accepted her award, a shellacked hamantasch pastry spray-painted gold. Mordecai won for "Best Supporting Jew."

As I left the synagogue later that night, I felt giddy and a little baffled. Since Rosh Hashanah, I had been cataloguing my sins and adopting the appropriate attitude of remorseful sorrow. I had prepared myself mentally for this very serious mission, one that would culminate in several weeks with Passover, when Jews remember being freed from slavery. I had not anticipated my very first stop would be a boisterous, partylike celebration. I did not realize Jews had a holiday where the point is to be loud and dress up and get drunk if you want to. It reminded me of the Catholic tradition of Carnival or Mardi Gras, the wild public partying before the somber season of Lent. Some historians suggest that Purim and pre-Lenten celebrations developed in tandem as a result of Christian and Jews living for hundreds of years in proximity. They capture parallel moods: a burst of fun before the dutiful weeks leading to Easter or Passover. It seems to be human nature to crave levity, especially in the midst of a serious journey.

I have my eye on the door of the restaurant because I'm nervous about Nina showing up. But as soon as I see her, I know it won't be like that. I spy all five feet of her, but she might as well be the biggest person in the room from the size of the smile on her face. We hug, and I am flooded with relief. After tonight I'll e-mail her and hopefully set up a get-together with just the two of us to catch up on the more serious aspects of the time we've lost. But tonight isn't for that. We laugh and swap lighthearted stories. I relax and focus on how good this is—how wonderful to be reunited with Lisa and Nina. I've struggled with moving past my feelings of fear and guilt to carve out enough space where a sense of thankfulness and joy might flourish. Life is its own serious journey, and these moments of fun can help grow gratitude—if you let them. Tonight I'm just appreciative for my old friends—people who know firsthand the terrible mistakes I'm capable of, but who smile anyway when they see me.

The Tabernacle

After the golden calf debacle, Moses returns from his second trip to the top of Mount Sinai with another set of commandments and instructions to create a special place in which the people can worship God. It's a nice compromise: a location to help people dispense their anxiety without sullying the notion of a single unifying divinity. The people can't have icons, but they can have a place. Perhaps God cannot be touched or seen, but God can be experienced. Of course, this edifice needed to be portable—a tent or "tabernacle," as it was called—because these people were on the move.

All synagogues are modern incarnations of that first tabernacle. The ones on my list to visit in L.A. were often so nondescript on the outside that I took to driving past them hours, even days, before the service I planned to attend. More than once I was convinced the synagogue in question had gone out of business—the office building or warehouse it once occupied was abandoned, the small Hebrew letters a forgotten remnant of its former life. Even after being reassured by phone that the place was indeed in operation, I was never fully convinced that I had found my destination until I crossed the threshold into a sanctuary as vibrant as the exterior was dormant. The contrast between inside and outside made me wonder if modern-day synagogues have also inherited the emotional legacy of the original tabernacle; when translated into a stone structure in Jerusalem and renamed a temple, it was destroyed—not once, but twice. In the plain facades, I sensed a reluctance to invest too much energy into a physical structure, an acceptance of impermanence, and a desire to go largely unnoticed by the city at large. Even a synagogue with a lavish exterior like the Sephardic one I visited in a ritzy neighborhood—with its facade of white limestone and intricately carved wood door announced its purpose quietly: a simple metal menorah affixed to one of the blocks of stone. As I approached, I believed it was likely I would find the entrance locked, a small sign announcing the congregation had packed up and moved away.

My second Sabbath in L.A., I arrive for services just before the front doors open at nine a.m. This is the synagogue I had stared at from the dinner table with my friends the week before, where I celebrated my first-ever Purim. It is also where, the night before, as a group gathered to welcome the start of the Sabbath, I had been reprimanded for holding a pen. In the middle of the night, a storm rolled in, and I awoke to find the usually blue skies blanketed in grey and rain pouring down. I head toward the building protected by an umbrella. As I approach, I see that the entrance is crowded with people trying to stay dry under the overhang above the doors. I get closer and realize the people have camped here for the night, a dozen young men and women who are now folding makeshift bedding and tarps. A few worn-out signs say "Occupy Wall Street." They are part of a protest movement started in New York City in 2011 that symbolically claims power for the "little guy" when ordinary people dare to inhabit a public space. I join them at the top of the steps just as one of the front doors opens and the rabbi sticks his head out to check on their progress. As they hoist their packs and sleeping rolls and take their leave, the rain dissipates and the sun emerges, a trick that seems almost as remarkable as the parting of the Red Sea.

For as many years as I've been orbiting this synagogue, I find it remarkable that I have never seen its sanctuary. I've passed by countless times on foot and by car, and now I've celebrated Purim here, which took place in the basement, and participated in the Friday evening Sabbath-welcoming service, held in a small adjacent chamber. This will be my first time in the main room, and I feel as if I've passed some small test and proven my mettle to gain access to the holy of holies. In the foyer I greet the rabbi, who says, "Good morning," with a smile even as his eyes offer a less enthusiastic, "Oh, you again." This rabbi has all the traditional trappings: full beard, spectacles, black coat, and stern expression. Only his *kippah* is unexpected. It is like a little pillbox hat stitched from a rainbow of fabrics.

I grab a flyer that details the history of the building and step through a second bank of doors. The most surprising aspect of the sanctuary is how massive and plain it is. In my imagination it sparkled like an opulent Catholic cathedral, but in reality it looks like an auditorium for a large high school, with dozens of rows facing a stage. I find a spot in the middle toward the front and settle in to read my flyer, which explains that this building, the oldest synagogue in West Los Angeles still in operation, was constructed after World War II. To save money, the design was borrowed from a military base theater. It doesn't appear to have been updated in any way. It's as if these walls claimed this enormous space and then froze it in time.

The flyer explains that Venice Beach was once "a haven" for Jewish families and retirees—"the Coney Island of the West"—and, at one point in the fifties and sixties, the boardwalk was lined with Jewish delis, kosher butchers, bakeries, and tailors. I take a moment to imagine this version of the boardwalk—fedoras and suits in place of the oily limbs of bodybuilders and sunbathers. Most of these Jews would have come through New York and made their way across the country by train or plane drawn by those age-old magnets: sunshine and Hollywood. Here was an unlikely end point to the diaspora.

A man I recognize from Purim and the Friday service spots me and waves. At those events, he was outgoing and friendly and elaborated on certain aspects of what I was witnessing. Today he takes the seat next to me and fills me in on a tidbit not included in the flyer. "See how there's this middle section of seats and then smaller sections on the left and on the right?" I nod, noticing how an aisle on either side of where we're sitting separates us from a narrower bank of seats. "That was a compromise. The middle section is for men and women who wanted to sit together and then for those who still wanted to sit with only their gender, the two sides." He explains that when the synagogue was built, some congregants were starting to embrace the idea that not all the traditional rules were necessary. This more-relaxed approach was formalized in the 1950s when the synagogue joined the conservative movement. Members of the congregation who wanted to remain orthodox broke away and started the synagogue located directly on the boardwalk. Since then, the rule-following spectrum has expanded further to include the more lenient reform movement. The seating arrangement in the auditorium offers a snapshot from this evolution. All three sections are now coed.

Today's Torah reading covers the remainder of Exodus, which focuses on God's instructions for the tabernacle tent. I'm surprised at how detailed they are: according to Moses, God has outlined the exact components for every part of the tabernacle, their precise measurements and even what material each feature should be built from. God has also made it clear that everyone who is able to contribute resources or skills must do so. The people are eager to comply. Carpenters, blacksmiths, weavers—everyone chips in. Even the "working women" give up their precious scraps of metal for the cause. During an informal question-and-answer portion of the service, the rabbi acknowledges that this may be a reference to prostitutes surrendering the small reflective surfaces they used as mirrors. This small detail, he explains, indicates how even those with very little were willing to sacrifice items essential to their livelihoods.

Once the people understand what the tabernacle is for, they dedicate themselves fully to its construction. I believe they were soothed by the specificity of the instructions, the lack of ambiguity. Just as the history of being enslaved helped them grasp how time can be used to draw closer to the sacred, being homeless had made them keenly aware of how a shelter can be used for that same purpose.

With all this focus on homelessness and tents, I can't help but think about the young people who camped on the synagogue steps. Freedom is the ability to say "no," whether it's "I won't work this day" or "I won't vacate until I'm ready." It's why the Occupy movement is so powerful—people are refusing to leave an area that technically does not belong to them. With their tarps and tents and bedrolls, they draw attention to social and economic inequality by claiming power. It's not all that different from what the Jews did as they trekked across the desert thousands of years ago, taking ownership of time and space.

The parallels are not lost on the rabbi. At the end of the service, he explains the events of the morning to the members of the congregation; most had showed up after the porch was cleared. I don't know what he could have done differently, but he obviously feels that kicking the Occupiers off the porch wasn't the best choice. "We must ask God for forgiveness," he says. "We have to right this wrong." He doesn't elaborate on what restitution might entail—whether something impersonal like cutting a check to a homeless shelter or more intimate like opening the basement as a shelter on stormy nights—but it reminds me once again what I admire about religion. It doesn't automatically make you do the right thing, but it helps you imagine that there might be a right thing, lighting the way from what is to what could be.

o

A replica of the biblical tabernacle is temporarily on display in the Los Angeles area. That it's been constructed at a church is not too shocking, as the adoption of the Jewish Torah as the Old Testament makes all the stories and characters it contains vital to their history as well. That the tabernacle is at Saddleback Church is a bonus as far as I'm concerned since visiting a megachurch headed by a celebrity preacher is a gaping hole in my Christian experience. The wisdom of this opportunity presenting itself smack in the middle of my Jewish journey revealed itself only after the fact, leaving me with a greater understanding of the ways that Christianity and Judaism are different and, yet, how each speaks to a universal need.

It's a strange dance Christians and Jews do around one another. When I first started attending church, I was surprised at how often Christians casually mentioned Jews during their services. Looking back, I don't know why I should have been surprised or how it could be avoided, as most readings from the Old Testament mention Jews directly or indirectly. I suppose I still had Martin Luther in the forefront of my thinking. Earlier in his life, he treated the Jews kindly in his writings, expressing hope that they would soon come to embrace Jesus as the human incarnation of God. I don't know why he thought Jews would choose to accept Jesus during his lifetime, but when they didn't, he grew disillusioned and angry with them. In 1543 he wrote a booklet called "On the Jews and Their Lies," detailing all the reasons he believed Jews deserved to be despised. That this hateful propaganda circulated in the region that is modern-day Germany is not lost on most historians, and some suggest it fueled contempt that simmered for four hundred years and came to a head with the Holocaust. Today's Christians have distanced themselves from this hatred; genuinely horrified by the Holocaust, they tend to be more attuned to the debt Christianity owes Judaism. Jesus himself was a Jew, and some of Christianity's most vital tenets—the belief in "one God" and the idea that each person is valued deeply by a creator—were clearly bred by Jewish thought.

Still, some awkward tension remains. During my months of churchgoing, I was cautious enough not to mention being married to a Jew, even one as lackadaisical as Phil, until the morning I felt compelled to, then quickly regretted the decision. I was at a Presbyterian church. After the service, during the coffee and cookies part, a group of women gathered around me—the first recognized me as a visitor and approached to make conversation; others joined until we formed a substantial circle in the middle of the room. Several of the women were wearing name tags, and one in particular caught my eye. On this piece of plastic affixed to the lady's chest was a decidedly Jewish surname. Years of Jewish classmates have made me aware of names common among Jews—like Cohen or Bernstein—and on this morning, in front of my very eyes, was one of these names—as strange and exotic, given the setting, as, say, "Sally Goldberg."

"Are you Jewish?" I asked her. I couldn't help it; I was curious. Obviously she wasn't a practicing Jew, but I wanted to know what twists and turns of history might have led her here.

"No!" she practically shouted.

Our coffee klatch was silent, the air gone faster than a whoopee cushion stomped with both feet. It occurred to me that perhaps my tone had sounded accusatory.

"My husband is Jewish," I said. It was as lame as if I had followed a racial slur with "some of my best friends are black." Apparently it only made matters worse. The whoopee cushion might as well have been the real thing. Suddenly everyone had important matters to attend to. I was left wondering which had been the bigger faux pas: the question or the revelation? Of all the ladies, Sally herself seemed the least fazed. Before leaving, she returned to me and gave my arm a tender squeeze. "I hope we see each other again," she whispered.

Now that I'm among Jews, I am cautious about mentioning my husband for an entirely different reason: guilt. Judaism is transmitted to children via mothers, and even though Phil and I have no children, the notion that if we did my non-Jewish status would rob them of a vital birthright is enough to make many Jews, even those on the more liberal side of the spectrum, uneasy. According to some orthodox strands of thought, the question exists as to whether my marriage is even valid. The only thing that could potentially rectify the situation is if I convert. It doesn't matter that Phil considers himself a None: the onus is on me as the potential vessel of life. When I do mention Phil, I can tell it is a question on people's minds—do I intend to convert?—though they are too polite to ask. I have a feeling that how they perceive me hinges on the answer to this question. It doesn't matter that I am the one within the marriage who is interested in Judaism, more eager to understand, and the only person who may eventually soften Phil's heart toward a religion that currently makes him bristle; in my current state, I am an agent of harm to the Jewish people.

Non-Jews who wish to officially convert must receive formal education under the guidance of religious leaders. By contrast, it's far easier to become a Christian. I don't have to do anything; I just have to accept Jesus as "my savior"—though, frankly, I still don't know exactly what that means. I suppose it has something to do with my acknowledging that Jesus sacrificed his life to absolve my sins, but the details of this transaction remain hazy. Luckily, I arrive at Saddleback on the perfect day.

The Saddleback campus is strewn with large tents. In addition to the main sanctuary where most congregants will attend services, supplemental worship areas are housed beneath canvas canopies. Each tent seats its own hefty crowd and will receive a broadcast of the sermon from the main chapel supplemented with unique music and other touches. I stroll past a tent for gospel lovers, another for Spanish speakers, and one called "Overdrive," where fans of hard rock can crank it up a notch.

I had to dig around on the website to find out that officially Saddleback is Baptist, as the denomination is overshadowed by the star power of Pastor Rick Warren, author of the *New York Times* best-seller *The Purpose Driven Life* (a book that has apparently sold more copies than any other nonfiction book *ever*) and frequent Christian commentator on various cable news programs. Online I find I can choose between three times for Sunday services, given at two-hour intervals to accommodate the estimated twenty thousand people who attend in person or via video streaming from all over the region, the country, and even the world. Apparently it's become something of a tourist destination—the Sunday plans for families visiting other local hot spots like Disneyland and Sea World. From my dad's house, it's about a forty-five-minute drive south on freeways blissfully free of traffic. As I near the destination, I see the massive roofs of high-end housing developments in every direction. Once I exit, signs clearly mark the direction of Saddleback. At a final stoplight, I have an option: turn left to take the road that leads to the church, or make a right away from the church; a sign declares this "Rocky Road." It's a joke, as Rocky Road doesn't actually go anywhere, but dead-ends into a patch of land that appears yet to be developed.

Volunteers direct the stream of cars. I make my way past various parking lots, different sections, with someone at every turn to point me to the appropriate slice of asphalt. I arrive twenty minutes early, with enough time to explore. I buy a cup of coffee at an outdoor café and stroll past the book and keepsake kiosk. Uplifting music emanates from speakers hidden in rocks. I've never seen so much creative use of concrete. It's stamped into boulders and walkways; it cradles water in meandering streams. Smoothed and polished, it forms the glassy floor of an industrial-looking building called "the Refinery," which houses big open rooms, like lofts in some urban dreamscape; teens are currently gathering in its cavernous spaces. Outside the building the concrete swoops and dips to form the necessary surfaces for skateboarding tricks.

On a big lawn behind the gospel tent, I spy the tabernacle. A high fabric fence surrounds it, just as historians say it did back in the desert, a measure taken to protect the sacred site and ensure that everyone entered through the same designated opening. In this re-creation, the fabric is a fine mesh, sheer enough to see through. If this tabernacle had been built according to God's exact specifications, all of the items would be made of precious metals and rare woods. The materials here are more ordinary, but the way it looks—the precise dimensions of each item and how they are arranged—is true to God's instructions. The tabernacle itself is not that big, less than half the size of the modern worship tents and much simpler in format—just a basic rectangle with fabric panels draped over posts. Inside, the space is divided into a few simple rooms, each dark and bare save for key objects: a large candleholder, a stand for food offerings, and a tray for burning incense. At the far back, in "the holy of holies" where only high priests were allowed, is the Ark of the Covenant, a fancy trunk for the stones with the Ten Commandments.

What's surprising is the size of the box-like dais for sacrificing animals. It sits directly in front of the tabernacle, the very first thing you encounter as you approach the tent's opening. Taller than the average person, a small ramp leads to the top where sheep and goats were tied to the "horns" at each corner. Originally made of bronze, today's version looks like plywood spray-painted to mimic a charred patina. I knew killing animals as a show of gratitude to God was an ordinary practice, but so much time has elapsed since it was abandoned that it's easy to overlook or downplay this history. With this re-creation, it's impossible to ignore. The proof stands front and center.

o

It's a little jarring, the transition from the dark and quiet ancient house of God to the big, bright worship center of today. The main sanctuary looks like a building one might find on a college campus—not the older, more distinguished stone structures but the brand-new ones that go up in a year and have tons of windows. They may not last as long, but they offer a breath of fresh air after you've been cooped up in the dim classrooms of yesteryear. Light floods in from the walls on either side of the stage; they are made almost entirely of glass, with doors that lead to additional rows of outdoor seating if our ranks swell. If this were an academic building, it would be the biggest lecture hall on campus, the one where huge mandatory courses like Organic Chemistry 101 are taught. The auditorium is quickly filling up as the band plays, and I find a seat closer to the back, where the rows are raised. On the way in I was handed a packet of materials, glossy and packed with colorful pictures. Today's sermon is the second in a multiweek arc given by Rick's wife, Kay Warren, entitled "All Access," which ties to the theme of the tabernacle. Here, the sophistication of the marketing is bumped up a notch—not only does the church have its own logo, but this series of sermons has a logo too—it looks like an old-fashioned ticket stub, the kind that gets ripped in half before a carnival ride.

At first I'm disappointed that Rick isn't giving the sermon, but then I see Kay, blond and confident, and that dissolves. Her eyes shoot laser beams of intensity, and suddenly I understand that hers is the steely determination of a woman like Hillary Clinton whose drive propelled her man and made all this possible. She emerges from the back of the stage like a benevolent queen at the end of our singing, the last lines from the final song lingering on the big screens as she greets the audience, her voice amplified by an invisible mike. "The tabernacle and what it represents has always been one of my favorite portions of the Bible," she says. "It gets to the heart of what Jesus did for humanity." I would never have guessed that a portable worship tent was the key to understanding the significance of Jesus, but if Kay says so, I believe it.

She lays the groundwork with a recollection. When she was eight years old, she tells us, she ate candy from her Easter basket after being told not to, and for the first time she was shaken to the core by the knowledge that she was a sinner. I smile because this jibes with my own experience; I was the exact age when shame began to haunt me. I didn't have to look far to find evidence of my deviation from perfection. It was presented to me via my parent's divorce. Though, if hadn't been that, I'm sure I would have found confirmation elsewhere. Something tells me Kay did the same thing—and if it wasn't sneaking candy, she would have invented some other proof of her sinfulness.

The Jews built into their system of worship an answer to this sense of unworthiness, an attempt to repay God. This, Kay explains, is where the bronze altar that stood outside the tabernacle comes in. She tells us to find the guide to her sermon in the printed materials. I get mine, which is a four-page supplement with sentences that have blanks where I can fill in the words like a biblical Mad Libs.

The first sentence that needs my attention is this: "The altar represented the claims of a holy and righteous God which must be _____ before he can meet with man and bless him." The missing word is "satisfied," but I need a moment to locate my pen, so it stays blank. Farther down: "Any deviation from perfection must be punished by the person or a _____." I fill in "substitute." Kay explains that during the time of the tabernacle this substitute was an animal, provided as an offering. "Why did God require a blood sacrifice?" _____. I write the words I hear Kay say: "Because blood represents life." The size and prominence of the bronze altar is no accident; it really was a hugely significant component of the tabernacle, perhaps even the most important element. Blood had to be shed for God in an attempt at restitution: the gift of life for the gift of life.

Now Kay's talk turns to the act that birthed Christianity from Judaism. "Jesus was the _____." I stare at the blank, knowing full well that "ultimate blood sacrifice" is the answer but unable to bring myself to write the words. Jesus was a human sacrifice, a concept that feels too big and powerful to reduce to a fill-in-the-blank response. His death didn't occur on a bronze altar, but his bloodshed is interpreted by Christians as the last say in the "life for life" transaction, officially nullifying the need for further animal sacrifice and rendering all the other Jewish "rules" obsolete. To flesh out the story, my study guide provides several quotes from the New Testament, like this one from Acts 13: "In this man Jesus, there is forgiveness for your sins! Everyone who trusts him is freed from all guilt and declared righteous—something the Jewish law could never do." I have to wonder at this particular translation, as the wording seems a bit rude, but I get the gist. Each of us senses an indebtedness to creation or God; in Christianity this debt has been paid by Jesus and our job then is to believe in the power of this transaction. "Acceptance of Jesus as my substitute makes me _____ to God." In tiny letters I write "acceptable."

At the end of the service, Kay has an exercise for us. She asks us to find a small rectangle of paper that has been placed in each of our packets. This piece of paper has been made to look like an old-fashioned luggage tag, with a hole punched at the top and a string through it to tie to an imaginary suitcase handle. She tells us to write our sin at the bottom of the tag and, on our way out of the building, she wants us to rip the sin portion off and toss it in the red bins placed by the doors for this purpose. Audience members rise and begin to leave, but I stay seated and struggle to come up with a good sin to write on my luggage tag, an appropriate label for my emotional baggage. I decide to write "not feeling worthy" because isn't that what each of us struggles with on some level? The ultimate sin that causes self-destructive behaviors that masquerade as the real sins? The crowd streaming out has thinned by the time I join its ranks. The red bins would be hard to miss. "Forgiven," each announces. Is it really so simple? I suppose if I believe it is, then it is. I go to the nearest bin and feed my paper into the slot. I peek in as it flutters down and lands on the mound of other people's sins.

On the way back to my car, I pass the tabernacle again. Now there's a line waiting to get in, and headsets are being provided for those in need of audio guidance. I stand outside the mesh fence and watch the scene for a few minutes. A group has formed around the bronze altar, and they are taking turns climbing the ramp and looking into the opening where an animal would have been tied. I think about how, for Christians, Jesus took away the need to engage in this practice as well as myriad other rituals. Christians created a system for believing rather than doing, whereas Jews continued to trust in the power of everyday acts both personal and public to soothe anxiety and draw closer to God.

o

I've always loved the Venice boardwalk first thing in the morning before the fog has burned off and it's just locals milling around and shopkeepers prepping. Today I can almost imagine what it would have been like in the fifties and sixties when this was a Jewish main street with the occasional Gidget in a sea of black fedoras.

I'm dressed like a throwback to an earlier time when bathing beauties came to the beach completely covered. I'm wearing a dress with opaque black tights and a blazer. I approach the synagogue, a simple stucco building that doesn't even attempt to take in its unobstructed view of the Pacific. I read on the website that once inside the first door, I'd encounter a second set of doors. I'm relieved I remember that the entrance for women is on the left because I feel awkward enough without having to be escorted out of the men's section. I'm the first person to arrive on the lady's side, and as I take a seat, the men begin to chant prayers in Hebrew. I catch glimpses of them through a thin strip of lattice that runs across the top of the room divider.

Soon, everything comes to a screeching halt. The men stop praying. A woman who has taken the seat next to mine whispers, "They're waiting for the minyan," when she sees me looking around, confused. Almost no prayer in the Jewish prayer book is recited from the first person. They are generally offered from the perspective of "we." Among the orthodox, only men count toward the minimum of ten worshippers needed for a valid "we." Not enough male congregants have arrived yet.

As the minutes tick by, I feel a little like I'm dangling on a frozen Ferris wheel. Luckily, I'm not alone. My companion is also here for the first time, though she is an actual Jew. Her grown children live in Los Angeles, and whenever she visits a place, she likes to worship with the local Jews. "My kids call me a 'synagogue slut,'" she says. I snort my approval. We have such a good time swapping stories of religious tourism that I'm a little disappointed when the Ferris wheel cranks back to life after fifteen minutes or so.

Today's Torah portion includes the first chapters of Leviticus and covers the rules governing sacrifices. Again, God's instructions are surprisingly detailed: what kind of animal to offer for different purposes and how to handle the various parts right down to the "entrails." The level of specificity churns my stomach, and I get why this topic is controversial among Jews today. When the Temple in Jerusalem was destroyed the second time, in 70 CE, and never rebuilt, the practice of animal sacrifice was officially suspended, and contemporary Jews disagree about whether the Temple should be rebuilt and the practice resumed. In general, Jews who belong to reform congregations see these options as impossible and unnecessary. A mosque is located on the site of the old Temple, and slaughtering animals for God is an outdated concept. Conservative Jews would like to see the Temple reconstructed in some form, but they are fine with not resuming the practice of sacrifices. Among these groups, prayers that reference the Temple and sacrifices have been modified to reflect current views. In general, orthodox Jews are in favor of rebuilding the Temple and reinstating all its functions, including the original purpose of the bronze altar; they believe a future leader, a messiah, will succeed in accomplishing both, perhaps making the instructions in the Bible as relevant as the day they were written.

At the end of the service, the congregation gathers together on a back patio for the prayers over wine and bread. A table is spread with snacks of the dairy persuasion; I sample the banana pudding and soft cheeses. A woman in a red dress and gold sun hat sits perched on a low wall like some exotic, radiant bird. I smile at her. "Are you coming to my house for lunch?" she asks. She seems to be looking at me when she speaks, and I think she must have me mixed up with someone else, as we haven't exchanged introductions. The people I've met these past weeks have been friendly and welcoming, but no one has invited me to come home with them. Maybe she forgot her glasses?

"Do you have lunch plans?" she asks. This time, I realize she is definitely addressing me. She stands, and I'm surprised at how tall she is. The hat puts her well over six feet.

"I . . . I . . ." I don't know what to say. I hadn't planned on lunch, especially in an orthodox home whose customs I understood only vaguely.

Before I started attending synagogues, I thought it would be obvious I wasn't Jewish based on my looks alone, but I had come to realize this wasn't the case. Certainly my freckles and stubby nose made me an outlier but not out of the question. "Oh, they'll know," my friend Lisa's mom said when we stopped by her apartment in Marina Del Rey. I mentioned how I had blended in so far; maybe I would blend in among the orthodox. Although not observant, Lisa's mom is extremely knowledgeable about Jewish genealogy and history. "How?" I asked. The smile that spread across her face was priceless; I saw in it the memory of a dozen lessons learned the hard way. "The second you do something wrong." Of course she was right and I found I did just about everything wrong.

"I . . . I . . . I'm not Jewish," I say. More than wanting to protect myself from humiliation, I'm hoping to shield her home from my ignorance. I understand enough to know that a Jewish home's dining room has, without the temple and bronze altar, increased in significance. Food on a table, especially on Sabbath, is a sort of offering to God. I explain my situation in a nutshell: how I am married to a Jew who feels alienated from the faith, that I am interested in Judaism and religion in general, how the visit to her synagogue is a tiny step in an effort to educate myself.

She nods slowly. I can see her considering my words, measuring them with private weights. Perhaps she consults God. Whatever the case, the result is in my favor. "So you'll join us? We don't mind if you drive."

Now it is my turn to consider. If she is willing to put up with me, how can I refuse? "Okay," I say. "Yes. Thank you."

"Wonderful," she says, offering the first smile of our exchange. She tells me her name is Barbara and gives me her street address; I repeat it to myself over and over again, as I am not writing on Sabbath. She tells me: "My husband and I will start walking home in about ten minutes, so give us a half hour."

About thirty minutes later, I approach what I hope is the right house. I repeated the address to myself at least twenty times, but now I'm not so sure. The newspaper is rolled tightly on the front walk, left there either because no one's home or Sabbath rules. As I get closer, I spy Barbara through the screen door, sitting with others around a dining room table. "Hello?" I call, marching in, not even thinking to stop and press my kissed fingertips to the little mezuzah posted at the doorframe. This gesture is meant to remind all those entering of the unifying presence of the divine. Instead I offer my toothiest grin as everyone turns to watch me ignore God.

Four men and one other woman besides Barbara sit around the table. As Barbara introduces me, I make sure to nod a polite greeting to the men, congratulating myself on knowing that orthodox men and women do not shake hands upon meeting. Barbara directs me to an empty seat on the lady's side of the table. Barbara's husband occupies one head, and the oldest gentleman present sits at the other. Two younger guys roughly my age sit directly across from the women. The table is set beautifully for seven, and knowing it would have been prepared the previous afternoon, it suddenly makes sense why Barbara pressed me on whether I would be joining them. Mine is the spot left empty in case God sends a lone traveler; feeding me is a mitzvah, or good deed.

The conversation resumes as I take my seat. It's a heated debate about current events and Israel. I'm familiar with the tones of this discussion, the impassioned voices that make it sound like no one at the table is agreeing when actually they are all nodding vigorously. As a teen I was exposed to this aspect of the Jewish dining ritual, which alarmed me at first until I realized that each person is simply practicing his argument against an invisible foe. The only difference here is the politics, which are decidedly right wing. I had heard that some Jews, particularly those on the orthodox side of the spectrum, are conservative Republicans, an affiliation born at least in part from a die-hard support of Israel. So contrary is this to the politics of the Jews I know—who struggle with the complicated affairs of Israel and the role Jews play in the violence of the region—that I was inclined to believe they were creatures too rare to encounter during the course of this exploration, and certainly not likely to attend a synagogue on Venice Beach. I tried to maintain a polite expression of curious wonderment as they took turns bashing liberal politicians. If I closed my eyes, I would have thought I was sitting with far-right Christians, who also adamantly support Israel, though they do so because the "gathering of the Jews" there is an essential piece of New Testament prophecy to ensure the return of Jesus. Both groups' opinions overlap at this thin sliver of foreign affairs. During the conversation I busy myself sneaking peaks at the woman sitting on my right, thinking that one of the great ironies is how separating men and women can make it so much easier to check out members of the opposite gender than those of your own.

When it's time to eat, everyone takes a turn going into the kitchen for the ceremonial handwashing. The counters are crammed with the remnants of yesterday's meal preparations, everything left just where it was when the sun set. The oldest gentleman shows me the ropes: he pours water from a pitcher over my hands and then asks me to repeat the Hebrew words after him, feeding them to me a few at a time. It's the basic prayer before eating when the meal includes bread: "Blessed art Thou, Lord our God, King of the universe who brings forth bread from the earth." After washing, we return to the table and silently wait as Barbara's fills each of our plates from her slow cookers. Today's fare is beef stew with beans and root vegetables—nothing with dairy.

Over the course of the meal, I finally get the opportunity to unapologetically stare at the woman next to me when she takes a moment to tell the table about herself. She grew up in a Hasidic family in Brooklyn, she explains. Today, in her forties, she remains observant, though she's obviously taken the guidelines for attire and thrown them out the window. She has on a long-sleeved black top that would provide excellent coverage but for the fact that it is constructed entirely of mesh. Every detail of her leopard-print bra is clearly visible. Her scalp is crowned in long platinum hair extensions. I know this because from my vantage point I can see where each clump of fake hair is attached to her real hair. I try to imagine what her parents must think of this daughter who knows every Hebrew prayer by heart but looks like Paris Hilton. When she explains that her dream is to fall in love and get married, my heart breaks a little. I sincerely doubt hers is the typical profile on JDate. It's one thing for someone like me to visit this world for a short time, but it's another entirely for a person to have each foot firmly planted in two worlds seemingly so at odds with one another.

Barbara asks if I'd like to return just before sundown to walk with her and her husband to the small evening service that officially recognizes the conclusion of Sabbath. I'm happy for the invitation because earlier at the synagogue one of the rabbis mentioned he would be giving a brief talk that evening about the future of animal sacrifice; he promised it would "blow our minds." After a couple of hours back relaxing at my dad's house, I'm once again standing in Barbara's living room. The dining table is exactly as it was when I left, dirty forks dangle from plates that bear the remnants of lunch and glasses puddled with water and wine. At the end of the meal, I had started to take my dishes to the kitchen, but Barbara told me no, I should leave them, she would clean after sundown. I was momentarily paralyzed by a mental tussle between two sides: what makes a good guest versus what makes a good Jew.

o

Our destination this evening is not the synagogue but a small building owned by the congregation several blocks up from the beach. It's next door to a popular Mexican restaurant and across the street from a massive Whole Foods. It's about a half-mile walk from Barbara's house along the same route to the synagogue and, as the three of us set out, I think about all the times they've covered these blocks by foot. It's a busy road, not exactly the scenic stroll one might choose, but this has been their Sabbath routine for over twenty years; they raised four kids with this walk as a main feature of every week. Our pace is unhurried, and as Barbara answers my questions, I study the front yards of houses I've sped past a thousand times. I had always dismissed this street as no more than a thoroughfare, but I see now the care the residents have taken with their small front yards. "Why don't women have to go?" I ask when Barbara explains that even though she is not required to attend synagogue services, she likes to go as often as possible. This detail has been bothering me since I learned that in more conservative congregations women don't count toward the minyan or help conduct the public prayers. If women go to synagogue, it's frosting on the cake, but they aren't essential to the proceedings the way men are. "Because in Judaism women are considered more inherently spiritual," she told me as we came to an intersection. "We don't need the structure of the synagogue like men do." This was consistent with explanations I'd heard for why, in pictures, I've only ever seen men wear those tiny square top hats on their foreheads and the straps twisted up their forearms—they need these little reminders pressed against them when they pray. Even so, she must have read skepticism on my face. "It's true!" she cried, pressing the crosswalk button.

At the building, Barbara and I separate from her husband and enter through our own door. The women's side of the room is cordoned off by a thin curtain, through which I can see the silhouettes of the men, the outline of fedoras as they take turns leading the prayers. When it's time for the young rabbi's talk, the curtain gets pushed open just enough to give the women a view of him at the podium. He has a scraggly beard and an excited gleam in his eyes. He says he finds the subject of animal sacrifice incredibly fascinating because while it is suspended for now, at some point in the future, when the Temple is restored, a decision will need to be made about how the practice will be resumed. Rabbis and Jewish scholars all over the world debate the topic, and theories abound as to what might happen. Today, people expect their religious leaders and their butchers to be separate people. But, the young rabbi explains, this could change. One theory purports that the general public will come to see animal sacrifice as no worse ethically than killing animals for food and will embrace it as an acceptable practice.

Another theory proposes that new rules from God will materialize upon the completion of the Temple—and that perhaps some new thing, like sacrificing plants, will be an option. Finally, the rabbi arrives at the last theory, the one he promised would "blow our minds." He explains that some scholars suggest animals may evolve in such a way that they will understand the meaning and significance of being sacrificed and will volunteer for the privilege. A wave of chuckles sweeps the room, and I think we must be sharing the same cartoon thought-bubble of cloven hooves in the air with the caption "Me, pick me!"

What happens last is short and poetic, like a 3-D haiku that bids farewell to Sabbath. It's just me, Barbara, her husband, and three other men. While Barbara's husband straightens up the room, the other men gather around a plate. The oldest of the three lights the multiple wicks of a large candle. He pours wine into a cup and sips it. He opens a small box and inhales deeply. As he does this, one of the younger men unscrews the lid on a typical spice jar—the plastic kind you can buy at any grocery store—and smells the contents. He passes it to me and I put it to my nose, taking in the sweet aroma of cloves. I give it to Barbara who does the same. I'm mesmerized as the men study their hands in the light of the candle and utter a Hebrew prayer. Then the oldest one douses the flame with wine from his cup, which then collects in the plate. All three touch the drops of wine and then press their fingertips against their closed eyes. Each step is like a single line of a poem whose meaning is allusive but by the end conveys perfectly the joy and sorrow of life. This new ending, this new beginning.

In front of the building, the six of us say our farewells. The sun has set, and the sidewalk is bustling with Saturday-night revelers. Music and laughter spill from the Mexican restaurant. The eyes of passersby linger on our small group, and I recognize in their expressions the quiet curiosity I've felt on occasions when I've happened on a pocket of people engaged in something I assume is both sacred and private. I recall the awe with which I would consider my old orthodox neighbors as I watched them playing and how it was tinged with resentment at my exclusion. I think about the nuns at the convent behind their screen. I want to reach out and touch people as they pass and whisper, "I'm one of you." I would say, "This religion thing is not the impenetrable mystery you think, but so basic and beautiful you can grasp its meaning if you desire."

Later that week, Barbara and I meet for coffee at a nearby café. Previously we had been so focused on the Sabbath we hadn't chatted just the two of us. She confesses that her own religious explorations brought her full circle. It was difficult, she explains, during the years she spent as a practicing Buddhist in her twenties to sit cross-legged, especially given her above-average height, but the seated meditations led her to an overwhelming sense of thankfulness for life, which led to a deep desire to show appreciation to a creator. She realized she longed for the more formal means of expressing gratitude that were the foundation of her native Judaism. Then a little token Buddha statue she kept broke off at the legs, and that sealed the deal: she was a Jew. But, she says, if it hadn't been for Buddhism, she may never have come to understand the deeper significance of Judaism. Buddha made her a better Jew.

Her story reminds me of a realization I've recently made. I tell her that when I moved to the Pacific Northwest and started to take on freelance projects, my workweek shifted. Instead of starting on Monday, I would start on Sunday morning. My justification was I wanted to have drafts waiting in client in-boxes by the start of their official workweek, but I maintained this schedule when I had nothing due. I even had a new motto: "Sunday is the new Monday," I would proclaim if anyone asked what I was up to. At the same time, I began my weekend early, usually stopping work by mid-afternoon Friday to spend a couple of hours on household chores before evening. Without even realizing it, and while my ignorance of Judaism was still in full effect, I had adopted a Jewish week. What I believed was a decision firmly rooted in secularism had led me straight to the heart of Judaism.

Barbara wore the knowing smile of a person familiar with God's tactic of bait and switch. "Maybe you're a missing spark," she says and explains the Jewish concept of sparks. Over history, some Jewish families were alienated from the faith due to political pressure or the whim of a single generation—whatever the cause, the Judaism is never fully extinguished in these folks but smolders in their children and their children's children. I think about the Greek side of my family and how my ancestors could very well have been Jews before Constantine declared his empire Christian. Is it possible that Judaism has been burning in the bosoms of my foremothers for centuries? I don't think there's any way of knowing, but I love the idea—a hot coal inside me is drawn to the fire of Judaism due to epic forces working to reunite the errant embers. It gives me a new perspective on the role of observant Jews, how they follow the letter of the law not just for themselves but on behalf of the global community of Jews, even those no longer in touch with their Judaism. With the hope that every spark, no matter how small, will someday reignite, they keep the fire burning brightly.

Tikkun Olam

West L.A. is home to three Jewish-themed museums. The Museum of Tolerance is the West Coast's answer to D.C.'s Holocaust Museum, though less epic in scale. It's also a bit broader in content: from the Holocaust it branches out to displays on racism and genocide around the world. The Skirball's main galleries are dedicated to Jewish culture, displaying objects used in the homes, businesses, and worship places of Jews all over the world from the medieval era right up to the current day. There's even a room with catalogued snippets of home movies and audio interviews highlighting aspects of the American Jewish experience. While both of these museums are kid-friendly, only the last—the Zimmer—is designed specifically for children.

On a Sunday afternoon near the end of my Los Angeles trip, I meet Lisa and her six-year-old daughter, Sydney, at the Zimmer. It's not technically billed as a "Jewish" museum, just a regular children's museum, but its location on the first floor and basement of a high-rise called the Jewish Federation Building is the first indication that this play space might have a special message. When I arrive, Lisa and Sydney are already deep inside, and I get stopped by the security guard for being childless and then let through once Lisa comes to vouch for me. Beyond the ticket booth, a few items remain stationary in a blur of activity: a full-scale ambulance with spinning red lights, a make-believe theater stage with an exploding trunk of costumes, a replica of a jet with the bobbing heads of tiny pilots.

One display stands out. In the center of everything, the floor has been cut away so that it continues below. A giant wall of levers and gears and pegs sports a sign declaring this the "World's Largest Tzedakah Pinball." I've seen *tzedakah* translated as "charity" or "justice," and my sense is that it encompasses any generous or kind act. Pucks released at the top fall through the open spaces, ricocheting off obstacles here and there. I suppose it's meant to symbolize the complicated course of life, with each collision representing an opportunity to do a good deed. The pucks rain down on the roof of a little house below.

On the bottom level, I stroll down a tiny main street complete with shingled roofs and streetlights. Each lovingly rendered storefront invites playacting: wait tables at the Blue Bagel Café, organize inventory at Bubbie's Bookstore, wrap yourself in a prayer shawl at the mini-synagogue. Lisa and I take a seat as Sydney joins a group of kids on a boat in a sea of squishy balls.

"So, how did it go?" Lisa asks. She's curious about my dates with Nina, Becky, and Deb. I had been so anxious about the prospect, I'd considered abandoning my goal of seeing each of them but decided I had to do what was right, not what was easy.

"Surprisingly well," I tell her. I had met each friend separately so that I could provide my undivided attention and effectively convey my sincerest regrets for having disappeared so thoroughly from their lives.

Nina and I arranged to have lunch at a café we frequented in high school. As the time drew near, I thought about the last afternoon I had seen her, more than fifteen years earlier when I had been insensitive and she had left in a huff. At the time, I could not fathom how Nina's mother had been felled so swiftly from a brain tumor that first made itself apparent on a trip to Israel, of all places, when her disorganized thinking alarmed her travel companions. After her mother's death, Nina seemed to float aimlessly. It was as if Nina were a balloon and her mother had been the tether.

Nina and I decided to get a table in the section of the café with wait staff: a small nod to the years gone by, as we had never before sat in this area. I thought of how I could justify that long-ago afternoon and my subsequent failure to reach out. I wanted to explain that I had been paralyzed by denial and fear.

I waited for an appropriate time to unleash the torrent of apologies gathered on the tip of my tongue. The longer they sat, the more useless they seemed; at last I realized that whatever excuses I offered did nothing for Nina; they functioned merely to alleviate my own guilt. The best thing I could do now was not to say I was sorry but to show it: give her the undivided attention I had refused her before. She had a dozen wonderful things to share. She was studying to become a counselor and was close to being licensed. She told me about the teenagers she works with and her animal-rescue work and the dog she had adopted. She mentioned her boyfriend who had died since the last time we saw one another but only to tell me she stayed in touch with his daughter from a previous relationship.

When Lisa goes to check on Sydney, I wander over to the lower half of the *tzedakah* pinball display. At this level it is something called the "Tikkun Olam House." It's the shape of a little playhouse with windows. From my reading I know that *tikkun olam* means "to repair the world" and is a fundamental concept in Judaism, perhaps even the most fundamental, the reason underlying everything. Each time a person does something good or follows one of God's directives, he or she contributes to the ultimate goal of *tikkun olam*. This display's size and central location suggests that the lessons provided here could be more important than any other, the primary message kids are meant to take away from this experience.

A window at the top of the house asks, "Where is your help needed?" A series of backlit boxes reveal cartoon suggestions of beneficiaries: communities, other people, the earth, animals. At the very bottom, low enough for the tiniest tots to paw, three big slots await tokens. The first has a picture of a dollar so that feeding it is meant to represent giving money. Another slot is labeled with a clock, suggesting a second option for what you might offer: time. But it's the middle slot I find most interesting. It sports a big bright ball with beams radiating out. To put your tokens here is to give something akin to your energy or your light. Maybe it means giving both time and money, but it transcends these categories because what you impart is even more personal. It's your attention, your focus. It could be listening to stories of hardship, helping a person carry the burden of heartache, but it's just as likely to demand something that human nature makes more difficult: celebrating another's good fortune. Nina's accomplishments, Becky's little boy, Deb's paintings—my friends had wanted nothing more from me than to share in the joy of their unique contributions. I marshaled a positive force from the depths of my heart and soul and made a curious discovery: the more light I shined on their joy, the more joy I felt.

I ask Sydney to make one last stop with me. It's an exhibit that re-creates the Western Wall, the only part of the original Temple in Jerusalem that still exists (perhaps thanks to my old friend Nehemiah). Here it is called the Wishing Wall; blocks that look like ancient, weathered stones have been affixed to a regular wall. Just as I've seen in pictures of the real deal, small scraps of paper are stuck between the stones.

A nearby table has a stack of small papers that invite us to, "Draw or write your wish for the world and place it at the Wishing Wall." I tell Sydney to put her wish down and I'll do the same. We're quiet for a few minutes as we concentrate, and then Sydney shows me what she decided on. In the box provided she's written, "More play dates with friends." I laugh because mine's not so different really. I want joy, for me and my friends. I don't want to wallow in the sorrow; I want to help repair the world by shining my light on all the good too. Then Sydney and I fold our wishes into fat little squares and add them to the wall.

o

A circle is a powerful symbol. I think most Kabbalists would agree that a circle represents one of the most potent forces in the universe. The Jewish mystic tradition divides the world into two basic components: the source of all power, infinitely giving energy and light, and the repository of this power, which holds and gives it shape. In Kabbalah the latter is referred to as "the vessel," often symbolized by a circle, like a container's open mouth. I laugh when I remember that before I started this religious exploration I thought of myself as a shattered pot. Healing, in Kabbalistic terms, is the creation of a strong vessel. One might think that the source of power is the force in the universe that demands all our attention, but Kabbalists emphasize the critical role of the receptacle—without which the power would be undirected. Much of Kabbalah concerns the proper management of this power, and the word "Kabbalah" means "to receive."

After a regular Sabbath service at a conservative synagogue, I mentioned my intention to explore Kabbalah to a middle-aged man with gentle, watery eyes that widened like two pools swelling. "Be careful," he said, though whether he was warning me about L.A.'s Kabbalah Centre specifically or Kabbalah in general I wasn't sure. Kabbalah has a reputation for being unsafe, and stories abound about its ancient practitioners losing their minds, driven to madness during the exercises meant to tap into the power; these include chanting, singing, breathing, dancing, meditation, and visualization. More than just drawing the energy, the trick is to safely channel it. When this transaction is not mastered, a person may cling to the power, feeding unhealthy self-interest, or misdirect it, fueling negative objectives. For this reason Jewish leaders often say that only mature pupils under the guidance of the most skilled teachers should attempt to practice Kabbalah.

Yet Kabbalistic notions seem to permeate all aspects of Jewish life. Casual references to Kabbalah and Kabbalah scholars peppered the talks of rabbis at practically every service I attended. Basic Jewish concepts were described to me using Kabbalistic ideas: the emphasis on passive activities on Sabbath is designed to foster the receptive, rather than productive, aspects of our nature, and women are excused from many traditional practices because our vessel-like qualities are naturally more fine-tuned than those of men. I even encountered an explanation of the Messianic era in these terms: the period itself will be one of receptivity, which is the source of the peace that will prevail, like a Sabbath that extends indefinitely.

Without meaning to, I happened into a special Kabbalah-inspired service at a reform synagogue. I thought it would be a typical Friday night ceremony that welcomes the Sabbath like those I attended at other synagogues. I expected something bare bones, just a handful of people led by a lone rabbi, but this was different. The chairs in the large sanctuary were arranged in concentric circles starting with a small one at the center and spiraling out; by the time I arrived, the only spaces available were along the outer ring almost to the wall. A photocopied sheet explained that this "new model of worship" began a few years earlier; introduced as "Fifth Friday," it initially took place when a month had an extra Friday. A huge hit, it was incorporated as a regular monthly service renamed "Kabbalat Shabbat." If synagogue leaders were hesitant at first to label their new model Kabbalistic, they were emboldened by the congregation's acceptance. In addition to seating in the round, the entire service is sung by everyone present.

I found an empty seat sandwiched between two young families facing the boyish rabbi and female cantor in the middle circle along with the musicians, whose instruments included a harp, violin, and dobro. As I flipped through the pamphlet to lead me through the service, I thought about how ordinary everyone in the room looked—regular grandmas and grandpas and middle-class couples, not the eccentric elders one might associate with an ancient mystical tradition. These were people who shopped at Target and attended their kids' soccer games. Then the band started up, and all the voices joined together. My pamphlet had phonetic translations of the Hebrew and some English explanations, but I opted to play it by ear. These were the usual prayers but performed in a steady rhythmic fashion. I found I could join, particularly at choruses when phrases and words were repeated over and over in a beautiful hypnotic loop. At one point everyone stood and turned to face the doors of the room. Rising, I quickly consulted my guide and found we were at a prayer to greet the Sabbath. The explanation read, "The Kabbalists used to go out on Friday nights and dance as the sun was setting. It is traditional to face the entry of our prayer-space on the final verse to greet the Sabbath bride." I had seen this analogy before—Sabbath addressed as a woman, particularly as a wife-to-be—but in this context I understood the connotation on a deeper level. In a sense, we were welcoming our own ability to receive, nurtured by the vessel-like, feminine aspects of Sabbath.

Profound Kabbalistic tidbits arrived at unexpected times, like offerings dropped in my path, but the one time I went looking for them—when I visited L.A.'s Kabbalah Centre—I was given nothing. For years I had been reading about the Kabbalah Centre, usually in the captions beneath tabloid photos of celebrities exiting a building with little red strings freshly tied around their wrists. Or it was Madonna in an interview talking about her life-changing study of this ancient wisdom and mysteriously revealing that her "Kabbalah name" is Esther. I had no inkling what Kabbalah was, and when I decided to visit the Kabbalah Centre in the early stages of my journey, I still hadn't grasped the basics I know now.

I found the place on a busy street in what appears to be an old Spanish-style house. It was the middle of the afternoon on a weekday, and no paparazzi were in evidence. Inside, young women seemed to be running the show. One was at a reception desk, another manning the gift shop. A third was wandering around aimlessly. She approached me. She had a name tag and was something called a "Study Path Manager." She couldn't have been more than twenty-five years old; that she should be the first representative of an ancient wisdom I associated with hunched and wizened men struck me as strange. Maybe she's exceptionally wise, I thought.

"Can I help you?" she asked.

"Yes," I replied. "What is Kabbalah?"

By way of an answer she posed a scenario. "Say you gather the best basketball players in the world," she said, "but you don't give them the rules of the game. What happens?" I was confused, how did we know they were the best players if they didn't know the game?

I guessed at what answer was expected. "They aren't able to play?"

Her already bright eyes brightened further. "Yes! Kabbalah is the rules."

She handed me a shiny flyer that announced, "You Deserve Great Things" and invited me back for a free seminar on Tuesday night at seven p.m.

At the appointed evening and time, I sat in a conference room with eight other curious souls, and here is what I learned from three attractive young women: sign up for the Power of Kabbalah (POK) class and all the secrets to Kabbalistic teachings would be revealed and my paradigm shifted. Each ten-week course will take me further along my spiritual quest. POK 1 teaches that I create my own reality. POK 2 shows me how to remove my blockages. Finally, in POK 3, I learn to become a purer channel for the Light of the Creator. If I sign up for the complete series—POK 1, POK 2, and POK 3—I get a $770 value for $520. Payment methods include Visa, MasterCard, American Express, Discover, cash, or check (payable to the Kabbalah Centre).

So, from what I gathered, I could have everything I wanted in the world—in particular "lasting fulfillment"—if I knew how to properly receive these gifts. Except what I wanted at that particular moment was to know exactly what Kabbalah was, which no one would tell me. I also wanted to take a look in the Centre's main sanctuary, which I was told was off limits, and to sit in on a class in session—from which I was swiftly booted.

Yet at the Kabbalat Shabbat service in an ordinary reform synagogue just a few blocks from the ice-skating rink I frequented as a teenager, on an evening when I did not expect anything and yet was open to what might come, I happened on a group of people who were inviting, maybe even pulling, light into the world. No slick marketing materials, no fancy jargon, no pretty girls with evasive answers. Just a surprising number of old ladies and a bunch of other normal folks sitting in a big circle using their voices and imaginations to fill up with joy and gratitude and a sense of abundance so as not to be the sort of people who move through the world feeling needy or lacking—you know the sort, people who are willing to manipulate and lie and steal and hurt because they want more, always more. As I sat and sang, I understood a primary purpose of Kabbalah, if not all the specifics. It is this: to toil in the privacy of your own heart to know and feel that you are and possess more than enough so that you can show up to any situation with something to give. It might take an inordinate amount of work to acknowledge and meet your own voracious need, but it must be done so you're not, intentionally or unintentionally, looking to sources outside of yourself to meet that need. Instead you are able to offer empathy, support, forgiveness, or joy. Your light shines because your vessel is full and you have more than enough to share.

Partway through the Kabbalat Shabbat, the singing stops and the rabbi makes his way to the front of the room. Several individuals break away from the circle to join him. This is a joyous occasion, the rabbi explains, because tonight the newest addition to the family before you receives her Hebrew name. Only then do I notice that one of the women is holding a tiny bundle in her arms, and I put the pieces together: this is a naming ceremony, one of the most significant of the Jewish life-cycle rites of passage. Boy babies are normally named during a bris eight days after being born, but female newborns are named at the synagogue in front of the entire congregation.

The mom, holding the infant, huddles with both grandmothers. The rabbi wraps their shoulders in a single prayer shawl, pulling them in close. He speaks to the women, expressing sentiments you might expect to hear: how this baby is the future, the continuation of all of her ancestors who lived before her. Then he flips the script and addresses the baby directly. "You will one day be an ancestor like us," he tells her. I imagine this room seventy years from now, when most everyone here tonight is gone and this brand-new human is the older generation wrapped in a prayer shawl giving out special names.

I still have that image in mind when the congregants begin singing the Mourner's Kaddish. When I first realized this prayer for the deceased was a part of every service at every synagogue, I thought it was intended specifically for those who were grieving. When we came to it, all those who had lost someone within the last year or so stood, and sometimes the rabbi requested them to call out the name of the departed. I didn't know or understand the significance of the Hebrew words being recited by the congregation, but I sensed it was a sorrowful lamentation, the shaking of a metaphorical fist at the cruelty of death. I thought people stood because they were meant to see one another and thereby know they were not alone in their grief and to allow the rest of the congregation to identify those in need of our support. I believed the reciting of the Mourner's Kaddish was akin to other life-cycle ceremonies in Judaism—whether a naming or bar mitzvah or wedding—that act as markers in a person's life, tying her to millions of others in the past, present, and future. The ceremony might transform what feels like an ordinary occasion into one with extraordinary potential, or it might reassure a person who feels overwhelmed that what he is experiencing is actually very ordinary.

I was surprised when I saw an English translation of the Mourner's Kaddish and realized it doesn't even mention death. It's simply a collection of lines praising and thanking God. Only then did I learn the true purpose is to rise up and proclaim your joy and love at a time when you might feel bitter or lost or angry. But the Mourner's Kaddish continues to be spoken by the entire congregation day in and day out, long after the official grieving period for any one person has passed. The gratitude it expresses is offered on behalf of all those who are departed, giving voice to worshipful words they can no longer utter here on earth. Through future generations, the dead continue to honor God indefinitely.

I sensed how those who are no longer here rely on those who are here and are yet to be here to carry on expressing faith and continue the task of bringing light into the world. It's such a big job, no one generation can do it alone; it's an ongoing responsibility that rests on the shoulders of countless generations. Only together can the ultimate goal of *tikkun olam*, or repairing the world, be achieved. I learned that the literal translation of *tikkun olam* is something like "forever light." Each generation after the next working to shine light here on earth is how the healing takes place.

o

During my visit to the Kabbalah Centre, I bought a book called *God Wears Lipstick: Kabbalah for Women* by the wife in the husband-wife duo that founded the center. I hoped it would shed light on the Light. In it she explains that before the universe as we know it formed, all that existed was the light and the original vessel. Everything we perceive as matter was united in this single vessel until the Big Bang blew it apart. Now we think of ourselves and all we see as being separate, unique entities, when our true nature is really one of cohesiveness. The book says that in a sense, existence is a process of bringing the shards together again to "regain our former wholeness." With this idea fresh in my mind, I decide it's time to try to find my old Hasidic neighbors.

I study a map of the neighborhood and find an orthodox synagogue seven blocks from the corner of their apartment complex. Perhaps the family had moved, but it seemed likely that someone at the synagogue would remember them. I can reconnect with their community if not the family itself.

I call and make sure they are all right with visitors and to see if I need to do something with my hair. A rabbi with a rough Brooklyn accent says, "It's not important your hair."

By the time I am ready, the only thing showing besides my hair is a few inches of neck, my face, and hands. I arrive early. I thought parking would be a nightmare, but a space directly in front sat waiting. I wonder what the building was before being converted into a synagogue. A World War II dance hall? Inside looks like an old gymnasium. I spot a couple of elderly women behind a partition, and I join them. They are speaking in hushed tones, and they nod in my direction then return to whispering. I flip through a prayer book with no English or phonetic translation, just a sea of squiggles, and listen to the rain falling outside. Everything feels damp and dreary and not at all welcoming. I wonder how often they are visited by non-Jews. I review my motives hoping some element of insincerity will grant me good reason to flee. I decide I am coming from a genuine place and that the discomfort is a sign of this effort's importance.

No one pays any attention to me. Male voices chant on the other side of the partition. More women arrive, but they seem not to notice me. They set about chatting quietly with one another. Every once in a while, one will stand, bow, take a step back, and mouth prayers. Occasionally some kids wander over to say a few words to their moms before being ushered back to their classroom.

I sit mute and invisible for what feels like a long time. As the sounds and activities go on around me, I am painfully aware of my own presence, even more so because no one else seems to notice it. Maybe my childhood musings were accurate: I really do exist in another dimension from these folks. Eventually, a woman my age approaches. "What brings you here today?" She asks. I can tell she is trying to be friendly, but she doesn't smile.

Her name is Rachel, and she looks surprisingly normal. I know her hair is a wig because most Hasidic women use wigs to cover their real hair, but it looks like my hair, long and dark, except better. My hair is a fuzzy mess from the moisture in the air, but hers is perfectly smooth. I explain about living down the street and how I saw the kids but never spoke to them. "I've come back," I say. Spoken to a stranger, the endeavor seems bizarre, but she nods like it is the most natural thing in the world.

She says, "My husband grew up there."

I couldn't believe it. It was that easy. I had found them.

"He's the head rabbi here." She points at a man who had emerged from behind the partition to check on something at the far end of the gymnasium. He is dressed almost identically to how I remember. His little suit has gotten big. Even from far away, I spy faint traces of the boy my age through his enormous beard. "His mom still lives there."

After Rachel leaves me, I try to relax. I close my eyes and focus on the sound of the Hebrew words being spoken by the men. I imagine each one like a soap bubble, filled with love and gratitude, floating up and out beyond this room.

Midway through the service, two men pull apart each side of the partition. A glare floods the cozy dark of the women's side, and I squint. I felt uncomfortably exposed.

A rabbi stands behind a podium. He is the one with the mobster accent. He makes several announcements in preparation for Passover, which will begin the following Friday evening. Most importantly, he wants to remind everyone to get rid of all *chametz*, which is food made of grain mixed with water that has fermented or risen. This is given up on Passover in honor of the ancestors who fled Egypt and had neither the time nor accommodations to prepare such elaborate dishes. I always knew flat, cracker-like matzo was eaten instead of bread during this holiday, but I hadn't realized all the other things that are forbidden: beer, hard alcohol, pastas, cookies, and cereals—most of the items that are commonly kept in bulk in pantries. To avoid throwing away these often-costly goods, many observant Jews have developed a system whereby they temporarily "sell" them to a non-Jew and then buy them back after Passover. The leavened products may even stay in the house, though they will technically not belong to its inhabitants during that time. Rabbis generally manage this transaction.

The rabbi explains that this is the last chance to pick up the forms labeled "Delegation of Power of Attorney for Sale of Chametz" from a nearby pile. He invites anyone who wants to help sweep all *chametz* from every surface of the synagogue to come back on Thursday evening. When he is finished speaking, the men reclose the partition. The women's side dims, the words return to Hebrew, and I go back to pretending the source of the voice is the great and mighty Oz.

After the service, we do blessings over cups of wine and challah loaves. An older woman approaches me. Here is the mother, who has been told about me. Her wig is a chestnut bob. She says her name in Hebrew, a sound like a gurgle with a hiccup. I try to imitate her, but she looks disappointed. "Why didn't you ever come into our yard to play?" she asks in the wake of our brief introduction. I don't know what to say; I hadn't realized that was an option. I don't recall anyone in her family ever making eye contact with me, much less inviting me into their yard. She says, "The neighbors are always so standoffish with us." She seems angry at me.

She explains that for the past several years, she's been organizing a little street festival on the block for the Sukkot holiday. They construct a Sukkah hut, a temporary dwelling usually made of palm fronds that observant Jews build every fall to replicate those used by their ancestors after their exodus from Egypt. "We invite the kids from the street, but they don't come." Her eyes are accusatory.

Now I am getting miffed. Instead of recognizing me as a neighbor reaching out, she is seeing me as representing everyone who has failed to make contact.

The tension between us is palpable as she introduces me to her son, the head rabbi. It is a brief, awkward hello with no handshake. When we were kids, it would have been okay for us to talk and play, but now we are officially forbidden from touching and discouraged from engaging in unnecessary chitchat. "Hello," I say. "Hello," he says. With that, I suppose, a tiny corner of universe is mended.

The mother asks me to stay for the women's group, which is starting in a few minutes. I feel she is just being polite, but I accept. She and I wait for the others to join us around a big table; sitting quietly together, the air of resentment begins to dissipate. I tiptoe back to our previous conversation. "Maybe the neighbors don't realize you're open to social interaction with them." I am trying to be as gentle as possible. I think of how intimidated I had felt passing their yard, an extension of their secret and sacred world. She nods slowly, her gaze softening. She invites me to return to the synagogue the following Friday for the annual dinner they host on the first night of Passover. "Thank you," I say. "I'd like that." It would be my first-ever Passover. When the other women arrive, she introduces me as an old neighbor who has returned. "She didn't feel comfortable saying hello back then, but she's come now," she explains. Everyone raises tiny cups of white wine at me, and I say, "Better late than never."

Freedom Song

Before returning to celebrate with my old ultra-orthodox neighbors on the first night of Passover, I decided to take a self-guided tour of the Fairfax area, a section of Los Angeles known for its high numbers of orthodox Jews. Here the city is particularly gritty, the Jews particularly Jewish, and the juxtaposition particularly vivid. I was stopped at a light, thinking about how the only other place in the United States to offer this same cultural mash-up may be parts of Brooklyn, when a Hasidic man in full fuzzy-hatted regalia caught my eye and I turned to look just as he crossed paths with a scantily clad prostitute in Lucite heels, who, on closer inspection, also appeared to be a young man. So ho-hum was this encounter that neither seemed to notice the other. The area is also home to a cluster of Jewish shops, like a little main street with a deli, bakery, and a couple of small grocery stores. I parked and wandered up and down the street, thinking what it must have been like when the Venice boardwalk looked like this. One particularly expansive window front displayed a range of supplies: ram horns, menorahs, prayer shawls—all the odds and ends one might need to closely observe Judaism. I passed a bakery that I imagined had been cranking out matzo sheets for the last several days. I thought about the fact that even if you bought all your food from these establishments—kosher everything—being kosher still depends on the choices you make at every meal. Eating a kosher pastry made with butter and a slab of kosher meat together would render it non-kosher. Having all these goods available must be convenient, but you still have to consider what goes into each item and how they are grouped, combined, and presented. The rigors of this lifestyle are astounding; it requires the support of a community.

By the time I arrive at the synagogue for Passover dinner, it is dark outside. The gymnasium has been completely transformed for the feast. Fluorescent lights blaze over four long tables already populated with an odd assortment of individuals, men down one side and women down the other. Most of the guests do not appear Hasidic; they are a bit of everything, Jews from many backgrounds and countries. The rabbis and their families occupy separate tables on either side of the four main tables, whether to protect us from the world or themselves from us, I can't be sure. As I enter the room, I freeze to take it all in. I spot the rabbi's wife, Rachel, and wave; she smiles and waves back.

I notice that the corner of the room where there had been an assortment of liquor bottles the week before is now wiped clean, the spirits nowhere to be seen.

I find a seat in one of the last available spaces, to the left of a cluster of Iranian-American Jews, one of whom sports a platinum hairdo and ample bosom like a Persian Dolly Parton. Across the table is a young couple visiting from Israel and, to their right, a guy who appears completely out of place. He looks like a Vietnam vet with an American flag bandana tied around his head and a scraggily white beard. He must be a drifter who has come in for a free meal.

Long sheets of industrial-sized Saran Wrap cover each table, and atop this waterproof layer sits a jumble of plastic plates, cutlery, and cups, punctuated by bottles of wine and stacks of matzo. Within reaching distance of my seat, a small platter has been set with the Passover elements. I understand that minor variations might be found at Passover tables elsewhere, but here we had: a hunk of cooked meat with the bone still in, a single peeled hard-boiled egg, a blob of horseradish, a lump of apple cinnamon mush, and several sprigs of parsley. Next to this is a small Styrofoam bowl of water that is salted. As the proceedings officially begin, I turn my attention to my old friend and new acquaintance, the head rabbi, who is standing at his table holding an elaborate oversized wine glass. He pronounces this the "Cup of Elijah," the prophet whose arrival is supposed to herald the coming of the messiah. Tonight Elijah's drink awaits him, and the door is left ajar in anticipation of his grand entrance.

If you allow it, something happens on this night of storytelling and symbolic reenactment. I chew a bit of parsley dipped in saltwater, and I let it take me back. Passover isn't meant as a memorial to the events of a long-dead group of people; the Jewish sages wrote, "In every generation a man is obligated to regard himself as having personally come out of Egypt." Just as the living give voice to expressions of gratitude for the dead with the Mourner's Kaddish, we are to make the memories of being enslaved our own. Judaism collapses past and present: time is only an ever-changing now, and what we think of as different generations are merely a single people evolving and surviving. Tonight I let the sages' words ring true for a woman, as well as a non-Jew. The taste of salty water on the parsley is the sweat dripping into my mouth from the physical exertion in brutal heat, and my angry tears at having my freedom stolen. But my reverie of hardship is interrupted by the lively crunch of the parsley; freshness as vibrant as the color green itself floods my mouth, filled with life and hope.

From their stations at the edges of the room, the rabbis lead us through the steps. First, the recollections of enslavement: we scoop a spoonful of the apple mixture on to our plates to remind us of the adobe mortar we were made to mold into bricks, along with a dollop of horseradish for the bitter experience of forced labor. Then we are freed by the Egyptian leader, Pharaoh, after a series of plagues befall his land. Calamities including swarms of lice, flies, and locusts weaken his resolve. Water turns to blood, and the sun disappears, and his people develop incurable boils. One of the rabbis instructs us to spill a drop of wine onto our plates as he lists each plague. These are the tears we shed for the Egyptians because any human suffering is sorrowful, even if it is the price of freedom. The last plague, the death of every firstborn human and animal, finally sways Pharaoh to release the slaves, an event commemorated by the hunk of meat on the Passover platter. The Jews smeared a bit of blood from a sacrificed lamb on their houses so death would know which families to "pass over." The meat is a token of this gesture as well as a nod to the significance of animal sacrifice at the tabernacle and temple. I chew a piece of plain matzo, which turns into a flavorless lump on my tongue. It tastes like the nourishment of a fleeing people, the basic minimum to sustain life.

I watch my tablemates construct little sandwiches with apple mush and the horseradish by putting this odd combination of fillings between two shards of matzo bread. I build my own and eat it along with them. I am surprised by the overpowering sweetness, perhaps heightened by the contrast to the bitter horseradish. That's the thing about Passover: it's ultimately a celebration of freedom. The memory of slavery offers contrast that heightens the joy and gratitude we feel for the ability to live freely.

As the festivities progress, we consume the requisite four cups of wine and the atmosphere grows more jubilant. No one is required to fill her cup to the top but merely to take a hearty gulp each time, and a grape juice alternative is provided, but most people opt for wine, and some, like my Vietnam vet tablemate, take its consumption very seriously. We have been provided a small cup for wine and a large one for water, but he has swapped his water cup for the wine, filling it to the brim each time. Watching him, I abandon the notion that he is here for the free meal. He knows the Hebrew prayers by heart, and his enthusiasm for every aspect of the evening is contagious; when he eyes the people around him, their smiles grow. Each time we drink, everyone in the room tilts to the left like we are performing some synchronized dance movement. Per tradition, we are mimicking an angle of repose, as if reclining while drinking our wine, a luxury only a free person would enjoy. The Vietnam vet leans so far I think his wine might spill.

The entire room breaks out in a traditional song. The lyrics are an inventory of all the good things that have happened to the Jews before, during, and after Passover, but it's the single-word chorus everyone sings with such delight that it's impossible not to sing along. The word is *Dayenu*, and it translates into something like "more than enough." It expresses a deep sense of gratitude and satisfaction even when times are hard and means scarce. We sing the word *Dayenu* over and over again, clapping and shouting. At one point, three rabbis get up and begin to dance. Others join them, and for several minutes the joy bubbles over and the crowd cheers them on and grown men dance in a circle like ecstatic school children.

At that moment, as my tablemates and I grin wildly at one another, it dawns on me. "More than enough" is a theme that runs throughout Judaism; even Hanukkah has it: the lamp oil was only supposed to last a single night, but it lasted for eight. Hence the menorah's eight lights. The goal is to help us understand not only that we have enough but also that we are enough. Because the forces that rob us of freedom are just as likely to come from within, from our own thoughts and beliefs that prevent us from living fully. Many of us are imprisoned by the guilt and fear we haul around as birthright, the sensation of somehow falling short, which can provoke us to act in a myriad of destructive ways—aggressive actions, compulsive thinking, addictive behavior—that temporarily alleviate the suffering by blotting out our demeaning dialogue until they lose that power and become a private punishment, a prison built for us by us. Or maybe we disappear from the lives of those who love us because some part of us thinks we don't deserve that love. In this sense, the most radical religious undertaking is to work past these difficult and universal feelings to free ourselves from the confines imposed by our human perspective. Overcoming them does not come easily or naturally, which is why we call on the assistance of a supernatural strength, a higher power, God.

One of my favorite moments in every Sabbath service I attended came just before the rabbi's Torah reading, when he or she, usually with a few helpers, hoisted the holy book around the sanctuary. Members of the congregation would crowd toward the aisle to share a kiss with the Torah as it passed, either touching it with a prayer book or with the fringe of a prayer shawl and then bringing it to their lips—whether they were kissing it or letting it kissing them, I was never quite sure. Either way, I found it such a beautiful gesture that I always tried to participate. I would put my prayer book to my lips and then reach for the Torah and then bring it back to my lips so no matter what was kissing what, I had it covered. Even when the women were separated, the men would bring the Torah to an opening and we would rush to it as if to glimpse a rock star. Sometimes the Torah passed so quickly hardly anyone got a good kiss in, and a handful were left to toss a kiss in the air as the book whizzed past. I read that this practice of Torah smooching is considered an archaic custom by some, one that reform synagogues may have abandoned, but I found it in effect almost everywhere I went, lending credence to the theory that many reform places are embracing old traditions, even passionately so.

For the last Sabbath service of my trip, I went to a hipster synagogue I kept hearing about and was able to kiss the Torah not once but twice. Located in the middle of West L.A., this synagogue caters to young, cool Jews from all over the area and has a reputation for being particularly unorthodox; it was the only one I visited with a female rabbi. Yet besides the rabbi's gender, the main thing that seemed to distinguish it from more conservative places of worship was the level of enthusiasm with which the congregation performed even the smallest prayers and rituals. Something as minor as the Torah procession was performed so wholeheartedly that everyone was given ample opportunity to kiss the good book as many times as he wanted. I had rushed through the first kiss, trying to seize the moment quickly, so when it came back around, I went in for a second. This time I smooched that Torah like I meant it, like it was a dear friend I might not see again for a long time.

At the end of the Passover dinner, only the rabbis and their families remained; they had been serving the guests and were just now getting a chance to eat. I didn't want to leave yet, so I asked Rachel if I could stay to help clean. She showed me how to scoop up the plastic table coverings—plates, cups, cutlery, everything—into one big trash ball. I cleared the tables and then picked up items that had fallen on the floor—napkins, forks, shards of matzo. Underneath a table, I found a coloring book page of the ten plagues. Some kid had drawn little germs of pestilence with bright pink and purple.

The mother approached to thank me for helping. I reached for her hands and held them briefly between mine. It was a small gesture, but it was huge, too.

After she left me, I paused to appreciate the room: the rabbis and their families chatting and eating. This was their normal life and I was in the middle of it.

I was still congratulating myself on how well I fit in when Rachel approached and asked if I wouldn't mind helping with something in the kitchen. See, I said to myself, she and I are working together.

I followed her to the back where the burners on two industrial stoves were going. It was at least 100 degrees in there. "Would you mind turning them off?" she asked. I paused, considering the situation. I had read about observant Jews employing a non-Jew to stoke their fires and do the activities forbidden on Sabbath, but I had thought the practice was comical and old timey. Hadn't timers and slow cookers taken their place?

Sweat was beading on my brow. "Are you asking me to be your Sabbath Gentile?"

She laughed and nodded.

What would they do if I weren't here? I imagined the rabbi roaming the block explaining his need to passersby. It was almost midnight. Would he slip a $20 to a homeless person to do the task?

"It's nice to have someone who understands," she said.

Not exactly the high regard I had imagined, but she was right, I did understand—and maybe that was more than enough.

Buddhism

I am in the sanctuary of a Buddhist monastery "meditating." I put that in quotes because what I'm really doing is sitting in a chair, thinking. I've made a pit stop in Berkeley, California, on my way back to Washington from Los Angeles. It's a decision I came to because I would be passing right by on the freeway. Then I was offered the use of a guest room with free rein to come and go as I pleased for as long as I'd want. I tried to come up with a good reason to decline but could think of none. I plan to stay for a few weeks to explore Buddhism, which feels appropriate not just because the Bay Area is a hot spot for this particular faith but also because of how I behaved when I was going to school here. As long as I'm going back and staring down old demons, I suppose it's time to face the crappy karma I left in this place.

As a college student, I was not what you might call "lots of fun." I was the person who hissed at people for talking in the hallway past ten p.m., who scowled at merry pranksters for laughing too loudly. I was anxious about my grades and about proper behavior. I was an "old soul"—but not the beautiful, wise kind you hear about; I was more the grumpy, frowny kind. Somewhere out there existed a strict code of conduct, and it was my job to judge how everyone stacked up. I may have been only twenty years old, but my spine buckled from the burden of my role as "enforcer of all the rules" on a global scale. Looking back I can see how that old river of shame—the potent mix of fear and anger that had gone dormant in me for a time—bubbled just below. It threatened to seep up as anxiety or panic. Order was my only defense to keep it locked beneath the surface.

Wherever I was, I always thought somewhere else would be better. When I lived in the dorms, I imagined how much happier I'd be living in a student run co-op; when I moved to a co-op, I thought I'd really start enjoying life once I had my own apartment; when I had my own apartment, I thought a different, more happiness-inducing apartment was the answer. This discontent clung to me year to year, month to month, second to second. I would reflect on moments that were infinitely better than the one I was currently occupying, perhaps a moment I had lived in the past that hadn't seemed so great at the time but now, in retrospect, took on the romantic patina of life lived right. Or I longed for that fantastic future moment that I just knew, once I came to it, would offer up bliss as sure and solid as the ground beneath my feet. Of course, once I got there, joy eluded my grasp like a phantom.

The Thought Highway

The monastery in which I am sitting is just a few blocks from my alma mater. The building is actually an old church, the white steeple a reminder of its former incarnation. The pews have been removed, and the tall windows that line either side of the sanctuary have been filled with various stained-glass depictions of Buddha, some standing and some sitting. The altar remains, but now it has a gold Buddha statue several feet tall sitting on an intricately carved wood table. On either side is an orchid plant, the likes of which I have never seen; each boasts at least a hundred miniature yellow faces grinning out.

Before I entered the room, I obeyed a sign requesting that I remove my shoes. Other than that, I'm not sure what I'm supposed to do. I understand that it's okay for me to be here because the monastery hosts a public meditation hour every morning and evening. It also offers classes and interfaith roundtables and provides a home to a handful of Buddhist monks and nuns. But I'm the first here on this particular evening, so I take a seat in one of a few chairs at the back of the room. From this vantage, I can watch as people arrive, bowing even before crossing the threshold of the room and then, once they enter, bowing again toward the altar. Each selects a mat and a cushion from stacks along the wall and then arranges them on the floor before taking a seat. After several minutes, a gentle gong sounds, and everyone settles down, growing so still and quiet that the silence inside the room seems to magnify the sounds from the street. Rap music spills from a passing car, and a woman stands somewhere nearby chatting on her cell phone.

All I know about meditation is that it's meant to induce a tranquil state of mind. I command my thoughts to settle down, but they defy my orders and grow more active. I feel like I'm riding one of those mechanical bulls. I yell, "Slower!" and it speeds up instead. At times, I grow so deeply embedded in daydreams of my past, it's like I'm living them again—except through the filter of greater understanding, making them all the more painful. I feel guilty for how I behaved and upset at the angsty, angry young woman I was. Waves of shame and sadness wash over me, and tears sting my eyes. At moments it's almost too excruciating to bear, and I teeter on the verge of running from the room to find a private spot, a bathroom stall somewhere, where I can bawl my heart out.

Mercifully, the hour comes to an end with me still planted in my seat. People rise and stretch and return their cushions to the stacks. Their serene expressions seem to indicate that they've enjoyed a reprieve from the day's chaos. As I stand, I feel quite the opposite. I'm relieved that the bucking has stopped and I am walking away in one piece.

Later that night I organize the pile of books I brought and work out a flowchart of Buddhist centers I plan to visit. Any large university is surrounded by lots of places of worship, but Berkeley has an inordinate number of Buddhist options. They surround campus on all sides and represent derivations of the faith from Korea, China, Japan, Tibet, and Thailand. Some, like the monastery I visited earlier in the evening, offer a hybrid approach, emphasizing various aspects of different traditions. Most provide instruction sessions—orientations, classes, talks—throughout the week, and I hope to attend as many of these as possible. I'll take an aggressive approach to getting peaceful.

o

From my reading I'm beginning to understand that Siddhārtha Gautama, the real-life man who would become known as Buddha, or "the one who woke up," was something of a "do-it-yourself" neuroscientist. He realized that if he remained silent and paid close attention, he could observe how his mind worked. During his meditation, the present moment was free of activity, his body motionless, yet he could watch as thoughts arose like stories, their plots unspooling as if real, triggering genuine emotions. He discovered that to sit in a state of awareness of the thinking process was to grasp important truths about the experience of being human. This was how one started on the path to enlightenment.

This simple fact was the core of what he taught during his lifetime. Some of his students single-mindedly sought the answers this practice provided, retreating from ordinary society to dedicate themselves to the endeavor. Others decided to investigate this source of wisdom but remain among the general public with the purpose of helping regular people like me understand what Siddhārtha Gautama was talking about. The goal of this second type of devotee, according to an oft-used metaphor, is to help transport as many humans as possible over the river of life on the raft that is the Buddha's teachings.

The monk who answers the doorbell I ring is one such ferry captain. Roughly twenty-four hours after my first official meditation experience, I arrive at what appears to be a regular house in a residential area near campus. Upon closer inspection, a little sign distinguishes it as a Buddhist priory. A middle-aged man with a shaved head and long brown robe opens the door. It takes me a moment to register that he is white, not Asian; with his shaved head and smile lines, he more closely resembles a bald, laughing Buddha than an average Joe. As he greets me, I assume he knows why I am here, as it is just a minute or two before meditation instruction is set to begin and, well, here I am. But he stares at me expectantly, nothing taken for granted. His blank-slate expression throws me off, and I think I have gotten either the wrong time or place.

"I'm here for the meditation instruction?" I say, doing that thing I hate where the statement turns into a question at the end.

"Yes." He smiles. "Follow me."

We walk through what was once a large living room but is now a sanctuary with a shrine and meditation cushions arranged along the walls. He takes me through a kitchen and beyond into a small room with a single bookcase. "Wait here," he tells me. "We'll start soon."

I take a seat on one of a few folding chairs in what I imagine was once a child's bedroom, and the monk leaves. Like the monastery I visited the day before, this one offers morning and evening meditation periods. Once a week, an orientation is provided just before an evening meditation so that beginners can stay and practice what they've learned.

From where I sit, I can see through to the kitchen. I watch a cat saunter across the linoleum and rub its neck against a cabinet corner. This sight triggers a chain of thoughts: I wonder what it's like to be a pet among Buddhists, if he pretends to be a regular pet around the monastery but offers spiritual guidance to the neighbor cats in the alley like some feline guru.

My story is interrupted by a mellow-looking college-aged guy walking into the room. I wouldn't peg him as someone in need of meditation, but he's followed closely by a frazzled woman I would. She looks stunned to have made it on time, her blond hair sticking out in all directions.

The two newcomers join me on the folding chairs, and the monk begins his instructions. Mostly he tries to undo what might be our preconceived notions of meditation. You don't have to sit top-half ramrod straight, bottom-half twisted up like a pretzel. You should be comfortable, find a position that works for you. That might be cross-legged on the floor, but you can also use a little bench with your legs tucked underneath, or even a chair. Think of your spine more like a stack of coins than a broomstick, and just breathe naturally. You don't need to take giant, lung-bursting breaths—though if you want to take a few of those, that's fine. Really, the whole breathing thing is simply a way to place your attention on something happening in the present moment. Focus on the gentle inhalation and exhalation of air in and out of your lungs. The fingers of both your hands should come together roughly at your abdomen–ideally, thumb to thumb—so that your arms form a gentle loop, as do your fingers. Preferably, eyes are open, but relaxed—kind of a soft focus into the middle distance. If something noisy happens like a person outside has loud music or one of the meditators sneezes, try not to get upset. Actually, those are little meditation challenges. Let any irritation that arises be one more thing you place on an imaginary flatbed truck that sputters away.

All of this is preamble to the most important part. Your mind doesn't have to be "empty," he tells us. The idea is neither to pursue nor push away the thoughts that arise. He provides an analogy, further elaborated on in a handout he gives us. Imagine yourself standing on the shoulder of a freeway and the cars that pass are your thoughts. You see them coming but then you let them go. You may suddenly find yourself riding in one, and that's okay. Just try not to get too far down the lane. When you notice yourself being carried off, return to your spot on the side of the road.

It sounds a lot easier than it actually is, at least for a beginner. I know because for the next hour or so I try it. Out in the sanctuary, the other newbies and I join several seasoned meditators who had arrived during our orientation. We each select meditation pads and pillows. Here it is customary to face the wall during meditation, not the altar. I settle on a half-lotus, cross-legged but with one foot tucked beneath my thigh, the other resting on top. I wedge a firm, round cushion under my tailbone until my back feels sturdy. I practice a gentle gaze at the tiny nubs of white stucco. A small cymbal pings.

It's not hard to imagine my thoughts as cars because the sanctuary is near an actual busy street, providing the appropriate sound effect. It's much harder not to hitch a ride, especially when what I think is a flashy one passes—something that promises to sweep me away into a scenery of self-loathing. Like this time when I was a college senior, and a handful of people showed up at my apartment—invited, though not by me. They filed in and sat in the living room, happy and friendly. I was annoyed at them, and at my roommate, which I made obvious with my cold, standoffish demeanor. I couldn't just "go with it" and enjoy an impromptu party. I harrumphed around the kitchen within earshot of the guests.

Within seconds, I have been carried so far from my place at the side of the road that I am in the next county. I am so ashamed of how I behaved that afternoon—and a dozen others like it. I feel heaviness on my shoulders and constriction in my chest. I make that stupid jalopy bring me back to the present moment and drop me off. Go! I shout as it sputters away.

I watch the taillights on that particular thought recede, and it occurs to me to question what is going on here. If the road is my mind, and the cars are my thoughts—and I am standing off to the side, apart from both of those things, then where am I? How is it that my mind can observe my mind? Do I have two minds? Or does it have two parts? I seem to have a narrower one—represented by the road—and then something much bigger—the version that encompasses everything outside of the road, the one that can watch over the other one. It seems to be this vaster version I come back to when I refuse to let my thoughts take me away and opt instead to stay firmly planted in the present moment.

In Buddhism no deity exists in the way that many Westerners conceive of God, as a separate entity or creator. But I've noticed some Buddhists speak of an infinite source from which everything derives, of oneness and unity, descriptions that sound similar to how many

Christians and Jews speak of the divine. I'm seeing how this spot on the side of the road, the present moment, is a Godlike zone.

o

In the accounts we have of many religious figures, the events that occur after the person has embarked on his or her primary mission are what matter most. The story of Jesus really takes off when he leaves his life as a carpenter and begins a nomadic existence teaching and helping others. The Moses narrative gains momentum once he gathers up the Jews and leads them out of Egypt. For both men we have some biographical information from before they became what they were meant to become. But details about their emotional states in the months or years leading up their choice to act, to change their lives completely, are left largely for us to speculate over. I can only imagine that neither made his decision lightly, that whatever tug he felt in his heart was the result of careful consideration, sleepless nights, and maybe tears. Perhaps they even put off the final verdict until the prospect of not acting was more terrifying than facing the unknown that lay ahead.

In the story that's passed down of Siddhārtha Gautama's life, the part before he becomes "Buddha" is emphasized. Like what we know of Martin Luther, his private suffering takes center stage. Siddhārtha's father, the king of the region where they lived in India, wanted so badly for his son to be enamored with his life. He didn't want him to face any of the unpleasant realities of the human experience. The king built a high wall around the palace to block out the muck of the surrounding city; only vibrant people were permitted entry. If someone was injured while on the royal grounds, he was whisked away and not permitted back until he had made a full recovery. On the few occasions that the prince is allowed beyond the wall, attendants are instructed to prepare the route to prevent any chance encounters with disagreeable conditions like old age, illness, or death. The streets are swept clean, the facades coated in fresh paint, and the elderly asked to stay indoors. But small cracks in the shiny veneer do not escape Siddhārtha's keen eye. He spots a wizened, hunched man. On subsequent outings, he happens on a desperately sick person and sees a dead body being cremated in a funeral pyre. When he presses for answers, his attendant admits that no one is exempt from these fates.

The greater the effort to shield the prince, the more pronounced his suffering grows. What had been a twinge of dissatisfaction deteriorates into full-blown misery. He is terrified at the thought of his life one day being over and, at the same time, tormented by the very existence he is afraid to see end; he is bored by the pursuit of superficial pleasures, all the lounging and gazing on dancing ladies. On an outing, Siddhārtha encounters one of the many religious vagabonds who wander the kingdom. "Who are you?" he asks the man. The vagabond replies, "I am a recluse who, terrified by birth and death, has adopted a homeless life to win salvation." Something in this response rings true; Siddhārtha leaves the palace to spend time like the wanderer, searching for a solution to what he calls "the ever-present problem of life and death."

For a long time, the answers Siddhārtha seeks elude him. He studies with various wise men and practices different techniques. He stays with a group of ascetics who attempt to achieve understanding by eating as little as possible. In diminishing the physical, they hope to strengthen their grasp of the metaphysical. Siddhārtha starves himself, but this strategy only perpetuates his pain. He comes to see it as another expression of his discomfort with the ever-present problem of life and death.

This stage of Siddhārtha's journey reminds me of my own past struggles with food. Denying my body nourishment wasn't about vanity, as one might assume; rather, it was a response to a veiled conviction that I was not, and would never be, enough. On some level I did not feel worthy of the space I took up. To disappear was both punishment and solution. Yet I continued to suffer as much, if not more. I found no relief. Like Siddhārtha, I craved a different setting, a new version of myself—always something other than where and what I was. Starvation did nothing to address the real problem.

For six years, Siddhārtha continues in this pattern of discontent, unhappy in his life and miserable at the thought of death. He learns to make some concessions to his physical needs—sufficient food and a few creature comforts—but he still struggles with accepting things as they are, with feeling at peace in light of his human condition. He finds a pleasant spot under a tree, close enough to the trunk that he can lean against it if he needs to, and makes a nice place to sit, with a bed of straw. He commits to staying until he finds a way to end his suffering. For a time he falls into old habits: he gets caught up in the past; he worries about the future. Finally he manages to subdue those thoughts, to plant his feet firmly in the "now." At last, at the age of thirty-five, he arrives at "nirvana" or "the extinction of all concepts." He sees things just as they are, not filtered through memories or projections or ideas. His search for a more suitable place to be comes to an end. He settles into the simple peace that only the present moment can provide. For the rest of his life, he works to tell others about the peace of this simple state of being. His teachings, called "dharma," are repeated, handed down, and later written by his followers.

This newfound perspective transforms Siddhārtha into Buddha and eliminates his trepidation about life and death by providing him with a deeper understanding of the human condition. To communicate this insight to others, he used a number of analogies. One involves a single blind tortoise swimming in a vast ocean on the surface of which floats a gold ring. The tortoise comes up for air only once every hundred years. It is rarer, said the Buddha, to be born human than for the turtle to come up for a breath with its neck through the ring.

Jesus characterized the gate to life as narrow. Here, Buddha makes a similar point. To sense those infinitesimally slender chances and not put words to it is to feel overwhelmed, even to perceive its enormity as a burden. But to acknowledge it is to bring it into the open, to begin to embrace those slim odds, to start on a path from fear to gratitude. At the same time, the analogy hints at the countless eons before and after the turtle emerges to breathe the air; the time it may spend with its head through the ring is a brief flicker in a larger story.

Sangha

It's my head that's swimming when I arrive that evening. All day I've alternated between reading about Buddha and observing the highway of my thoughts. Now I'm joining a group, or *sangha*, that meets regularly to meditate. Like Christianity and Judaism, Buddhism emphasizes the importance of people coming together. Whether this speaks to the transformative alchemy of multiples or the importance of learning to put up with the guy with sniffles, or both, is hard to say.

Many *sanghas* are formed by the regular meditation periods held at the various Buddhist centers, but others are less formal groups of ordinary people who assemble on their own. I'm surprised to learn how prevalent these gatherings are—at the coffee shops and Buddhist establishments I visit around campus I pick up half a dozen little flyers advertising the different *sanghas* in the area. Some groups cater to a specific demographic or life experience, such as age range or gender or interest. Others, like the one I select, are more general. Anyone who wants to meditate is invited to this one. It is held once a week, hosted in the office space of a nonprofit organization during off-hours. When I show up, about twenty people are already sitting cross-legged on the carpet in a big circle. The majority here are males who appear to be in their first few post-college years. They have that particular dishevelment of young men newly introduced to the tug of war between late nights and a regular workweek. A smattering of young women breaks up the monotony of bedhead.

I join them on the floor. For several minutes, as we wait for a few stragglers to arrive, I feel exceedingly awkward wedged shoulder to shoulder between two strange boys. I fear that at any moment someone will pull out an empty bottle, place it in center, give it a whirl, and I will be forced to endure the most uncomfortable game of spin the bottle known to humankind. Thankfully, a young man whose crisp shirt lends him an air of authority, announces that it is time to begin. He claps together two wood rods and everyone settles into stillness.

The soft focus of my gaze falls midcircle; I can make out my fellow meditators along the periphery. It's a new challenge to see those bodies but not let them distract me from the task. I watch my thoughts approach and recede, resisting the urge to let them sweep me away. I start to enjoy the rhythm of my thinking, how the ideas rise and fall, rise and fall, like the surface of water. I'm so relaxed. I'm floating on the sea. I think of the popular Buddhist analogy of the ocean: each of us is like a wave. We think of ourselves as distinct and separate entities, but we come from, and return to, a common source. At this exact second, I understand this sentiment not just as an objective concept; I feel the absolute truth of it at the core of my being.

But it's too big a thought, and suddenly I'm terrified. I'm afraid of losing myself in this vast ocean. The idea of being alive and then dying is so overwhelming. A tingle of panic starts in my toes. My heart begins to race, and I can feel a burst of dread in my gut. It moves into my chest. It blocks air from filling my lungs.

I had been worried being here in Berkeley would make the old anxiety pop up and swallow me. Now what I feared is happening. I recognize these sensations as the onset of a full-blown panic attack. I think maybe I'm about to pass out. I consider grabbing the guy on my left and begging for help. He will understand. He will tell me to lie down and put my feet up. Everyone will stop meditating and come to my aid. One will fetch a cup of water; another will say it's going to be fine. The thought of the aid from my fellow meditators is enough to slow my pulse. I hang on another few seconds. I take a deep breath, and the lightheadedness begins to lift. I'm okay. Tears of gratitude come to my eyes; I am thankful to every member of the circle for helping me.

o

I'm starting to sense a pattern here: every so often someone comes along to suggest changes he believes will make a belief system more accessible to a greater segment of the population. Whatever new ideas such people present may have been brewing for some time, percolating in the minds of countless others and then, at last, circumstances converge; the time arrives to implement those ideas. The reform movement in Judaism is a good example—all those souls born Jewish, longing to observe their faith, but in a way they felt was more compatible with their contemporary lives. Sometimes a particular person gets most of the credit for the change: like Protestant reformer Martin Luther, who had the courage to act boldly first, or like Siddha-rtha, who dared to articulate concepts about our thinking. Regardless, both innovators wanted to open up faith to a wider audience; like Luther, Buddha offered his teachings in the common language (as opposed to the scholarly Sanskrit), and he shared his guidance with anyone, not just the elites who were more likely to have access to religious education.

Buddha taught that spiritual awakening is available to anyone who quietly looks inside, but years down the road, some who practiced his techniques reached the opinion that these teachings, while theoretically accessible, were not necessarily practical for everyone. One such person was a Buddhist monk named Shinran Shonin who lived in twelfth-century Japan. Even as a devout monastic, he did not feel satisfied with his religious accomplishment.

Shinran understood intellectually what he was supposed to do during his regular meditation—stand apart from the activity of his mind, observe the stream of thoughts, recognize them for the illusory stories they are—but in practice this seemed nearly impossible to achieve. If this was so difficult for someone like him, who lived apart from society and spent countless hours on the task, what about regular people who held jobs and raised families? Was the ultimate goal of attaining nirvana realistic for them? How could they hope to benefit from what the Buddha taught?

This line of thought gave birth to a new variation of Buddhism, called Pure Land. In some places, like Hong Kong and Taiwan, Pure Land is the most popular type of Buddhism. While this isn't the case in the United States, it is still a widely practiced version of the faith, as evidenced by the local temple whose services, held on Sundays, I decide to attend.

Pure Land offers a unique interpretation of the Buddha: he was the human incarnation of an immeasurable entity, sometimes called "Amida Buddha" or "Eternal Buddha of Light." Perhaps Shinran was also influenced by stories of Jesus Christ. This vast Buddha purposefully took human form to inspire humanity and someday, once the teachings of this human Buddha are forgotten, the eternal Buddha will once again walk the earth. The name "Pure Land" is a reference to a place that appears in the recorded teachings of this human Buddha, a fantastic setting where jewel-encrusted trees grow and lotus blossoms reach the size of city blocks. In Pure Land Buddhism, this location is an afterlife destination, a nirvana for anyone and everyone who maintained faith in the immeasurable Buddha during their lives.

o

Today's Pure Land service takes place in a midcentury building lined in hedges trimmed with bonsai precision. Though it is listed as a "temple," it is part of a network of "Buddhist Churches of America," so I suppose it is something of a bridge between two worlds. An Asian woman with a thick, swingy bob haircut welcomes me with the day's program. Inside looks and feels like a church, with pews and an altar, though the elegant simplicity evokes the Japanese design aesthetic. It may have a church-like shape, but the program reveals a decidedly Buddha-flavored filling. The congregation is called "the *sangha*," the choir is the "*sangha* singers," and kids attend "dharma school." We won't be singing hymns, but we'll chant verses of dharma called "sutras." A dharma discussion will take the place of a sermon.

A bell's chime indicates the beginning of service. A Japanese man in a Western-style minister's robe makes his way to a podium by the altar; in the program he is called "Reverend" though in person people address him as "sensei," the Japanese word for "teacher." While most people in the pews appear to be of Japanese heritage, some couples are mixed, and a few solos, like me, are non-Asian. The minister's assistant is a beautiful black woman with long dreadlocks.

After a few opening remarks by the minister, everyone falls silent and we enter a period labeled "Quiet Sitting." In Pure Land, the practitioner is not expected to strive for nirvana alone but to rely on assistance from Buddha. Chanting in unison with others replaces meditation as the primary means to awaken and express this unconditional reliance. Here, this peaceful moment is preparation for the central task, not the central task itself.

Together, we chant sutras called "Vandana" and "Ti-sarana." The first is a statement of homage to Buddha and is offered in Pali, the ancient language of India. Like some Christian and Jewish prayers that are voiced in a language other than the speaker's primary tongue, these are chanted in Pali not so much for the comprehension of the brain as the heart. Each syllable is broken down and drawn out so that it more closely resembles tonal breathing, like long exhalations with sound attached. Then everyone recites it slowly in English: "Homage to him, the Exalted One, the Enlightened One, the Supremely Awakened One." The second sutra is a declaration of the "Triple Treasures." Again, we recite it first in Pali and the air vibrates with syllables hummed loudly. Then we recite the sutra in English. Slowly, as if we are dazed, we say: "I go to the Buddha for guidance. I go to the Dharma for guidance. I go to the Sangha for guidance."

Like in many churches, books are tucked into the back of the pews, and the program tells us from what pages to read. Now it directs us to page 174 of the Large Service Book for "Namu Amida Butsu," which is perhaps the most important statement one can utter in this version of Buddhism. It's a proclamation of gratitude for Buddha's vow that all beings who call his name will one day be born in the Pure Land where enlightenment is attained automatically. "Namu Amida Butsu" is recited in fragments: *Na ... mu ... a ... mi ... da ... bu ... tsu*. The words translate approximately as "I entrust in the immeasurable compassion of Buddha." We intone them again and again; some notes dip and shimmy, and others step higher and higher slowly. It is said that to emit these sounds, and to listen as others do the same, is to receive a message, not to send one. Buddha has been calling to us since the beginning of time, reassuring us—at last, we are expressing that we've heard and understand and our appreciation is boundless. As the *sangha* chants,

I try to follow along, to slip my voice in here and there when I can find the right note. I want to offer my thanks as well.

After the service, members of the *sangha* convene in an adjacent room for tea. The treats on hand are made from rice flour and have a satisfying confectionary quality. As I chew one, I think about how food, particularly sweets, is a universal language that transcends all cultures and religions. Taste takes a back seat to the other senses during the worship services, and now our tongue gets in on the gratitude, those little buds pulsating messages of joy. It also gives people an excuse to linger, to exchange pleasantries, and to just be together.

As I walk past the sanctuary to leave the church, I pause; I take in a whiff of the lingering smell left from a lovely little ceremony called *Oshoko* when everyone who wished was invited to the altar to burn a bit of incense. I hadn't known what to expect as I stood in the line that formed up the center aisle. I could see each person bow, and then I saw a thin plume of smoke rise and chase after them in the wake of their departure. When I got to the front of the line, I bowed with my hands at my heart as I had observed others do. I was surprised to find that the incense wasn't a stick, but a heap of fine granules like sand. I took a pinch between my fingers and placed it in a box with a red-hot surface. Instantly, it smoldered and I inhaled the intense woody scent. As I turned, I could see the smoke bend in my direction. I followed the smoke from the previous person, and mine followed me. I could see it dissipating. Like the words of chants or songs or prayers, like appreciation itself that starts in our hearts, it was moving up and out into the world in ways I am only beginning to understand.

The Story

For most of my life, I've conceived of my past as something as solid and real as a ladder, and the events that compose it as true as rungs underfoot. Frequently I paused to consider the lowest treads, the particulars that made my early years a difficult climb—the broken home, the financial insecurity, the frequent moving, the spotty schooling—proof that I had suffered my share of hard knocks. In college I clung tightly to the handrails. I had to work harder than everyone else, I told myself, just to stay abreast. I had to hold down a job and study twice as diligently. I couldn't let my white-knuckle focus lapse for even an instant or I might lose footing. I was being nudged forward by the particularly sorrowful plot points. In a sense, the story was living me, not the other way around.

I was not fond of the ladder on which I stood. I wished for a different one. I thought if I changed my environment, then everything that had led up to that moment might be transformed, that I might shed my story like a snake does its skin. I remember junior year I decided what I needed, the one thing that would brighten my existence, was an apartment with a balcony where I could sit. So senior year I moved into a place with an outdoor space. But it was just a concrete slab with a few sad plants; I was no happier. My stupid story had followed me.

To pursue Buddhism where I went to college is a funny task because it is here where my investment in the story solidified, where I fine-tuned and polished it to sparkly gleam. And it is just this sort of attachment to story that Buddhism attempts to rid us of by encouraging us always to come back to the present moment, not to cling to the steady stream of thoughts that feed the story.

Still, being in Berkeley, a part of me can't help but feel teleported into the past, to sense my ghostly doppelgänger dangling precariously from her ladder. I see something, and suddenly I'm looking through the lens of the twenty-year-old me, which is exactly what happens when I enter a Zen center with a lush exterior courtyard. "Now, this is just what I had in mind," I think, referring to the outdoor space I thought could miraculously soothe me senior year. As the thought putters by, I am aware of how silly it is. Even if time collapsed and the old me somehow had access to this sumptuous garden, it wouldn't have mattered. My interior terrain would have remained unchanged.

o

The Zen center with the garden is on a residential street within walking distance of the places I lived junior and senior years—the one without and the one with a patio. It is made up of two houses next door to one another. Their separate backyards have been combined to create an oasis of serenity and to accommodate other structures. One is a zendo, a traditional Buddhist meditation hall that looks like a Japanese gingerbread house and adds to the charm of the courtyard. Long wood steps lead to the zendo's porch and offer a perch for removing shoes. When I arrive, the sun is only starting to rise. I have come fifteen minutes early, worried I would be late for the seated meditation that begins at six a.m. I enter the yard quietly, cognizant of the fact that several people live in these houses—a couple of monks who run the place, one of whom is married and raised his children here. As I sit on the zendo's steps, the garden slowly illuminates, and I listen to the reassuring rustle of people starting their days.

It's a full morning that's planned. Alternating periods of seated meditation with walking meditation, a dharma lecture, and a special ceremonial breakfast called *oryoki* served inside the zendo. So detailed is the style in which the food is presented and eaten during this meal that I was advised it would be best to stop by earlier in the week to receive instruction before attempting to participate, which is how I ended up at a twenty-minute tutorial on how to eat breakfast. Only this is no ordinary breakfast; it involves nesting bowls, a tiny spatula, loads of bowing and other small gestures to communicate in the absence of words, and a napkin that is generally a large cloth folded into points but, because I am a visitor, will be a small paper square—a difference that forces me to, as my instructor explained, "get creative with it."

As people begin to arrive, everyone makes their way into the zendo. Inside, exposed support beams create a series of lovely wood arches overhead. The windows are high up and designed not so much for looking out as for adjusting airflow and light; some are propped open, letting a gentle breeze circulate. A simple altar occupies one end; around the perimeter of the room, raised platforms covered in straw mats and cushions invite meditators to sit. Here it is customary to face the wall while meditating. I select a spot and hop up. After adjusting my pillow, I settle in.

The meditation period begins and almost immediately my cheek starts to itch. I try to ignore it. I've noticed that most people manage to stay absolutely still during meditation, which has been a challenge for me. I seem to require little readjustments—my knee gets a cramp or my hip twinges. But the face-tickle thing is new, and while this particular itch starts out mild, waiting for it to subside on its own quickly escalates into a tiny form of torture. I twist my mouth every which way, thankful to be facing the wall. As the sensation begins to fade, a series of itches erupts across my scalp. Suddenly I understand something more is going on here. Either I've contracted a rare case of chicken-pox-lice or my mind is playing tricks on me. I've read that the meditative task can create revolt from the part of your mind that oversees the thought highway. I spend the rest of the time engaged in the excruciating task of refusing to respond to the phantom itches that dance across my head. It is a battle of wills, both mine.

The morning's ceremonial breakfast is served in pairs, and I am coupled with the resident dad-monk, an older white guy in an elaborate robe. His eyebrows reach up and out into an impressive wingspan, making up for what he lacks in hair. He understands I am new to this and indicates with a slight nod to follow his lead. At some large monasteries, this elaborate breakfast is how Zen monks regularly take their first meal of the day. It is meant as a hybrid of meditation and eating, the idea being that you are so intimately familiar with the movements that they become second nature and you can relax into a tranquil breakfast ballet. The ritual also has a utilitarian quality; as part of the ceremony, every person washes his or her own dishes so nobody is stuck with all the cleaning. But as my instructor went over the nuances earlier in the week, I wondered how long it might take for a newcomer to feel at ease with this method of eating. Months? Years? For me, this wouldn't be an exercise in serenity; I just hoped not to botch it so badly that I ruined anyone else's serenity.

As previously instructed, I lay out my three bowls from big to small and arrange my utensils on my creatively folded paper napkin. When the server reaches us with her vat of oatmeal, the monk and I bow to her in unison. I raise my smallest bowl and bow again. I lift my cupped palm to indicate to the server that the contents of one ladle is sufficient. Small bowls of condiments sit between me and my monk. While we wait for everyone to be served, he sprinkles his oatmeal with a topping of sesame seeds and sugar. I think that sounds good. He bows and hands me the bowl. I garnish mine generously, only to find it is sesame seeds and salt. Everyone eats in silence. I had worried that I would eat too quickly, a problem solved by the taste of briny porridge.

The second course, served in the middle bowl, is a tofu stir-fry. Not a typical breakfast, but surprisingly flavorful. Finally the "Buddha bowl," the last and biggest, is filled with orange juice. I recalled the instructor saying that when I finished using the middle bowl, I should place my chopsticks across its rim. She said it with such firm urgency; it seemed like a vital piece of information. As I lay my chopsticks there, I congratulated myself on remembering this small detail.

After the breakfast we do a walking meditation; together, single file, we leave the zendo. I am near the back of the line trying to stay in step with the person in front of me. We walk out of the garden and onto the street. In the neighborhood, regular people are going about their mornings: an old man strolling and a couple of teenage boys practicing skateboard tricks. They freeze in their tracks and watch us snake up and down. When we return to the zendo, it is time for the dharma talk, but I can't help but replay an awkward moment from a few moments earlier. The front half of the line had doubled back on the sidewalk of the street; I could see everyone's gazes as they passed. Their eyes were cast down, a soft focus on the ground, looking at nothing in particular. It was the same middle-distance stare used for meditation but taken beyond the confines of the sanctuary. I couldn't put finger on it, but something about those blank stares sent a chill up my spine.

o

The day's dharma talk about gender in Buddhism is given by the dad-monk's wife, who goes by the official title of "senior student." Gender is a complicated topic in Buddhism, just as it is in other religions. In some Buddhist texts, women turn into men before they enter nirvana, fueling the argument that only men have the capacity for enlightenment. Buddha himself struggled with how to handle female followers and eventually concluded that they could practice just as men do. A male audience member declares sexism in Buddhism a "nonissue" and says, "We've evolved past talks of gender." The senior student concurs, explaining that society is a garden and Buddhism would have us all working to contribute to its upkeep and growth. "We are all Buddha's hoes!" she concludes.

Perhaps "being present" becomes a new story so powerful that you miss what's happening before your eyes. Buddhist exercises—the meditating, chanting, burning of incense—are meant to encourage the practitioner to recognize the truth. By reminding us to stay in, or come back to, the present moment, they help remove the veil of illusion. We are not the details of a story, good or bad. But the same exercises can just as easily strengthen illusions. We may engage in an act and think, "I am extraordinarily spiritual" or "I'm not spiritual enough." The exercise solidifies the story.

After the dharma talk, several people stayed behind to put away folding chairs and tidy up the zendo. I pitched in and noticed that every other person helping was female. As I stacked chairs with the other women, I wondered if some of us were Buddha's hoes, while others were perhaps a different kind of tool. Some aspects of gender bias are so subtle; to claim the issue dead is to believe another version of the story. This realization brought to mind the last moments of the ceremonial breakfast, when we were cleaning our bowls. The server poured hot water into the biggest bowl. We cleaned that bowl and then poured some of the hot water into the next bowl, and then repeated this procedure for the last bowl. At the end, the water was dirty with leftover bits of breakfast, but we were invited to drink it as everyone offered a final chant that included "the water with which we wash these bowls tastes like ambrosia." I sipped and said these words, but I didn't believe them. The water didn't taste horrible, but I would hope nectar of gods would have a pleasant flavor.

I was glad then for what I did during the walking meditation. The old man out on the street who stopped in his tracks to watch us glide hypnotically by looked baffled. As the front of the line doubled back, it passed feet from where he was standing. I could see that no one was even glancing at him. It didn't seem right to maintain a trancelike state, unable or unwilling to acknowledge other members of society right in front of us. So when it was my turn to pass him, I caught his eye and offered up the goofiest grin I could muster.

Theravada

Not every Buddhist temple is set up for outsiders wishing to saunter in and grab a meditation pillow. Just a few doors down from the Zen center stands a Thai temple. I couldn't find a website, so I called the phone number and spoke with a resident monk. I asked if there was daily mediation. In a thick accent, he explained that meditation and chanting took place in the sanctuary twice a day. I asked when and he offered the hours, and I thanked him.

A few minutes before the evening session on a weekday, I arrived at the temple. The openings in the high gate—one for foot traffic and one for cars—were both shut tight. I loitered in front, thinking someone would come to unlock them, but no one did. A few days later, I phoned again to make sure I had the times right. The same monk answered. "You called before," he said. He assured me that my information was correct. Then it occurred to me to ask, "Am I permitted to attend?" "Of course," he said, though he seemed surprised by the request. "Tomorrow?" I asked. "Of course," he replied.

The following evening, the opening in the gate for cars was ajar. Beyond was a scene of hustle and bustle. I could see through to a kitchen as two young men worked diligently scrubbing pots. Another attended to a small pond outside while still others carried large tables from one end of the courtyard to the other. Some wore ordinary Western-style clothes, and some donned the traditional marigold robes. These were unlike the robes that the monks wore at the Zen center, which were subdued hues but ornately layered with folds as complicated as origami. The robes here looked to be a single swath of fabric wrapped around the body and casually tossed over one shoulder, leaving the other bare in the mild afternoon air. The color shocked in its vibrancy, but the loose drape was relaxed. I stood watching them, but no one paid me any attention. Finally, I approached the kitchen door and caught a young man's eye. He was wearing shorts and flip-flops. "Meditation?" I called to him. His English was not so good, but he understood what I was asking. He came out of the kitchen and motioned for me to follow him. We went around to the back of the building, and he pointed to a door up a flight of stairs.

Inside, I was greeted by the older monk I had spoken with on the phone. He bowed slightly and welcomed me. At last it dawned on me what was going on. I was being permitted to observe their spiritual practice, not participate. I suddenly realized that this monastery is of the Theravada tradition. The monks here do not seek to hold off attaining nirvana for the sake of teaching others about that egoless state. Unlike the Mahayana tradition, these monks strive daily to dissolve their individual identities. This effort is their unique contribution to society. While not so prevalent in the United States, this type of Buddhism is the most practiced in some countries like Thailand, Cambodia, and Laos. Many young people, some just children, spend a portion of their lives working in monasteries and ascending the various monastic ranks. They receive education and Buddhist training. Most will leave eventually to rejoin mainstream society and have families; others will stay on. It's a bit like the military in the United States, only theirs is a different method of obtaining peace.

"You may sit here," the monk said, pointing to a section of floor toward the back of the room. A photocopied prayer book lay at the spot. I sat directly on the carpet, which was so magnificently plush there was no need for a meditation mat.

Several younger monks, also in orange robes, filed in. They arranged themselves along with the older monk on the floor at the front of the room near a tall gilded statue of Buddha. Radiance from the setting sun flooded in from west-facing windows. I pressed my palms to the carpet, which was a rich crimson hue. Everything was glowing gold: the sun, the statue, the robes. The monks alternated between periods of quiet and chanting. From the snippets in English, I understood they were paying homage to the Buddha, dharma, and *sangha*. Their deep tones vibrated the air and lingered. Light and sound saturated the room, spreading a buttery warmth. I felt so wrapped in brightness and heat that I wanted to squint or lie down for a nap. Apparently, I was not alone. One of the young monks began to nod off, slumping forward by degrees. He would catch himself and sit tall, only to slowly melt again.

I had no idea I would be witnessing this sight—completely ordinary in the lives of these monks but extraordinary in mine. I've operated under the impression that worship practices of the Theravada tradition are too private to have much effect on society at large. This experience gives me a new perspective. Like contemplatives or hermits of other traditions, they are working diligently to capture all that is bright and good and, through sheer force of concentration, send that energy out into the world. I'm overcome with gratitude for their commitment to this taxing exercise meant to benefit us all. Even if most of us never see it, it is happening on our behalf every day.

Big *Me*

Despite my experience at the Thai temple, most of the Buddhist institutes and monasteries around campus are set up for the purpose of teaching Westerners dharma. Many offer a variety of classes, workshops, and retreats to encourage ordinary people to incorporate Buddhist practice into their lives. While meditation sessions may be free, the classes usually are not, and most have various skill levels to ascend. At one, the full series of meditation courses from beginning to advanced would cost about $700—which is why I chuckle when I flip over a book I bought there to see the word "freedom" in the title has been misprinted on the back flap as "feedom."

This particular center is perhaps the most prominent of its kind due, in no small part, to the canary-yellow building it occupies very visibly against a green hillside less than a block from campus. Its roots in the area stretch back to the 1970s, making it part of the earliest formal efforts in California, if not the country, to expose Americans to Eastern religion. In particular, it claims to be the first institution in the United States to provide education about Tibetan Buddhism. This branch of Buddhism has its own unique qualities, the most notable of which might be the tradition of locating the reincarnated souls of departed spiritual leaders in children who, after passing a series of tests, are groomed for their special roles. The most famous example is Tenzin Gyatso, who was identified as a child as the fourteenth incarnation of the Dalai Lama. The center I'm visiting today was founded by another spiritual leader who was similarly chosen, though he represents a different school within Tibetan Buddhism, a distinction that seems more sociopolitical than theological.

Tibetan Buddhism is also distinguished from other types of Buddhism by its distinctive paths to enlightenment, based on the last burst of writing about Buddha's teachings, called "tantras," recorded around the seventh century. In tantric thinking, the body is made up of seventy-two thousand channels through which subtle energies, called "winds," flow. Some of the primary passages in this network meet up at intersections called "chakras." One of the main goals of spiritual practice is to loosen the circulation of the body's currents to create heat and light that helps melt the boundaries we see as separating ourselves from others and the world. Practitioners employ various methods to kick up these winds. They might visualize a seated Buddha with absolute focus and repeat a short series of words called a "mantra." Unlike prayers chanted in unison, a mantra is usually a phrase spoken privately again and again. These exercises are meant to encourage extraordinary shifts in awareness—though it's difficult to communicate how with words. For example, a mantra can drive all perceptions into a single point, producing a level of insight so profound that the Buddha suddenly has your face. But these are advanced techniques—and I can see why a student might want the help of a teacher to traverse this mysterious terrain. At its introductory levels, the differences between this and the practices of other types of Buddhism are less obvious.

The Tibetan Buddhist center occupies a majestic former fraternity house; steps up the hillside to the front door offer a small taste of trekking the Himalayas. At the top I pause to catch my breath. Above the gracious porch, squares of cloth in primary colors hang like scarves drying on a laundry line. From up here I can see for miles toward the San Francisco Bay and Golden Gate Bridge. I've been so busy looking inward, hemmed in by the tight confines of my own being, that to look out at such great distance feels like emancipation. I almost don't want to turn away and go in. But I must. They are letting me sit in on a class that starts soon.

Just beyond the ample foyer sits the base of a grand staircase. The wood floors are beautifully worn. I try to imagine how much beer was consumed in this space during its previous incarnation. The ghosts of keggers past have been cleared in favor of a reception desk and a couple of comfy chairs. Off to the right sits a dining room with long, family-style seating. The wavy glass in the old windows makes the outside world appear to be dissolving.

I hear a repetitive mechanical churning and am drawn to the long, thin sun porch beyond the dining room from which the noise originates. Inside, a series of oversized spools spin. These are shiny gold Tibetan prayer wheels with small script along their facades. They look like the drums of a printing press designed to emboss words on a surface—only the paper is missing and the writing goes around endlessly, adhering to nothing. The turning is meant to help disseminate the sentiments contained in the text. The movement is key (before electricity, Tibetans rotated their prayer wheels mechanically and many still do). The same principle applies to the squares of fabric that dangle and the numerous flags hanging from poles around the property; printed on these are important words from Buddha's teachings. The wind animates the ideas, more effectively sending them out into the atmosphere.

From a newcomer's perspective, these are the biggest differences you notice: saturated colors everywhere you look; the constant, creaky hum of prayer wheels; the dance of fabric. If much of Buddhism as practiced in the United States is conceived as something that subdues with neutral tones and natural materials, here is a brand of Buddhism that goes the opposite direction. Buddhism like Zen is considered cool and calm, but here it's fiery. It may be a hot road, but the destination is the same.

The dharma class that I'm joining is taught by one of the center founder's longtime devotees, who is both a Westerner and a woman. It's a beautiful, sunny day, and I've been told that class will convene on an outdoor patio. As I make my way to the backyard, I catch a glimpse of a bright red gazebo that appears to contain some sort of merry-go-round. I step into a wonderland for my senses: the fragrance of blooms, the chirping of birds, the bouncing of sunlight off bright surfaces. A footpath wraps around a koi pond, and I realize on closer inspection that the gazebo is a carousel—only the riders are more prayer wheels. Against the hillside sits a shiny stupa, a memorial statue to Buddha that is believed to generate good karma; it doesn't show a figure but looks like a jaunty crown for some larger-than-life being. Its presence adds to the playful, otherworldly vibe.

On a wood deck, several students have gathered. They are mostly women, all ages, a few Asian. I join them. As we wait for the instructor to arrive, the group alternates between polite chatting and stark silence. Five minutes turns into ten, and ten tick-tocks toward twenty. I begin to doubt our teacher will show. In college we had a firm, unspoken rule: if a professor failed to show in the first ten minutes of class, the students made a celebratory, mass exodus from the room.

Today no one seems fazed by our leader's tardiness, and because they remain seated and content, I do the same. The enchanting yard and karma from the stupa must be positively affecting me because I have never in my life been so unbothered by lack of punctuality. After thirty minutes, our instructor climbs the steps to the deck where we sit. She mentions something about traffic and apologizes. She laughs and says that having to wait is the best beauty treatment: all the anti-aging serums in the world are not as effective as cultivating patience. "So, you've all just paid a visit to the Buddhist beauty parlor!"

I think there must be something to what she is saying because she is radiant. Objectively, her looks are ordinary. Perhaps nearing seventy, her hair is white and her features are makeup-free and yet, somehow, it adds up to stunning. Her eyes are clear, her smile is wide, and her face is animated with interest. For several minutes she covers the day's message about dharma. What is she saying? I hardly notice because I am so focused on how she says it. It's as if each phrase she speaks is being uttered for the first time—like the words astound even her. Every time her eyes land on something, she seems to take in the sight with fresh curiosity. I've heard people explain about "staying in the present," but I've never seen it so clearly demonstrated. She is not flogging herself over the past or worrying about the future: she is right there, occupying each new moment. She is the lesson.

After the talk it's time for a bit of walking meditation. This is a different style of walking meditation from the more militaristic type I experienced at the Zen center. Today, our instructor explains, we should make our way slowly around the garden, each according to her own whim, pausing every few steps. She tells us to look around and try to gaze on everything as if we have never seen it before. "Each time," she tells us, "create a never-heard story for how that vision came to be."

I'm not entirely certain what she means by this, but I get the gist: we should practice moving through the world like she appears to.

My classmates and I set off in all directions like dazed sleep-walkers. I begin my trek toward the koi pond, stopping along the way to take in the golden curves of the stupa and a flag with squiggly script. "What is this amazing new sight?" I ask myself. It's not so hard; I find these items fascinating. I try objects that are more familiar: an open rose and, then, a stone from the path. "Wow, look at that," I tell myself.

I try to feel all the wonder of seeing something like the Grand Canyon for the first time. A simple flower, a chunk of rock—these things truly are remarkable if you look at them like that. It's good to remember. But what would happen if I tried this with mundane things from my everyday existence like a piece of junk mail or an empty skillet? For a moment, the spell is broken. I think how nuts this group would look to an outsider who saw us meandering the yard like overly medicated patients. Then even that gets a lens through which nothing has a set explanation, and I slip back into my hallucinatory dream.

When the class reconvenes, it's time for seated meditation. I get comfortable in a plastic deck chair. I lower my eyelids to half-mast and focus on the sensations playing all around: the breeze against my skin, the gurgle of a fountain, the earthy smell of sun-soaked vegetation. I don't know if it's sitting outside or if the teacher's example has nudged me forward, but today I see more clearly the essential dichotomy of being human. Each of us has a "little me," what we conceive of as a distinct self, hungry for us to believe that's all we are. The contours of its identity strengthen when we are caught up in ideas; memories of the past, worries about the future: the highway of thoughts is its domain. Our individual stories strengthen the idea that we are a thing apart. When we step away from the thinking and plant our feet in the present moment, we become a part of something immeasurable, a piece of the larger whole, the "big me."

Suddenly what I feel is more expansive than the view to the ocean out front. I see that I can choose to let the "little me" have the power or I can challenge its authority. I breathe in a beautiful state of bliss. All around is space, and I am a part of it. I am nowhere and everywhere. "Here it is!" a voice shouts. I feel like a runner who has been struggling for miles and then, miraculously, hits her stride. I could go and go and go. Has it always been this easy? I want to hold this feeling forever.

What if I can't hold it forever? A thunderbolt of panic rips through me. My chest constricts and my heart beats wildly. I had been falling with no end in sight, and now the ground has risen to smack my back. It's awful to have the bliss slapped out of me, yet a part of me is relieved to return to the familiarity of my smaller self.

How to Pray to Buddha

"This is how you pray to Buddha," says Betty, who hails from the Philippines. She is an acquaintance who has offered to take me to a service at her temple. We are in her car, driving to Oakland. She is instructing me about praying to the main Buddha. Her version of Buddhism is also occupied by lesser Buddhas. A few minutes earlier, as I strapped into the passenger seat, she pointed to the laminated picture dangling from her rearview mirror. "Medicine Buddha," she said.

"You bow. You tell Buddha your name." Betty seems excited that I've agreed to accompany her. She is in her mid-forties, a single mom to a teenage boy. She works as a caretaker to an elderly gentleman, an atheist who gives her Sunday mornings off but playfully teases her for wanting to use them to attend religious services. She continues: "You tell Buddha where you live, the year you were born, if you have kids. Remind him. So many people on earth. You jog Buddha's memory."

I smile. I like this idea. This is the first I'm hearing of engaging in dialogue with Buddha like a Christian might God.

She glances at me, very serious. "After you introduce, then you talk. But don't ask Buddha for material things. Don't say, 'Buddha, I want money.' You ask for 'success,' you ask for 'piss.'"

I turn to her. "Piss?"

She nods emphatically. "Yes, you ask Buddha for piss. You say, 'Please, make me pissful.'"

"Oh, peace."

"Yes, piss." She flashes a look like, boy, does she have her work cut out.

o

Betty's temple is part of a Buddhist order that prides itself on practicing a version of the faith that integrates many types of Buddhism. It accommodates monastics, both male and female, and caters to laypeople all over the world with universities and schools. Its temples may hold services on Sundays and engage in many similar practices to the Buddhist church I attended, but here the Pure Land concept gets an official tweak. Instead of worshipping with the hope of being reborn in paradise, the goal is to create a Pure Land on earth by working to improve oneself and society. This Buddhism is sometimes referred to as "humanistic," and some scholars say it marks a turning point—a sort of "reformation" in which the faith addresses the needs of a modern world. Using the goodness of the human Buddha as a role model, the leaders in this sect promote social responsibility and religious dialogue.

I marvel that so grounded a vision of Buddhism can be flexible enough to oblige Betty's way of thinking—which, from my perspective, is somewhat "magical." Apparently this is not uncommon among the faithful whose belief systems from previous generations merged with Buddhism. Betty speaks casually of spirit beings visiting her in the dream realm. She explains that burning incense opens a channel, either to an upper-level world or to a lower-level world, depending on the intention with which it is lit and if proper prayers are offered. She warns me to be cautious because people who use incense just for the smell may end up on a slippery chute to some place they never intended.

We come to a part of town where the street signs are Chinese characters. As we park, Betty points to a small square structure with a pagoda-style roof. The sanctuary's doors open directly to the street. Activity spills on the sidewalk at a busy intersection. We pass through smoke rising from a large metal bowl holding incense sticks and then we are standing inside. The room is packed with people squatting on low benches arranged with a single aisle down the middle.

The altar at the front of the room is occupied by a tall Buddha statue, just as I've seen in other locations. Here the main figure has a buddy on either side, smaller versions or other incarnations. Around these are fresh additions: impressive pyramids of mangoes and apples. Everywhere my gaze falls on a new, stunning object, some item like a flower or a tree cast in metal or carved in stone. Bright, fantastical images adorn the walls. I've entered a life-size jewel box, a tiny patch of Pure Land.

Women in monastic robes mill about, preparing for the service to begin. Betty spots two free benches side by side, and we squeeze our way down a row and take seats. I am the only non-Asian present. I feel privileged to be a guest. For her part, Betty seems very pleased to have brought someone, especially someone so ill informed. For each person who turns to look at me, she puffs a bit with pride. She makes a fuss to secure a folder of the phonetic versions of the prayer sutras. She hands it to me with great aplomb, as if to accentuate to all that she has obtained this item on behalf of her clueless companion.

The service kicks off with chanting. Perhaps because the sanctuary is full and the room is not so big, the sound of the voices is particularly powerful. Betty turns my folder to the appropriate page, but it is just a long series of phonic fragments (*na mo ho la ta na to la yeh yeh*, etc.) that every once in a while fall into an arrangement that could mean something in English (*cher la cher la*). I'm amazed that everyone here has committed this complicated sequence of syllables, with its intricate intonations, to memory, but, then, this is the heart of worship. This exercise improves karma—not just of people in the room; it's for everyone in the city, the state, the country, and all around the world. I chime in when I can, but even when I have the pronunciation, I don't have the tone just right. Luckily, my mistakes are drowned out by the collective. Certain syllables resound so deeply that the walls seem to vibrate.

On the other side of me is an older gentleman whose full head of dark hair is salted just so. Age has bestowed on him the rugged good looks of an Asian Marlboro Man. During the chanting, when he notices I've grown silent and Betty's not looking, he points to my open page—as if my failure to join in were as simple as having lost my place. He continues to make sure I know exactly where we are in the chant. At first he does this surreptitiously so Betty doesn't notice. Eventually his effort grows more brazen, and Betty shoots him a look. He gives her one back, as if to say, "It's not my fault you're slacking on the job."

This little power struggle continues through the dharma talk, for which my Marlboro Man elects himself the superior translator. Perhaps because he better understands the Cantonese in which the talk is given, Betty concedes. It takes me a while to determine that the person giving the talk is female. Her head is shaved, and her robe is a variation of the ones worn by the nuns who have hair. Baldness is a great gender neutralizer, as are robes for that matter. I imagine she is the abbot here or some other high-ranking position. She is the spitting image of the founder of this sect, whose picture hangs on the wall, and I notice she is addressed as "master."

"She talks about desire," my Marlboro Man tells me about one minute into her speech. "How it's not good for you." He goes silent, so I elaborate in my mind. I imagine she's explaining how that feeling of wanting, craving, grasping—anything other than satisfaction with your immediate situation—removes a person from the present moment. Several minutes go by, and I'm tempted to ask what she's saying now, but I decide not giving in to that impulse is sort of the point of the talk. Finally, he leans over. I can see him struggling to find the right words. "She says desire is bad . . ." I wait for him to elaborate, to offer some new twist or detail, but he doesn't. Fifteen minutes go by and the speech winds down. My Marlboro Man shrugs. "Don't worry, you don't miss much."

o

Betty is excited for me to have my fortune told. After a lunch of stir-fried tofu served soup-kitchen style in an adjacent room, I follow her back to the main sanctuary. The rows of little sitting benches have been put away, and Betty drags out a bigger prayer bench. This one has a slanted top, allowing for easier up-and-down movements required for sequences of prostrations. She positions it in front of the altar.

"Remember I told you how to talk to Buddha?"

I nod. I hadn't realized she intended me to use those instructions today.

"Good. You do it. At the end, ask an important question."

She points at the bench, and I assume the position. I had been instructed the previous week by a young monk on a proper bow. He had spoken softly with a bit of hesitation, and I imagined his exotic backstory took place somewhere like the jungles of Cambodia. Then I asked him where he was from. "New Jersey," he said, clear as day.

I rest my knees on the platform and bend at the waist so that my forehead presses against the taller edge closest to the altar. I turn my cupped hands palms up as if I were holding the feet of baby Buddha. Just as Betty explained, I formally introduce myself. I provide the year and location of my birth, my current whereabouts, and a few details about my home life. I wrack my brain for a significant question. Finally, I decide on an issue that's been weighing heavily on me: should I write about these religious experiences I've been seeking? So far, I've taken notes here and there, but I haven't committed to undergoing the long, arduous effort of arranging it on paper. I feel extreme trepidation. As a None, is this even a topic about which I have a right to write?

When I open my eyes and come up, Betty is standing before me with a jar filled with small bamboo slats, a big grin on her face like she is presenting a bouquet of chopsticks.

"Pick," she commands.

I pull one out and look at it. Burnt onto the tip is a number.

Betty takes it. "Come," she says.

I follow her into an adjacent room. Along the wall is a series of little drawers like you might see in a garage to organize nuts and bolts. She opens the one with the same number as my stick and pulls out a slip of paper no bigger than a receipt. She studies it before letting me look. On it, are the Chinese characters for a Buddhist sutra; even if I could read it, there's no guarantee I'd understand if or how that ancient poem answers my question.

"Let's find a nun," Betty suggests. "She'll tell us."

I try to keep up with Betty as she hurries around, scanning for a particular nun. We find her out front, wishing visitors well as they depart. Betty hands her the piece of paper and points to me. I hadn't planned to put too much stock in the outcome of this exercise, but now I start to worry. What if Buddha puts the kibosh on my project?

For several minutes, Betty and the nun go back and forth. Betty looks very serious, and the tone of their conversation seems heated. This cannot be a good sign, I think. I suppose if Buddha said no, I'd still give the endeavor a shot. I mean I can't just throw up my arms in defeat based on a sutra I got from pulling a random bamboo stick from a jar. That would be bonkers, right?

Finally, Betty turns to me. I brace myself for the news.

"The answer is yes," she announces.

She continues, "But so much work. So hard. You must be strong for it to be yes. Otherwise, it's no. So much struggle. Barriers to overcome. So hard."

All the way home, Betty repeats how difficult whatever it is I've asked will be, how easily it could tip to no if I'm not tough as nails. She seems apologetic, as if she wishes I had received a rosier fortune on her watch. But I'm satisfied. I never expected it would be an easy undertaking. Already it's been the most difficult thing I've ever done—and the most rewarding. I can only imagine how much more challenging it will be to try to tell it in some coherent fashion.

I'm happy with a hard-earned yes. Thank Buddha.

Karma

The Buddhist leg of my journey is nearing its conclusion, and I have yet to step foot on my old college campus. I have skirted it these last weeks, like some skittish satellite refusing to leave orbit. I know this story won't be complete unless I go there. I start gently: strolling the sidewalk that lines the southern perimeter. I pass the building that houses the library where I worked all four years, the outdoor café I frequented for their frothy lattes, and the art museum whose facade has always reminded me of concrete steps sized for a giant; while climbing, the giant dropped bits of neon that shine and blink when it's dark out.

Since graduating, I have visited campus, but never in the middle of the day when school is in session. I've cut across a corner at night or on the weekend, tossing a cursory glance at one of my old haunts. "Wow, looks the same," I might say, or, "Goodness, a new building." Then I'd turn tail and skedaddle out of there.

It's a sunny Thursday afternoon, and spring semester is in full swing. I pass a series of tennis courts and a parking garage, both of which are unchanged since my days here. Then I get a few butterflies because I'm close enough to see the main entrance, the pedestrian thoroughfare that leads from Telegraph Avenue onto campus. A river of students flows with currents in both directions.

As I walk it comes back clear as if it happened yesterday: the first time the floodgates keeping my anxiety at bay burst open. Sophomore year, spring semester, finals week, dusk. I was in the library studying in my own little cube with a book wide open, but instead of looking at its pages I couldn't take my eyes off the smooth white desk around it. It was so perfect, so devoid of color or texture. I hated it. I wanted to mark it up or smear it with mud. I had that weird tingling sensation starting in my feet; this time, it short-circuited something in my brain. I popped my head above my cube's little walls. I hoped the sight of all the other studiers might make everything settle back to normal in my mind—make a desk just a desk, not some blank canvas begging to be fouled. Instead, seeing so many heads in their own little boxes made matters worse. The silence, the fluorescent light, the linoleum floor—I wanted to scream, I wanted to push stacks to the floor, hurl books into the air. I gathered up all my things quickly. If I laid eyes on something familiar, like my bed, this world would make sense again. The jigsaw puzzle had been put together wrong. I couldn't understand the picture.

As I hurried home, the tingling sensation traveled up. My legs were too heavy—or was the sidewalk undulating? It occurred to me that I might not make it, that I might collapse. Was I dying? I couldn't catch my breath. I continued to lumber forward, thankful for the dark. I arrived just in time to heave the contents of my stomach into the toilet. Only then, depleted and sweaty, did the ground begin to feel solid again. I spent the rest of the night lying down, letting the pieces fuse into a coherent whole, too exhausted to wonder why it had all come undone.

Today I approach campus slowly, casually, as if almost two decades hasn't slipped by since that first panic attack, although at the time I had no idea what it was. It would take years for me to unravel that mystery and learn how I might prevent anxiety from spiraling out of control. Back then I had to double down my efforts to keep the world from shaking loose.

As I let the tide help carry me, I can almost feel the weight of my old industrial-strength book bag being added to my shoulders. I kept that thing packed to the gills at all times, a cross between the protection and burden I believed I needed and deserved.

Soon, I'm standing in the belly of the beast: Sproul Plaza. A stream of students stretches as far as I can see into the center of campus, but smaller tributaries branch off here and there, and everywhere eddies of greeting and conversation pool. The entire area is teaming with life, just as it would have been on a beautiful weekday afternoon when I was here. I find a clearing on the steps of the student union and take a seat.

o

I can track my college career by tragedies. A few weeks into my freshman year, we were jolted by a surface-wave magnitude 7.1, the largest earthquake in the region's modern history. I was walking to class when it hit; I tripped and blamed the uneven sidewalk. It collapsed a section of the Bay Bridge and part of the freeway in Oakland, flattened houses, and set businesses ablaze.

Sophomore year began with a fire in a fraternity house that killed three students. Just a couple weeks later, and a few blocks away at a local bar, a psychotic gunman took thirty-three hostages, mostly students. After seven hours of terror, police managed to bust in and the deranged man was shot dead—as was one student who took a bullet to the chest.

How does that kind of terror and tragedy affect us? Some are touched directly. The victims whose time was cut short, their family and friends—those lives are obviously altered. What about everyone else? As Buddhists conceive of events, nothing occurs in isolation.

According to "dependent origination" or "Buddha's theory of causation," everything is a result of something else and, in turn, has consequences. A particular domino's collapse may command our attention, but its fall was preceded and followed by countless others. Technically, the quake killed sixty-three people, injured almost four thousand, and left many homeless (some estimates were as high as twelve thousand). But in ways difficult to fathom, none of us was left unscathed. Aftershocks of that and the other misfortunes rippled out.

Fall semester of my junior year, a fire tore through the Oakland and Berkeley hills. I watched its progression from the window of my second-story apartment south of campus on Telegraph Avenue. Residents were asked to prepare for evacuation. We waited for further word, our radios dialed to pick up what our eyes couldn't. I saw the fire come around the bend from Oakland, toward the houses on the hills like some hungry dragon laying waste to everything in its path. It was sneaking up on a dwelling I had always admired, a Victorian painted crisp white against the dark hillside. I told myself the fire would stop before it got there; that home was special, it deserved to survive. Then the trees around the residence ignited as easily as birthday candles and a few seconds later the roof was smoking. Too soon, it was nothing but the outline of a house, everything but its frame consumed by an inferno, leaving its skeleton against a bright light. The only other time I can remember feeling as helpless and heartbroken over a destroyed building was watching live footage of the twin towers collapse on September 11, 2001.

Pieces of burned things rained down for days after the fire. Even once the sky began to clear, slowly turning from dark grey to hazy orange, bits of blackened stuff floated through the air. I snatched one of these items as it fluttered past me on campus. It was part of a page from a book, charred illegible and so delicate it crumbled in my hand.

Had we somehow brought these events on ourselves? Related to Buddha's theory of causation is the concept of "karma." It's the application of Buddha's theory on a personal level: an individual's actions and thoughts affect the events that occur in that person's life. According to this idea, the students and the people of this community, area, and region were responsible in some way for the misfortunes that were befalling us. Had the twenty-five people killed in the fire done something awful to deserve their fates? What about the thousands whose homes were destroyed? Taken too literally, the concept of karma can seem to blame those who suffer tragedy. Cancer patients grow their own tumors. Jews caused the Holocaust. Thankfully, I'm told that's far too simplistic a take on karma. There's personal karma, but there's also collective karma, which are social and historical forces too broad and complex for sorting through and allotting culpability. Personal and collective karmas crash and mix in unpredictable and mysterious ways.

I can begin to grasp the multifaceted ways karma plays out when I think about the saga surrounding "People's Park." The swath of undeveloped university-owned land just south of the main campus was weighted with so much emotional and political baggage before I was even born. Its story goes back to the 1960s when a group of students and community members occupied that lot as a gesture of defiance against the state government and its institutions. But its history goes back even farther than that—to an ongoing conflict between the students and administration over civil rights and free speech. Actions escalated from sit-ins and demonstrations to tear gas and wooden bullets. People's Park became a symbol of empowerment but also of rage and violence. Over the years it was taken over by the homeless, many psychologically unwell, who were drawn from all over the country to that rebel patch of grass. By the time I arrived, it had come to represent deep cuts to social programs, lack of affordable housing, and slashes in mental-health services.

In Buddhist terms, the karma of People's Park had been shaped by the decisions and actions of policy makers, activists, administrators, law enforcement, and countless others both past and present. Collectively it added up to something thorny and nuanced and potent. Our little personal karmas were drops in a bucket compared to that force, which seemed to have all the unleashed energy that hides behind the Hoover Dam. It felt volatile, bound to break through at any moment. That feeling of danger radiated from People's Park in ever-widening concentric circles consuming the community and campus.

Yet to admit that and agree with college officials that something better should be done with the land was to turn our backs on the other legacy of the park, the one about equality and freedom. So as the final chapter opened, some of us joined the demonstrations that flared up my junior year to demand the university shelve its plans to turn People's Park into a "sports complex." I participated briefly in a march that materialized one afternoon and lent my voice to the chant "Save People's Park!" My fist was up, but my heart wasn't in it.

Maybe Grace's murder was the final straw. Although I didn't know her personally, she and I had started school at the same time and would have graduated together if she hadn't been murdered. She was stabbed to death at the start of the second semester of our junior year while she was working in a building on the edge of campus closest to People's Park. A janitor found her body in the student offices of the Pilipino American Alliance. To this day the case remains unsolved. Every person who knew her was eventually eliminated as a suspect; the best guess was someone had wandered in off the street. A sick and angry stranger simply happened on her. It didn't matter how virtuous Grace's personal karma. It was eclipsed by something bigger and darker.

All this thinking about karma makes me wonder about what I left for the students who came after me. That's the beauty of the concept of karma—it forces you to examine your thinking and behavior, to take notice of how you interact in the world. Even if you can't control other karmas, both individual and shared, you can take responsibility for your own. Doing so contributes in a positive way to the collective. It's one way you can make difference—not just in your own life but in ever-widening circles of peace and joy.

I've come to campus today to try a "loving-kindness contemplation," an exercise to improve both personal and shared karmas. I was introduced to it a few nights earlier during a "joy class" at a center directly across the street from campus. This particular organization teaches a version of Buddhism tailored for a secular audience. While its founders claim that the practices are rooted in the traditions of Tibetan Buddhism, they have been tweaked and elaborated on to appeal to Westerners, particularly those who might want to focus on the benefit to society at large. Individuals are taught a variety of contemplative tools to help create a culture of kindness, generosity, and courage.

The students streaming past me on Sproul Plaza today are exactly as we were then: the hipsters, the nerds, the jocks, the aspiring politicians, the activists. I left, but the river never stopped flowing. It's these never-ceasing tides that make our institutions karma repositories in need of care. I even see an updated version of me—the serious, scowling girl sitting by herself in the shade. I'd like to tell her what I've learned: that it's impossible to keep the tide back forever, so you'll need to learn to ride the waves or drown. I would whisper this in her ear, but I know she's not ready to hear it. For now she needs the hard exterior she projects; it's her armor, shielding what's tender underneath.

The main difference with this new batch of students is the technology they carry in their hands and pockets and bags. We didn't have cell phones, and now they have smartphones with Internet—instant access to the world from everywhere. If anything, these devices require us to pay even more attention to our thoughts and actions; they're like little karma accelerators: speeding up how quickly our intentions are added to an ever-widening collective.

The instructors of my joy class called those who engage in karmic exercises like the loving-kindness meditation "spiritual warriors." I can see why they say it requires bravery: to do it properly one must face painful realities. Before I start I have one final chapter of the past to revisit. My undergraduate career was capped by events I find particularly troubling.

After Grace's murder, school administrators made good on their promise regarding People's Park. Their timing was clever: they waited until summer, when most students were gone. I had stuck around to work my library job, so I saw it unfold. As I rode past on my bike twice a day, I witnessed the earthmovers rumble into People's Park and scrape up big swaths of lawn. I watched the machines dig deep holes for the posts and then dump heaps of sand. By the time students returned for the academic year, the middle of People's Park had been transformed into a beach-like setting complete with a series of volleyball courts. The park's regular inhabitants were forced to move along the grassy edges, eyeing those pristine additions like sharks circling an island.

The start of my senior year, the fury over the administration's actions was palpable. The student's sense of betrayal fueled the outrage. I suppose now it was full-on war; it was the opposition's move. In the middle of the night on August 25, 1992, a twenty-year-old woman who went by the nickname "Rosebud" broke into the chancellor's on-campus residence. She was not a student; in newspaper stories about what happened next, they refer to her as an "activist." What else could they call her? She was one of the many people drawn to the intoxicating force of People's Park, for whom that land was a powerful idea. It makes me sad because what she needed was real help, not some symbol to hasten her demise. It pains me to think of her vulnerability and disadvantage. Rosebud's rage was mixed with delusional thinking. She thought what she was doing would somehow save People's Park. At the chancellor's house she crawled through a window, tripping a silent alarm. She was carrying a machete. As the police arrived, she huddled in a bathroom. When they burst in on her, there she was: sick, tiny, homeless—and clutching a large weapon.

What choice did they have but to open fire?

o

I had thought reviewing my past behaviors and actions would be the hardest part of this task, but I see now that those never existed in isolation. My private dramas were unfolding alongside these communal events, their causes and effects crisscrossing and overlapping in mysterious ways. Did those events influence my feelings of anxiety? Did my thoughts and actions contribute to them? A Buddhist would answer "yes" to both—though no one can know precisely how or to what extent.

Having come to the end of my recollections, my heart feels battered and sore. This, I am told, is a good place to start. In my joy class I learned that spiritual warriors are those willing to wade through the muck turned up by their own tender hearts. It is important to keep going even when the journey gets tough, to learn to dwell in the discomfort. This is fertile ground for compassion.

A loving-kindness contemplation transforms the pain into something positive. You might channel it as contentment or goodwill or the absence of suffering, but the idea is to share the feelings that radiate from an open heart in some systematic fashion; experts generally suggest starting with a recipient for whom it is easy to summon kind feelings and move out from there.

In the version we practiced in class, guided by the instructor, we were told to start with ourselves by thinking these words: "May I enjoy happiness and the root of happiness." For about a minute I concentrated on that sentiment, but I couldn't feel any tenderness for myself. My heart softened when we were told to repeat the statement but replace ourselves with someone we love. Then we were instructed to direct happiness to those for whom our emotions are "neutral" and, finally, to those we find "challenging." I was able to scrape up a sense of compassion for both categories—certainly more so than I had for myself.

Sitting on Sproul Plaza, I put my own spin on the exercise. My recollections have left a delicate ache in my chest, and I know I must use that sensation. As uncomfortable as it might seem, I must kindle it—cup my palms around that spark and see if it will ignite. Because I've been thinking about Grace and Rosebud, I start with them. I project the tenderness I feel onto their memories and extend it to their families and friends. After several moments I turn that raw softness to the victims of the other tragedies I've recalled today, those whose lives were ended too soon by the earthquake and the fires and the senseless acts of violence. I expand my feelings to encompass everyone affected by those events, all who were attending school here at the time or lived in the region. Then I think of the participants in my joy class, some of whom seemed so sad, and I send them this warmth that radiates from my broken heart. I offer it to all the students, every drop of the river that continues to flow through this institution. I blanket my family and friends. The flame is stoked; now I picture a map of the United States, and I visualize a glowing love spreading like honey out from where I sit. It oozes across the land and over the ocean; it travels north, south, east, and west. I keep going until the light that emanates from my heart wraps around the entire globe.

At the end, I have one person yet to be officially included: me.

Then I realize there's no reason to treat myself separately. By extending my compassion to everyone, I've included myself. I'm part of the network of humanity. When I see it like that, I feel a surge of sympathy for the girl I was and the woman I am. I'm just another person doing the best she can—as vulnerable as Rosebud, as innocent as Grace.

Dharma Interview

I don't know what to expect from a private meeting with a Zen master. Part of me hopes it will be like sitting with Buddha himself. He will say some phrase that will ping around my skull, releasing profound wisdom. Or maybe he won't say anything, just put a hand to my head and pass on enlightenment via touch. I've been told that my "dharma interview" is a chance for me to ask a question regarding my spiritual practice, which seems like good timing because I have one that's been brewing.

I want to see if he understands why, at times, when it seems I'm finally getting a hang of this meditation thing, I'll be rudely yanked out of my peaceful contemplation by some awful sensation. It's the sharp crack of panic or some other random feeling like an explosion of itches. They seem to come out of left field, in response to nothing; I'm not considering anything troubling when I'm stricken with the anxiety. In fact it happens when I'm especially absorbed in the meditation practice, which is why I find it perplexing. The Zen master will probably say I just need to ramp up my efforts to stay on the side of the metaphorical "thought highway," firmly planted in the "big me" zone. When I get lazy, I must wander into oncoming traffic.

This particular Zen master is a Jew by birth and psychotherapist by trade—two characteristics that apparently lend themselves to being a good student of Buddhism; I've found they are not uncommon among practitioners in the area. My consultation with him is part of a one-day meditation retreat. I became familiar with this opportunity and the master a few nights earlier at the weekly lesson for newcomers held at this particular center, which occupies a historic schoolhouse in the middle of a residential neighborhood. The Buddhism practiced here hails from Korea and often employs seemingly mysterious combinations of words or strange little questions as part of the path to enlightenment. The master told us that during his own meditation he favors a silent statement for each inhalation and exhalation. "Clear mind," he says, breathing in; "Know nothing," he says, breathing out. He invites us to use these words or come up with others.

This Buddhism bears a resemblance to the type I experienced at the other Zen center, which came to the United States via Japan. At both, those further along in their practice are distinguished by robes, bowing is frequent, decorations are subdued, and walking is orderly. However, seated meditation here does not take place facing the walls. The cushions are set up so that we sit side-by-side looking toward the middle of the room. I've watched others coming and going, so I know to bow as I enter the room and then again before I sit. Today I am assigned a spot between two more experienced practitioners. I bow to my cushion and take my place.

It's not difficult to imagine the Zen center's main sanctuary as an old-timey classroom like the kind in *Little House on the Prairie* where kids of all grade levels sit together. At one end, where a chalkboard might have hung, sits a simple wood altar with a statue of Buddha. The school desks have been swapped for low cushions, offering occupants a shift in perspective, one in which the windows on both sides look exceptionally tall and the ceiling far away. The floor seems to stretch endlessly and must be from a redwood tree because it glows a rich rosy patina.

Today will be the longest I've sat in meditation at one time, though the hours will be broken up by periods of walking. What's in store is nothing compared to the agenda of some retreats, which can go on for days, but for me, today is a huge challenge. I've never spent so much time cross-legged. You wouldn't think sitting could be so physically demanding, but doing it with nothing to lean against requires a surprising amount of strength in the muscles of your back and belly. I've realized this the hard way—by discovering my core is extremely achy. By the end of the first hour of the retreat, I'm eager for the part where we get up and move around the perimeter of the room in a line.

In the middle of the second hour, my spine droops, and I begin to question whether I can sit upright for much longer. An older woman across from me has dragged a folding chair to her spot, and I consider doing the same. The discomfort becomes so acute that I even think about getting up and leaving—just walking out the door and not looking back. Forget trying to watch my thoughts, I'm just struggling to stay seated; I'm barely holding on, inching from one painful second to the next. Then I remember a tip the Zen master told us in the meditation instruction a few days earlier. He said when your energy flags, sometimes it's helpful to imagine a hose—a big one like the kind firefighters use—going into your stomach. He explained that this shouldn't be too difficult if our arms are in the traditional stance with the tips of our thumb and fingers of one hand lightly touching the tips of the thumb and fingers on the other; this forms a loose circle that rests just below the belly button. He told us to picture this as a feeding tube of sorts, one that can nourish us with energy from the universe. In my moment of desperation, I try it. I imagine it like a pipe pumping fuel. I breathe in a tiny bit of strength. Slowly, I feel my spine straighten, and a second wind blows into my core.

o

The Zen master isn't in the room with us. He's in a small room that shares a wall with this one, accepting his consultations. When the last person comes back, the next goes. In the meantime, the rest of us continue our meditations. At some point, I begin to notice a crashing noise that sounds like a two-by-four being dropped. At first I think construction is going on nearby. But, no, it's perfectly silent in the space between crashes. No hammering. No buzzing saw. Just "thwack!" out of nowhere. It dawns on me that the crashing might be coming from the little room where the meetings are taking place. If this is the case,

I hope it is a technique reserved for the most advanced students. As people reappear, I surreptitiously study them for signs of trauma.

My turn arrives. I bow to my cushion upon standing and again to the altar as I leave the room. I enter the dark hall and then open the door where the interviews are being held. The Zen master is sitting cross-legged on his cushion. I scan the area for a two-by-four but see nothing. I walk in and perform the "sandwich bow" that the abbot showed me earlier. It is made up of two bows at the waist with a single prostration of forehead to floor in between. Although it is optional, I was told it is the traditional way of greeting a master. I am hoping my performance of it lessons the severity of my beating should one be in store.

The Zen master invites me to sit opposite him. "Do you have a question?" he asks.

I nod. "I've noticed that sometimes when I'm meditating . . ." I search for the right words, wondering if what I'm about to say will make any sense. "Something will happen. I'll be really aware of my breathing and the present moment, and then suddenly I feel like I'm about to have a panic attack. Do you understand why this happens?"

He nods knowingly. "That's your 'little I.' "

"My 'little I'?"

"You begin to occupy the space of the 'big I' and then your 'little I' gets scared. Before, the 'little I' is who you thought you were, and now you have the understanding that you are more. She is threatened. You are making progress, and you might not need her. That feeling of anxiety or panic is her tool. You have no choice but to come back to her."

I'm amazed at how effortlessly he presents his answer, as if this issue was brought to him regularly. Then I remember a small detail I read about the Buddha. In recalling the years leading up to his enlightenment, when he was meditating in the forest by himself, he said fear and terror became his "constant companions." They could be aroused by the smallest things like "a peacock dropping a twig and the wind blowing the fallen leaves." That must have been Buddha's "little I" rebelling against his increasing awareness.

So maybe these sensations aren't a sign of my going backward, as I had believed. I recall the moments of panic, not just on this trip but at other times in my life, too. Perhaps they were all fueled by the dawning realization: I might be more than this individual identity. Maybe I was starting to sense that vast space outside the thought highway.

"So how do I get rid of her?" I ask my Zen master.

"Who?"

"My 'little I'? How do I kill her off for good?"

A look of concern washes over his face. "You don't."

"I thought that was the point."

"No. You need her."

"I need her?"

"She takes care of you. She gets things done. Be compassionate to her."

"But . . ." I was about to say that I thought she was the enemy when it occurs to me what a bizarre thing that would be to admit. She's me . . .

"Be aware of her. That's enough."

I'm staring at the nubs of the natural-fiber carpet between us trying to recalibrate my perspective when my Zen master asks, "What is all that exists?"

I look up. It's a koan, a Buddhist brain-teaser meant to slap me upside the head so I can see things with fresh eyes.

"Truth?" I say.

He slams his open palm against the floor, making the thwacking sound I've been hearing all afternoon.

"If you can name it, you've limited it," he says. He's transformed into a Buddhist drill sergeant. "This," he hits the floor again, "is all there is. It has no words!"

He tries again. "What do you see?"

Now I'm worried. I don't know the answer. I'm looking into his eyes. "A soul?" I say. The second it comes out, I know it's wrong.

He looks disappointed. "You see a soul?"

"Uh . . ."

"Come on!"

"Love?" Another stupid answer. That's a concept, a mental construct.

He bulges his eyes out at me. "What . . . do . . . you . . . *see*?"

"Eyeballs! I see your eyeballs!"

He smiles. "What color are they?"

"Grey."

He looks pleased. "That is what you see." He smacks the ground. "All there is with no thinking."

I've read that Buddhism is as much about unlearning as it is about learning. It offers a process of removing "the veil." We can begin to see the world with fresh eyes, without all the interpretation and beliefs we're accustomed to glopping on top of everything. I think all religion, at its best, strives to offer a path to a new perspective. There's a saying about this. Before studying Zen, mountains and rivers are mountains and rivers. While studying, they are no longer these things. Farther down the path of enlightenment, they are again mountains and rivers.

Yet I'm not ready to abandon my thinking—the jurisdiction of my "little I"—altogether. Like my Zen master pointed out, I need it and her. What would I write about if not for the realm of ideas? How would I get it written? Like people with jobs to hold down and kids to raise, my ability to function in society depends on the language of concepts. But I can see the importance of coming back to the present moment, which offers an alternative state of awareness: my true nature is more than a "little I." Maybe, then, she panics and lashes out because it is like a death for her—and what if I never come back? Inevitably I do. Something draws me away from "the now"—some dissatisfaction or distraction or task. I return to the thoughts, and my "little I" is reborn. These cycles of awareness may happen a few times a week or many times a day.

When I started this exploration of Buddhism, I thought the concept of reincarnation was cut-and-dried: my body would die, and my consciousness or soul would appear in some other life form. It would be me, only looking out from the eyes of, say, a turtle. But this path encourages realizations inside of realizations. Now I see, like karma, it can be more subtle and more complex. Perhaps Buddha was referring to cycles of awareness when he said every life contains countless deaths and rebirths. Each time our attention leaves the present moment is a death, and each time our awareness returns is a birth. The thoughts and actions in one affect the thoughts and actions in the next, and so on down the line, because nothing arises independently.

On the morning before I begin the drive back home, I wake up before sunrise. I'm all packed and ready to go. Before taking off, I plan to return to the center where I had my meeting with the Zen master. Early every morning at least one person at the center performs a series of prostrations. These are not normal bows but a far more challenging move where the practitioner goes from standing to forehead-against-floor and up again in a matter of seconds. The custom is to execute 108 of these in a row, a number that is powerfully symbolic in Buddhism, as an expression of deep gratitude. Today I wish to complete the exercise to honor the conclusion of this leg of my journey.

I've been warned to come prepared for a surprisingly difficult cardiovascular workout. The first rays of sun are showing by the time I get to the center, and I'm chewing the last bite of a banana. I'm greeted by a young man in robes whom I recognize from the retreat. He is the same abbot who taught me the "sandwich bow" I performed for the Zen master. He and I will carry out this morning's prostrations together.

He tells me to pick any spot in the room. I bow to the altar and again to a cushion just a few feet down from my previous spot. It offers a slight variation on my earlier view, which feels appropriate. He dives into his first prostration, literally: falling as if to kiss the floor. Following his lead, I drop to the ground, remembering when my head is down that I should also turn both outstretched palms up. Then I flip them back so I can use my hands to push myself to a crouch from which I can leap to a standing position. I hardly have time to congratulate myself on one down when my companion collapses for the next.

At first I'm counting each completed prostration. Somewhere along the way, I lose track. I focus on what I'm doing. I try to stay in the moment. I decide not to worry about the end. I'll know when I get there. My leg muscles burn, and my back dampens with sweat. I let the effort be my thanks for the tools and experiences and the change in perspective Buddhism has given me. Our individual stories strengthen the idea that we are a thing apart rather than a piece of the larger whole. They keep us focused on the past and worried about the future. I imagine energy spent as appreciation for the present moment, my labor as an engine that generates compassion radiating up and out. I do the movements as best I can, over and over again, each one starting anew when the last one ends, an ever-evolving now.

Islam

As I wrapped up my trip through Buddhism, I started to get nervous. I knew the time to explore Islam was fast approaching. Unlike the places of worship of the previous religions that had allowed me to tailor my explorations to ease into a particular faith by degrees, theological variations among Muslims are less apparent. Perhaps this is especially true in the United States, where congregants who gather under one roof may hale from a range of countries and represent a spectrum of belief. In all likelihood I would have no way of readily identifying the individuals whose convictions put them at the extremes of Muslim faith, a fact that further strained my already stuffed emotional baggage.

Back at home I gave the matter more thought. My tiny town serves as home to a surprisingly diverse Islamic community, many of them young men and women from countries across northern Africa and the Middle East who are earning degrees from the university. The absence of a busy urban environment seems to render them more conspicuous here, and I watch with interest. One day I witnessed a man and his two young sons pause to offer afternoon prayers at the local mall. They knelt on small rugs facing a Bath & Body Works, their backs to the walkway. I wondered about the trust it took to assume such a vulnerable position in public. Their faith was as enveloping as the sweet fragrance from the store.

Phil and I encountered a group of Muslims at a remote county park. Ours was the only car in the lot when we arrived, but after our hike we happened on two picnicking groups. One was a cluster of men sitting and eating. A hundred yards away, several women were stretched out together on a blanket in the grass, laughing and relaxing. We knew they were Muslim because of the scarfs fastened securely at their chins. So unexpected was this sight that I felt Phil and I had entered the forest in rural Washington state but had emerged somewhere on the other side of the planet.

I was forced to consider what seemed like an irony: Islamic female garb may be worn to conceal, yet it never fails to identify. This might not be the case in places where the population is predominantly Muslim, but in other countries, Muslim women stick out. Often, if it weren't for the women, the Muslims in my midst would have gone unnoticed. A guy in the pasta aisle at Safeway was just a regular dude until I spotted his wife in a face-concealing hijab draped from ear to ear; she had a bare band around her eyes, like the opposite of a masquerade ball. Her features may have been hidden, but the collective identity to which she belonged was on display. I wondered what it must be like to bear the brunt of public scrutiny, to have your presence function as a symbol. I once walked behind a woman wearing a full burka that rendered the person inside as invisible as a ghost. Meanwhile the fabric of her garment rolled and snapped so wildly that it appeared to contain its own weather pattern. Outside a breeze blew gently; perhaps a storm raged underneath.

Ramadan

The holiest month in Islam, Ramadan, was quickly approaching, and my goal was to participate. Ramadan is the four weeks out of each year when every adult Muslim who is healthy enough is expected to refrain from all eating and drinking from sunup to sundown. It falls according to the lunar calendar and therefore migrates a bit annually. This year it would start in the second week of July and last through August.

Obviously, not consuming anything—not even water—during daylight hours is a difficult challenge. But in communities and countries where many are observing the fast, it can also be a festive experience. Maybe in part because of the demands of the task, fun elements are added in. The work day is shortened, and restaurants open late so people can gather to feast after sunset.

Before Ramadan began I hoped I might find a Muslim who would be willing to take me on as a friend—not just to offer me a few pointers on logistics but to help me feel less alone in this daunting endeavor. I imagined we could provide a bit of support for one another and, perhaps, celebrate together. I was on the lookout for a female roughly my age.

The Muslim community in my town in the Pacific Northwest is served by a single mosque, a simple brick structure whose small dome and arched windows give it an Arabic flare. I phone but get no answer. Knowing that their services are held on midday Friday, I choose that day to stop by. I selected a time I thought would be late enough for the service to be over but early enough for activity to still be going on in the building. I suppose I was taking cues from other places of worship I had visited, where for several hours after an official gathering, people can be found milling around. I thought I might happen on a community elder attending business or perhaps a group of students meeting for discussion. At the very least, I hoped for some straggler whose acquaintance I could make.

When I arrived I was undeterred by the empty parking lot. The mosque is close enough to the neighborhood and student housing that many congregants can walk. The front door was unlocked. I removed my shoes just inside and tucked them on a shelf provided for that purpose. Mine were the only ones, but I had noticed a back entrance and thought some could be there or maybe people put shoes back on after the service.

No lights were on inside, but it was bright enough from the windows to see. On my left was a large area separated by a wall of glass; to my right a few rooms with doors that looked like offices. "Hello?" I called loudly. I went into the area behind glass that appeared to be the main sanctuary. It was plushly carpeted in pale blue, a small niche in the wall at the front of the room looked like it should contain some sort of statuary or artwork, but it was bare. Aside from a small bookcase in one corner that contained Qur'ans, there was almost no furniture. A few folding chairs were propped off to the side. I stood quietly hoping for the sound of voices or some movement in the building; aside from the occasional car passing out front and the hum of insects from the surrounding trees, I heard nothing. I thought maybe I had come on an off day—summer had just begun—so I tried a different Friday with the same result.

During a haircut, my hairdresser mentioned having another client who was Muslim, an unmarried woman who had converted to the faith from Christianity several years earlier. I thought the universe was sending me a friend, the ideal person with a foot in both worlds who might even need a Ramadan companion herself. I jotted out a heartfelt note asking if she would meet me. I wanted her to feel safe, so I wrote out my cell phone, my e-mail, and my street address. That same week, our mutual hairdresser passed the note along. I never heard back.

I put out feelers again. This time I learned of a lady through one of Phil's coworkers. She came from a Muslim family but was born in the United States. Our mutual friends contacted her first, and she agreed to help me. They gave me the green light, and I phoned her. She seemed really nice, and I thanked her profusely. I had thought the previous woman from my hairdresser would be my perfect Muslim mentor, but now I realized I had been wrong. We set a place and time to meet. Just before our date, she texted saying she couldn't make it. I tried a bunch of times to reschedule, but she grew more and more evasive.

o

It looked like I would be on my own for Ramadan, even more so since Phil would be on a work trip for the first two weeks. I searched the Internet for tips on fasting. I downloaded an app to my smartphone that uses GPS to alert you when the fast begins and ends each day based on the precise rise and set of the sun where you are.

Two things I hadn't thoroughly considered worried me. This Ramadan was falling smack in the middle of summer, and I happen to live far north of the equator. The daylight hours at this time of year are extremely long. They may not be as intense as summer days in Canada or Alaska, but they are much longer than places where day and night stay more evenly divided throughout the year. Here we can have about eighteen hours of light during the peak of summer. That this particular Ramadan would be my first was a bit like deciding to start my mountain climbing with Everest. How would I make it so long without even a sip of water, especially as the sun blazed and temperatures climbed well into the nineties?

I set those concerns on the back burner to focus on the logistics of coffee consumption. Normally I drink two large mugs of coffee when I wake up in the morning. I usually sip them slowly, over the course of a few hours as I'm working. With my new schedule, I had a couple options. Online, I learned that many Muslims change their days to wake up early during Ramadan and go about their morning routine before the sun comes up. I could see how this might be a nice alternative even if the sun rises as early as five in the morning. According to my app, my first day of fasting was to begin at 3:01 a.m. This meant I would have to start my day at about 2:30. Ramadan day one, I set my alarm to see how I felt at that hour. When I heard the beep, I turned on my light and sat up in bed. I guzzled a tall glass of water and downed a container of yogurt I had left on my nightstand. I snapped off the light. No way was I getting up at that hour and starting my day. For me, the only possibility was going cold turkey.

I suppose I have the raging headache to thank for distracting me from thirst and hunger on the first day of Ramadan. The morning started okay. I was able to work for a few hours at my laptop, though my thinking felt muddled. The pain set in at about noon and built over the next several hours. By seven that evening, I was horizontal on the sofa, eyes shut and a hand at each temple, wondering if my brain was actually pulsating or if it just felt that way.

I had read that if one's health is threatened, Muslims are permitted to relax the standards of fasting. Allah wants people challenged, not packed like sardines into local emergency rooms. After seeing that, I determined I must listen to my body throughout this experience and respond accordingly, even if it meant bending the rules. I felt my headache was bad enough to do something about, so I choked down two aspirin with a tiny sip of water.

All day I had been focused on the exact moment my app said the fast could be broken: 8:43. I had fantasized about the foods I would consume when the time came. I was planning on making at least two grilled cheese sandwiches and letting my heart's desire guide me in scooping out my ice cream. I'd chase it all with big bowl of granola before bed. Instead, 8:43 came and went with me sprawled on the bathroom floor, intermittently dry-heaving into the toilet. The situation I had created by taking aspirin on an empty stomach was worse than the original pain. As the waves of nausea reached a sickening crescendo, I moaned pathetically and wondered what purpose, if any, my suffering was serving and if this was anywhere near a typical Ramadan experience. I felt an overwhelming sense of gratitude as the queasiness subsided enough that I could eat a piece of toast. I was content to simply crawl into bed and say goodnight to day one.

o

By far the hardest part of Ramadan for me was abstaining from fluids during the day. Even in my normal life, I'm preoccupied with the importance of proper hydration. We live in an era of constant media reports that our bodies need at least eight glasses of water daily. If you don't meet this quota, they warn, you might land in the hospital with an IV in your arm. Over time, if health and beauty magazines are to be believed, you'll wind up shrivel-brained and pruney-faced. I don't know if all this sensationalism has made me more in tune with my thirst or if I'm just a particularly thirsty person, but I like to keep a glass of water nearby. Even on a day that I've had free access to water, I wake up in the middle of the night for a few extra sips and then reach for my glass first thing in the morning.

I increased my middle-of-the-night fluid intake from two tall glasses to a container that holds thirty-two ounces. I used a jug given to me by my mom printed with the slogan "Life Is Good." I thought it might make the task more cheerful. A sip of water on a parched throat at two a.m. can be a beautiful thing. Forcing one hundred times that amount down your already satiated gullet is less so. I would lay back down, my belly like a balloon stretched to its limits. I shifted carefully, my gut sloshing its swollen girth. A series of trips to the bathroom fragmented the night's remaining sleep.

As my Ramadan experience progressed, I found my decisions increasingly governed by physical need. I drank all that water at night not because I wanted it but because it was my only option if I hoped to make it through the next day. I felt a little like a contestant on some survival-based reality show. I grew calculating. I avoided sun exposure and strenuous physical activity. I stopped going to the gym; my yoga class was out of the question with no water. When the sun went down, I focused on the bare essentials: walking the dogs and replenishing my body.

I had never given much thought to my stomach's precise capacity. I suppose I considered it more or less bottomless. I put stuff in whenever I wanted. Every so often, I registered its being full as pain, and then I stopped putting stuff in for a while. Now with Ramadan, I became extremely mindful of each item that entered and what purpose it served. With food vying for space with water, I learned through trial and error. One night early on I wolfed an enormous bowl of pasta and discovered that while gut-busting, its substance petered out too quickly. I came to see my stomach as valuable real estate; I had to select and pace wisely.

I was forced to acknowledge the wisdom of guidelines that nutritional experts cram down our throats. I still daydreamed about downing an entire batch of cookie dough or a huge stack of pancakes dripping with syrup. But when the time came to eat, those options were no longer appealing. Perhaps I would have gone in for a bite or two, but filling up would have been reckless. I couldn't afford to live out any Willy Wonka fantasies.

I needed a small amount of carbohydrates in conjunction with protein. I found that eggs and high-quality yogurt provided long-lasting hunger suppression. My body craved nutritional powerhouses. Black beans, walnuts, and spinach were good, as was whole-grain toast smeared with peanut butter. I read that dates, a rich source of vitamins and natural sugars, are a popular Ramadan treat. I began to eat them nightly, craving their compact goodness first thing after a long day of fasting.

Even with all the effort I put in, I struggled—especially with thirst. Each day was a test to see how long I could go with no water. The first few hours were never too difficult. At about noon, the dry spot at the back of my throat would begin to creep down my esophagus, and I imagined cracks forming in its walls like a defunct pipe running through the desert. The saliva in my mouth would evaporate; my tongue became a rough seabed. I grew obsessed with the texture of my naked taste buds, wooly against my upper lip. At some point, my thirst would morph into a low-grade anxiety. Still, I held tight as the first signs of panic prickled up my legs. But when the alarm bells in my chest caused my heart to race and my breathing to quicken, I drank. It was usually late afternoon or evening: five or six or seven. By then I didn't see water as a source of rehydration so much as an elixir to calm my nerves. Of all the days of Ramadan, I made it only once to the official end without a single sip of water—helped, I think, by a light summer rain that dampened the air.

I became familiar with the nuances of hunger. There's the super-ficial discomfort when your belly growls. Most of us in the course of our normal lives will never get far beyond this feeling. But past it await ever-intensifying shades of deprivation. Eventually the burning want dulls and radiates out. Your limbs grow heavy and less adept. Several hours in, it reaches your brain and your thinking slows. In the late afternoon, putting my body in a horizontal position seemed like a good decision; in fact, most days it felt like the only option. I thought how difficult it must be for Muslims who had to work throughout Ramadan, especially those with manual jobs. I was fortunate to have the freedom to rest.

The fasting is meant to shift the normal power dynamic between the two components of our dual natures: the physical side is stripped of dominance, and the spiritual side gains it. Muslims are known to spend extra time during Ramadan reading their Qur'ans. Religious leaders also emphasize that time spent in reflection and prayer can be particularly fruitful during this time of year. But on practical terms alone, I can see why these tasks are favored. There came a time in the late afternoon when reading was about as physically demanding an activity as I felt I could manage. I studied passages from the Qur'an. Much of it was reminiscent of the bible, surprisingly similar stories, some with a slight twist. I also made my way through books about Muhammad's life, the history of Islam, the political narratives of predominantly Muslim countries, and the significance of religious practices such as Ramadan. But eventually even reading felt too challenging. My eyes didn't have the energy to track the lines; my brain didn't want to process the words. I would fall asleep or just lay there lethargically, my thoughts puttering. Without gas, the traffic of my thought highway slowed considerably, as had my ability to hitch rides.

Much to my surprise, I learned that the purpose of Ramadan is not, as I feared, simply to discipline the body. The goal is actually to increase one's compassion and gratitude. Such a trial elevates one's consideration for hungry and thirsty people. Around this time of year, devout Muslims are expected to make charitable contributions, especially of food. The willingness to give is hopefully rooted in deep understanding.

Ramadan showed me the complexity of hunger. It seems counterintuitive, but the more time that had elapsed since the last time I ate, the easier it became to not eat. At some point each day, my stomach ceased signaling that it even wanted to be fed. It must be some sort of protective mechanism: your stomach stops bothering you. It's pleasant to be free of the nagging, but this is when the mind-body connection starts playing tricks on you because you don't realize how in need of nourishment your body is becoming. Of course, it's when hunger stops hurting that it's doing the most damage.

o

A few days into Ramadan, I suddenly remembered why this creeping empty feeling was familiar. I recalled the interest with which I made a discovery during my early stages of anorexia: at first not eating is hard, but it gets less difficult until, at last, it's almost too simple. People think it takes amazing willpower not to eat, and it does in the beginning. The less frequently you eat, the easier it becomes. It's this sleight of hand that allows anorexics to ignore their bodies' needs, perhaps even convincing themselves food is unnecessary. When I realized the similarities between my past struggles and Ramadan, I got scared. I felt like I was inviting one of my worst demons back into my life. Would we tango once again?

As if to address this precise problem, Ramadan guidelines are equipped with a safety measure: one is obligated to eat immediately after the sun sets. Breaking the fast is as much a requirement as the fast itself. As the minutes ticked closer to the time for food, I found that my hunger would kick back in. Just knowing I'd eat soon seemed to reengage some vital link between my belly and my brain. I worried, then, about those for whom hunger is a real problem—the kind of challenge that recurs, persistent and corrosive. What would happen if I didn't see an end in sight? How devastating to face hunger again and again without knowing if or when you'll eat again. It's not just a physical toll, it's emotional too.

I was being afforded the opportunity to approach the precipice of starvation and look out. It wasn't the same as when I had suffered from anorexia, when I had stepped over the edge and was in free fall. Now I could stand firmly. From this vantage I saw how food is understood by our bodies as hope and joy; its absence can lead to despair and sorrow. At times I felt its abandonment as if it were an actual friend. It didn't help that my human pals seemed to be steering clear of me, saying we'd catch up after my Ramadan experience was over, as if our friendships were based on cramming goodies into our mouths. One day I felt so lonely and depressed that I convinced myself a small snack was a medical necessity to cheer me up. I ate a few almonds hoping they might function in my system like Prozac.

If this experience was designed to heighten my gratitude for food and drink, it did that in spades. I began to think of water as "beautiful, beautiful water." I ran an errand one afternoon during Ramadan, and the cashier was enjoying an icy beverage from a to-go cup—the clear kind with matching lid and a straw. The liquid inside was amber; I imagined it was herbal tea of some sort. I made believe it was mint-flavored. I waited in her line, mesmerized by the sight of the frosty condensation gathered across the plastic. I could not look away as she picked up the drink.

The spots where her fingers gripped displaced tiny beads of moisture causing larger droplets to snake down. Outside the temperature was a bone-dry ninety-five degrees, and I was approaching my thirteenth hour with no water. I stared unabashedly as she lifted the straw to her lips and sucked. The sight caused a slight dampness to bloom at the back of my tongue, but not enough to swallow.

After having been apart from water, my very first sip back offered instantaneous relief and pleasure. It was an uncomplicated homecoming. With food, the reacquaintance process was more measured, as if the time away had somehow damaged my trust. Even though the last thirty minutes or so before the fast's end were usually some of the most difficult mentally—a point at which my Willy Wonka fantasies often kicked into overdrive—when the hour finally struck, I approached my meals cautiously. I would start with something small like toast or dates and graduate to items with more substance. I would eat methodically, over the course of many hours, my satisfaction building gradually until, at last, I felt absolutely content.

I was so excited by my normal routine when Ramadan ended. No more middle-of-the-night water chugging. I could hydrate whenever I wanted. I resumed drinking coffee, a ritual I hadn't realized was so vital to my productivity and sense of well-being. My appreciation for lunch and midday snacks soared. To eat before one's energy flags struck me as a revelation. My thinking was sharper, my limbs more adept. I could take walks in the middle of the day. I was instantly more cheerful.

Finding Khadija

The religions I've explored all have central figures that faced a period of deprivation. Jesus retreated to the Judean desert for forty days, consuming nothing but water. The Jews experienced forty years of isolation and adversity in the desert. Siddhārtha Gautama sat for forty-nine days under a bodhi tree. In each case this time of hardship is an essential component of the story. It precedes a breakthrough, a vital step before a vision is clarified, the homeland is reached, or enlightenment is achieved. The suffering is designed to purify and to prove. It forges the key actors into what they are supposed to become: Christ, Israel, Buddha.

I didn't go anywhere, but Ramadan had brought the trial to me. I had walked through a desert of my own creation for thirty days. I had spent hours with my cheek against the bathroom floor. I went days with dogs as my only company. I shed copious tears. I came face to face with despair. I emerged several pounds lighter and a bit weary. But I was tougher and more fearless.

After Ramadan, I redoubled my efforts to find a mentor who could help me with the practical aspects of Muslim worship. This time I e-mailed my appeal to the president of the Muslim Student Association on campus. I explained a little about myself, that I was exploring religion, and that I was looking for someone to teach me to perform the daily Islamic prayers. Then, just in case he wasn't sure I meant business, I wrote that I had completed the most recent Ramadan. He wrote back immediately. Within a week, I had plans to meet a female graduate student from Egypt.

Mandisa suggested via e-mail that I come to the mosque at eight p.m. on Saturday night. I wasn't sure what to expect—if it would be just the two of us or if I was showing up for an already-planned event. Either way, I wasn't about to quibble. I told her I'd be there.

I pulled into the parking lot a few minutes early. I had only ever seen one or two cars here, and now it was full. People were also arriving on foot. I sat frozen, watching for several minutes. I had dressed in what I hoped was appropriate attire: a skirt to my ankles and a long-sleeve shirt. It was the same outfit from my time spent among orthodox Jews. I had also brought a plain white scarf big enough to cover my hair and hang past my shoulders. I tossed it into my bag just in case. I thought if the circumstances seemed to demand it, I'd drape it loosely over my head. Now I could see that all the women had their heads wrapped tightly. I pulled my scarf out and used my rear view mirror to put it in place. When I was done, I hardly recognized myself.

I finally got out of my car. An older woman stood nearby, staring at me. She must have watched me struggle with my scarf. She looked like someone's sweet granny, her ample frame obscured by bundles of fabric, only the precious moon of her face exposed. She smiled and said, "You go this way." Thank you, I responded and went in the direction she pointed.

The women were streaming toward the back of the building, the men to the front. I got in line behind a few women and ahead of a couple more. I walked right in, and no one said a word. I thought it must look like I belonged—that my attire was communicating the fact that I was a Muslim—and I was suddenly worried. I was donning this garb as a gesture of respect, but now I realized it might also function as misinformation. Were my clothes telling a lie? What I thought I was saying and what I was actually saying weren't necessarily the same. It was a problem I hadn't considered until now.

The women's entrance led into the basement of the building. At the end of a short hall, I came to a rack filled with shoes outside a room where the women were sitting family style at long tables. This must be some sort of party, I thought. I bought a few minutes by very carefully removing my shoes and arranging them on the rack. I wondered if I should remove my head scarf too. By recognizing customs, was I being respectful or deceitful?

I decided to leave my shoes off and my scarf on. I would be as forthright as possible when I spoke to people. I couldn't help what assumptions were made about me from across a room. I preferred this scenario to the risk of offending.

The women were sitting around the tables talking. I wondered if Mandisa was here yet. I made my way to an opening across from two women, one older and one younger. Their faces appeared Asian.

"I'm looking for Mandisa," I told them.

"From Egypt?" the older one asked. I nodded, and she looked around the room. "I don't think I've seen her yet."

"It's your first time here?" the younger of the two wanted to know. I nodded and sat. "I'm not Muslim."

They seemed not at all surprised.

Someone announced the food was ready; I'd had dinner at home, but I wanted to participate. We filled our paper plates buffet style in the hall and returned to our places.

The two women and I exchanged some basic information while we ate. They were both from the Philippines. The younger was a student. The older was married to a professor and had lived in the states for twenty years. She pointed at the ceiling. "My husband's upstairs."

They wanted to know what brought me to the mosque, and I explained my quest. Now I was exploring Islam. Specifically, I was hoping to learn the daily prayers.

The older woman looked at me sheepishly. "I don't do them. My husband does, but not me. Maybe when I get old I will do them all the time." She shrugged. "Not right now."

"Corinna?" A beautiful face framed by a hot pink scarf was peering down at me. "Mandisa?" She grasped the hand I had extended and wrapped her other arm around me. We hugged and shook hands simultaneously.

Like mine, her clothes were Western-style pieces that just happened to provide full coverage: an ankle-length skirt and a shirt with sleeves to the wrists. Many of the women wore long caftans, most in dark colors. Some topped off their outfits with regular-looking scarves while others used special wraps with a cut-out for the face. The ways the women presented themselves were surprisingly varied.

"Shall we go to the library?" Mandisa asked. Her accent had just a whisper of British; it spoke volumes about the history of colonialism in her country. She seemed sophisticated and fashionable, and it suddenly made sense why my other mentors had fallen through. All along, it was meant to be Mandisa.

I followed her out to the hall and up the stairs to the mosque's main floor. I could see through to the sanctuary. Men and older boys were milling and chatting as casually as the women downstairs.

We entered a room that looked like a makeshift library. Shelves filled with books and pamphlets lined the walls. Mandisa shut the door, and we sat across from one another at a table. Mandisa looked very serious, and I wondered if my Islamic instruction was to begin promptly. She seemed to be considering where to start when the door opened and a third woman joined us. The latecomer was as drab as Mandisa was colorful. She wore a solid grey caftan with an extra snug topper; not one hair peeked out. Her scarf was the same grey material as the rest of the outfit, as if she had made both pieces on her own. I wondered about the fabric she had used; it looked rough. When she got close, I could see sweat beading across her brow and upper lip as if she had just completed a physically demanding task. I didn't know it right then, but the teacher I had been looking for had finally made her entrance.

Mandisa introduced the new woman, giving me her name and her country. I recognized her name immediately from my reading: it was the same as one of Prophet Muhammad's most beloved family members. Among Muslims, disagreements abound over which of Muhammad's relations was closest to the Prophet, but this was a woman whose significance and goodness is undisputable. Every Muslim holds Khadija, Muhammad's first wife, in highest esteem.

"Khadija!" I said because I recognized it. The way it came out, I realized it might seem as if I thought we had met before.

She smiled. She understood. "You know it."

I nodded. Her country, on the other hand, I knew little about. I had never met anyone from there. I hated to admit it but, in my mind, its name was synonymous with violence.

As Mandisa hunted the shelves for literature I could take home, Khadija beamed at me—as if I was an answer to her prayers, as if she had been waiting for me to come into her life not vice versa. "I am so happy. Allah makes all things better. You will see." It occurred to me that this meeting was not as haphazard as I had assumed.

Mandisa handed over recent copies of an American Muslim magazine, and Khadija invited me to return to the mosque the following day. She told me that classes are held for women and children in the afternoon on Sundays. She repeated several times, "I will be there. *Insha'Allah.* God willing." I thought she was hedging, perhaps giving herself a little wiggle room in case she decided not to show. I fought my impulse to ask, "What happens if you aren't there? Who will help me?"

The night prayers were about to begin, and the three of us hurried back downstairs. Women were congregating in a small room adjacent to where we had eaten. This one was free of furnishings, and the floor had extra-plush carpeting. I asked Khadija if she thought it would be okay if I joined. Of course, she said. She would do the prayers on her own later, but I should go. Wait, she said, fix your hijab first. She tucked my bangs into my headscarf like a doting mother.

The women were lining up shoulder to shoulder. I got in next to the younger of the two Pilipino women; the older was nowhere to be seen. In this room the carpet had designs like little built-in prayer rugs to indicate where to stand. The orientation of the main squiggle put us with our backs to the windows. A man's voice from upstairs played from small speakers hidden in the ceiling. I didn't know the words, but I recognized the way he spoke them. All the women bowed. I followed along. We dropped to our knees. We pressed our foreheads to the ground. We squatted. We kneeled. We stood. We did it all over again.

Prayer

To achieve my goal of worshipping with Muslims, I needed to understand the prayers. When Muslims gather at mosques, their primary undertaking is prayer. The group activities one might recognize from services of other faiths—like singing or chanting or listening to a reading from a holy book—are, for Muslims, contained within the act of prayer. A service at a mosque will usually include a speech roughly equivalent to a sermon or Torah lesson or dharma talk in which an imam or elder addresses the congregation and imparts bits of wisdom. Other than that, it's all about the praying.

In general, praying is one of the most important acts in the life of any Muslim. Of the five pillars, or deeds, to which a Muslim is expected to remain faithful, praying is the only one that must be done every day. Two other pillars—fasting during Ramadan and a donation to charity called *zakat*—are annual (though a Muslim may fast or give more frequently). The remaining pillars need only happen once a lifetime. The first is the confession of faith or *shahadah*. By saying, "There is no God but Allah and Muhammad is his messenger," a person officially embraces Muhammad's message of the unifying one God. It's the same monotheism promoted by others whom Muhammad himself recognized as messengers and prophets—Moses and Jesus, among other notables. Here, Islam brought the idea to a whole new group of people, and the Qur'an is taken to represent the synthesis and completion of previous scriptures. Finally, before he or she dies, every Muslim is expected to make a special trip to Mecca, located in present-day Saudi Arabia, but only if health and finances allow it.

Prayers, however, are required a minimum of five times from sunup to sundown. Some historians say the number may have originally been three during Muhammad's time and increased after the Prophet's death. Either way, Muhammad is said to have personally negotiated with Allah to have the number reduced from fifty. Each of the five daily prayers has a designated time slot according to the position of the sun. *Fajr*, the first prayer of the day, is set for dawn. The noon prayer, called *zuhr*, is timed for just after the sun passes its highest position in the sky. After these comes a prayer in the afternoon (*asr*), at sunset (*maghrib*), and around nightfall (*isha*). While each prayer has a precise start, which moves by a minute or so as the days shorten or lengthen, you actually have until before the beginning of the next time slot to do the prayer, so the times provide more of a window rather than a strict on-the-dot engagement.

Before the Internet, most Muslims probably relied on old-fashioned means to meet daily prayer deadlines: word of mouth, the sun's trajectory or, for those living within earshot of a mosque, the call to prayer. Now we have high-tech options. I was able to download a free app that displays the day's prayer times for my precise location based on the GPS in my smartphone. For a small fee, I had the option to set a chime in advance of each prayer. While most prayers are conducted privately either at home or wherever a person happens to be when the time comes, Muslims are encouraged to complete a slightly shorter version of the noon prayers as a group at the mosque on Fridays. On this day only, the congregational *jummah* prayer takes the place of the *zuhr* prayer.

o

The next afternoon I was sitting in the same basement room where the women and I had eaten the night before. Now it was a classroom. A bunch of kids were sitting around a long table. I sat at another table by myself. When Khadija told me classes are held for women and children, she may have overdone it on the plurals—it was just one class, and I think "woman" would have been more accurate. If you didn't count Khadija and the other instructor, I was the only person older than ten. I thought back to the beginning of my explorations, when my sophisticated tome about Protestant reformer Martin Luther arrived in my mailbox as an illustrated children's book. God may have been going by Allah here, but the sense of humor was unchanged.

When I first entered the room, Khadija's co-instructor seemed unpleased with my presence. She wore a dark caftan and even darker expression. Then Khadija welcomed me with an embrace and a kiss on both cheeks, and the other lady's attitude appeared to soften. She opened a folder and handed me a photocopied sheet as if it were a peace offering. Single-spaced and printed on both sides, it was labeled "Steps of Prayer." It spelled out the precise movements and words to utter. It was exactly what I needed. "Thank you," I said as if she were giving me a precious gemstone.

As we waited for more kids to arrive, I read the instructions carefully. It explained how to do a *rakah*, which is one cycle of standing, bowing, prostrating, crouching—the building blocks of a prayer. Depending on the time of day, every prayer has two to four *rakahs*. Start, it read, by facing in the direction of Mecca. Declare your intention to perform the prayer. (For example, "I intend to offer *fajr* prayer for Allah.") Then cup your hands to your ears and say, "*Allah Akbar*," which translates as "God is the greatest."

So far so good, I thought optimistically.

Next, the instructions continued, place your left hand over your stomach and then grasp the wrist of that hand with your right hand. Say,

"Glory be to You oh Allah, and praise be to You. Blessed be Your Name, exalted be Your Majesty and Glory. There is no God but You." But really I was supposed to say this in Arabic and, luckily, a transliteration was provided: *Subhanaka Allahummah wa bihamdika, wa tabarakasmuka, wa ta'ala jadduka, wala ilaha.*

I tried to form those sounds. I got halfway through and began to worry.

I skimmed ahead.

I had a few more phrases to say in the standing position. Then I needed to recite the first chapter, or sura, of the Qur'an, which is very short and, ideally, another short sura or section of a longer sura—prayer's choice.

Now came the bowing part I knew from the night before. A quick *"Allah Akbar"* and bend at the waist. In this position, I was to say three times: "Glorified my Lord, the Great." In Arabic it sounds like *"Subhana rabbiyal Ajhim."* I got excited. I thought this was something I could probably master.

Stand. Say, *"Allah Akbar."* Then come swiftly to my knees. With palms and forehead to the ground, I am to say three times, *"Subhana rabbiyal A'ala,"* which means "Glory be to Allah, the Exalted." Awesome, I thought, this part I could definitely do.

With an *"Allah Akbar,"* come out of the prostration and sit with posterior on the heels of feet, which is like a crouch with knees on the floor. This position has a special name: *jalsa.* From here, repeat *"Rabbi-ghfir li wa arhamni"* three times. This looks really hard to say, but it simply means, "Oh my Lord, forgive me and have mercy on me." I suppose, if one must, this is a good phrase to butcher.

After this and another *"Allah Akbar,"* one's forehead returns to the floor for another three repetitions of the phrase, *"Subhana rabbiyal A'ala."*

Now do it all over again—once, twice, or three times depending on the location of the sun.

At the end of the series of *rakahs*, regardless of how many and while still seated in *jalsa*, one recites something called the Tashahod. This appears, for the most part, to be a summation of the compliments given to and requests made of Allah throughout the rest of the prayers. It is customary to point one's index finger toward Mecca while saying it.

Finally, you turn your head to the right and say, *"Assalamu alaikum warahmatullah."* Then you turn left and repeat this phrase, which translates as, "Peace and mercy of Allah be on you."

Khadija explained that today the children would be practicing saying the Tashahod in Arabic—and that maybe I could read along and get a feel for how it sounded. In English the words are straightforward: "All salutations, peace, perfection, omniscience, and prostrations, prayers, and blessed deeds are for Allah. The peace of Allah be upon you, O Prophet, and His mercy and blessings. Peace be on us and on all righteous servants of Allah. I bear witness that there is none worthy of worship except Allah, and I bear witness that Muhammad is His servant and messenger." The phonetic translation cloaks it in mystery, at least to my untrained ear: *At-tahiyatu lillahi, was-salawatu wattaiyibatu. Assalamu alaika ayyuhan-nabiyyu wa-rahmatu llahi wa-barakatuh. Assalamu alayna wa-ala ibadi llahi s-salihin. Ashhadu alla ilaha illa llahu wa-ashhadu anna Muhammadan abduhu wa-rasuluh.*

Every student took a turn as I listened carefully. A few were too young or too shy and didn't make it all the way through. Their voices trailed off, or their presentation ended in a face-plant on to the table. Khadija gently prodded and corrected. One kid who was a bit older performed exquisitely, his annunciation clear as bell. It sounded beautiful and otherwordly, like the music of a concerto played at double time and backward.

When the other instructor took over, Khadija and I retreated to the upstairs library. She wanted to explain a little more about the guidelines regarding the Tashahod, so she got a pencil and began to diagram something on a piece of paper. She wrote numbers for each of the daily prayers depending on how many *rakahs* they required. Starting with the *fajr*, she created a column: 2, 4, 4, 3, and 4. She explained that what the children were practicing was really only half of the Tashahod; the second part, which some people refer to as the Durud, is another variation of a request for Allah's mercy and blessings. Next to the 4s, she wrote: 2, ½, 2, whole. She said after the first two *rakahs* of these prayers, you recite half the Tashahod, then complete the next two *rakahs* before reciting the entire Tashahod. For the morning prayer with only two *rakahs*, you can do the entire Tashahod at the end. However, for the *maghrib* prayer at sunset that only has three *rakahs*, it goes like this: 2 *rakahs*, ½ Tashahod, 1 *rakah*, whole Tashahod.

I stared at the marks she was making on the page. I could feel my eyes surrender focus; soon I was watching through two filmy blinds.

Maybe it was time to throw in the hijab. Like the other faiths I had explored, the primary ideas weren't so difficult to grasp, it was all the stuff that had sprouted up around them: the customs and rituals, many of which developed after the main messengers were long gone. A few of the essentials regarding prayer and other behaviors could be found in the Qur'an, but the rest was based on the daily habits and practices of Muhammad himself as recalled by the people who had known him. This extensive compilation of guidelines, called the Sunnah, supplements the Qur'an.

Something about the Tashahod being chopped in two pushed me over the edge. I could not believe the intricacy of these procedures. How was any newcomer expected to understand, much less adopt them as her own? Do religious people see how intimidating it is to approach their belief systems? For believers, all these rules and formalities wrap them in a warm, familiar blanket; for an outsider, this same stuff creates a barrier that can seem impossible to penetrate.

Khadija could tell I had hit a wall. I couldn't take my eyes from the paper. "I think that's enough for today," she said. She put her hand on my arm, and I reluctantly lifted my gaze. "Don't worry," she told me. "Allah wants it to be easy for you." I tried to smile, but I wasn't convinced.

For several weeks I sat in on the children's class. I got used to arriving in the mosque parking lot, putting on my headscarf, and making my way to the back entrance that led to the classroom. The sound of Arabic as performed by squirmy students grew familiar. I began to recognize certain phrases and to know what they meant. I wasn't sure that I could ever put all the pieces together and do the prayers myself, but I tried not to think about that.

o

Just as I was settling into the routine, Khadija suggested we switch it up. She wanted me to come to her apartment during the week for more one-on-one time. I continued to fasten my headscarf in the rearview mirror, only now I emerged into the busy parking lot of a student housing complex. I felt like Clark Kent making the transition to Superman. I walked the pathways to Khadija's building in hijab. I wasn't concerned about running into anyone I knew because I felt unrecognizable. I had never understood why Lois Lane couldn't tell that her superhero boyfriend was the same man as her reporter colleague, but it suddenly made sense. Identity is so much bigger than a face.

The personal details about Khadija I had gathered at the mosque were skeletal at best. She had come to the United States for her husband's graduate studies. She had two little girls. I also knew the basics about her homeland: colonial past; ruthless leader, initially supported by the West, brought down in spectacularly grisly fashion; roving bands of militants fighting for control. Its story was similar to at least a dozen other countries in that part of the world.

Now, with time spent just the two of us, I put meat on those biographical bones. Despite my preconceived notions regarding the status of women where she was from, Khadija had managed to obtain an advanced degree living there. She had been a professional working woman before coming to the United States. Her husband's degree in the sciences was being funded by her country's government—some aspect of which was obviously working well enough to finance such projects. But her family's efforts to broaden their horizons came with sacrifice. Since arriving in the United States more than five years earlier, they hadn't returned home once. Both of their little girls had been born here. Their grandmothers had only ever seen them on Skype.

I had met expatriates of countries like hers who fled and had no desire to return. Not Khadija. She longed to go back. She spoke of her homeland with a tenderness some might reserve for a dear loved one. She showed me pictures on the Internet of its most beautiful features. She called it "my country." She fed me its popular dishes. "This is food we eat in my country." She and her husband had visited another town in the United States that reminded her of it. "The temperature, the way the air smelled," she said with a serene smile. "I closed my eyes and I was in my country."

I wondered how she felt about the ruthless leader who had been killed—if his rule was as bad as the media here had made it seem. She hadn't been back since his death. Her gaze lowered to the floor; her expression went pensive. She nodded. "It was bad," she whispered. She told me about a cousin who was executed for carrying antigovernment propaganda in his car. "I'm sorry," I said. I meant for her family's suffering but also for whatever role my country may have played in creating the situation. "Thank you," she replied. I searched her eyes but didn't see any blame there.

Mostly Khadija and I practiced the passages I would need to perform daily prayers. We would go over the basics: the Tashahod and the Qur'an's first sura—both of which are part of every prayer. But she'd also had me print out the phonetic versions of the Qur'an's last three suras, which are only a few lines each. With these I would have options for the parts where it was "prayer's choice." This was the bare minimum I would need to do prayers correctly.

Khadija selected what we would practice each day. She would call out the words bit by bit, pausing for me to parrot her. It always reminded me of the famous scene from *The Sound of Music* where Julie Andrews teaches her young charges the basic components of a song by having them repeat the lines she sings. Only here it was called *The Sound of Prayer*. She sat next to me as we practiced; sometimes, she would move around her apartment, tidying up and checking on her actual children. With my eyes glued to the appropriate cheat sheet, I would try to mimic what she said, but often, even after we'd been going over the same line for several minutes, it would turn to mush in my mouth. When that happened Khadija would get close. It was the only time she was ever stern. "Look at my mouth," she would instruct because I was always reluctant to take my eyes off the translation. I never thought staring at her lips would help, but somehow it always did.

I adored practicing short phrases. After the twists and turns of the longer passages, "*Alhamdulillah*" (praise to God) and "*Bismillah*" (in God's name) were like little treats. I wanted to repeat them over and over again. I loved how "*Subhana rabbiyal A'ala*" felt like marbles rolling on my tongue. Khadija's favorite phrase was "*Insha'Allah*" (God willing). It peppered all she said, as natural as breath. She whispered it every few sentences even when discussing something as simple as what she planned to do that evening. But I noticed she said it more for big things like the approval of her husband's dissertation. "If that happens, we will be going home soon. *Insha'Allah. Insha'Allah. Insha'Allah.*"

One afternoon Khadija answered the door looking upset. Her concern was a recent headline about her country: an act of terror had killed a slew of civilians, some American. We sat together in her little living room. "I think it is worse now," she said, referring to the instability since the death of the ruthless leader. She squeezed her eyes shut. "My country," she said, swallowing a sob. Tears streamed down her cheeks. My own eyes welled up, and I reached for her hand. For several minutes, we stayed like that—just holding hands. I wished for something more to say or do, but I could think of nothing better than to make her pain my own.

Big D

When he first began to spread his message, Muhammad's focus was almost entirely social justice. He lived in a region where many prospered from trade while others struggled to meet basic needs. In Muhammad's time it was normal for the rich to provide loans to the poor. Equally common were unfair lending practices such as high interest rates and payment schedules that put debtors at a disadvantage. Borrowers who failed to keep up might suffer from another caveat to the agreement: being forced to work for their lender on terms dictated by the more powerful party. The households of the wealthy would expand as the disadvantaged lost their freedom, trapped in an indefinite loop of servitude.

Women and children were especially susceptible to this cycle. Custom did not permit women to accumulate resources in their own names or to inherit wealth. Even a widow was not the typical recipient of her dead husband's money. A woman who found herself with no male head of house would have no means of supporting herself or her children. If forced to borrow money, she would almost certainly be unable to pay it back. A needy widow might have no option but to attach herself to a wealthy household by whatever means possible, even as a slave. Children left without parents were also at risk of needing to trade freedom for survival.

Both Muhammad and his beloved first wife, Khadija, faced circumstances before they met that could have relegated them to lives of subservience. They managed not only to avoid the worst consequences associated with those stations but to go on to lead happy, prosperous lives. Muhammad lost his parents at a young age but was raised lovingly in his uncle's household. Khadija had been widowed but amazingly defied the status quo by obtaining her husband's wealth and his thriving trade business. But both she and her new husband must have lived with the "what ifs" of fates narrowly escaped.

Muhammad didn't start speaking out for social reforms until after he married Khadija. With her love and support, he argued for changing lending practices and abolishing interest rates so that the poor could have easy access to resources. The wealthy elite hated his ideas, but Muhammad didn't care. He believed women deserved the ability to accumulate wealth and receive inheritance. He insisted that the rich had a duty to care for the needy. While Muhammad's message evolved and expanded, it was rooted in these issues that troubled him.

The problems that existed around Mecca during Muhammad's life are not exclusive to that region or time. All over the globe and across generations, people struggle with the same things. The source of the disadvantage may vary—it might be race or education or illness or age. Women and children continue to make the list almost anywhere you go, though certain laws and government programs help.

After my parents broke up, I suppose my mom and I became a modern-day equivalent of Mecca's widow and orphan. We landed at the bottom of the barrel, resource-wise. Fortunately, we had my grandparents as a safety net. My mom's parents lived in South Dallas, in a mostly African American neighborhood. My dad's parents lived just north of downtown, in a much whiter and ritzier area. My mom and I were constantly driving back and forth between those two parts of town—between the "haves" and the "have-nots."

Dallas is where I first became aware of the difference between wealth and poverty. Even today, after living in a handful of other cities with similar income disparities, I still think of Dallas as particularly polarized by income. I attribute this association, at least in part, with the low-income status I shared with my mom when we lived there. Ours was a modest means. But the other part of my association is certainly tied to the "Big D" culture of wearing one's fortune. The rest of the country has since caught on—thanks to reality television, I fear—but Dallas was ahead of the curve: fancy handbags, head-to-toe designer labels, diamonds the size of ice cubes, expensive coats made from fuzzy creatures, cars that probably cost more than my mom would earn in a decade. Maybe the spectrum just seems so much wider when that extreme is flaunted.

I didn't think I'd have any reason to go back to Dallas for this story. My plan was to fly directly to Washington, D.C., and wrap it up there. If I needed more experiences worshipping at mosques, maybe I'd pop over to New York or Michigan, states that are known to have sizeable Muslim populations. I didn't think Muslims and Texas even belonged in the same sentence.

I was excited to revisit the nation's capital. I hadn't gone back for a long time, but I love that place. Dallas is another story. After moving to L.A., I would return to visit both sets of grandparents. Whenever I was there, my energy level plummeted and my desire to sleep spiked. I think most people attributed it to my being a teenager, but I knew it was something more. I felt physically unwell when I was there. I thought it was too real to be just psychological. I believed there must be an environmental factor, like the air was bad. Even when I got dressed and tried to circulate among the upright, I couldn't shake the lethargy. I didn't understand how others looked lively with so little oxygen.

I recognize my past pattern—leave a city and avoid going back—has been an essential aspect of my current explorations. I returned to L.A. and Berkeley to rifle through my emotional baggage and, with the help of a religion, hopefully lighten the load—or at least understand its contents better. But my Dallas baggage was different, I reasoned. With the other locations, my reluctance to visit had more to do with the person I had been or how I had behaved while living there. I had no beef with the places themselves. Los Angeles and Berkeley are pretty fantastic in my opinion. I was to blame. I felt my falling-out with Dallas had been the opposite—it was all Dallas's fault.

But signs were pointing me to Texas. First, my grandma's health began to fail. Second, I decided I really did need to visit another place besides D.C. to round out my experience. Then I learned that while I was busy looking the other way, Texas had quietly become home to a vibrant Muslim population. In fact, the 2011 U.S. Mosque Survey found that Texas now ranks third in number of mosques—behind only New York and California. Measures of attendance show that Texas mosques are cramming in more people than those of any other state. For Friday prayer services, the total number of congregants who show up at Texas mosques is second only to the total number in New York. But when it comes to Eid prayers, which are those associated with the two highest holidays in Islam, no other state in the country has more congregants attending mosque for worship than the old Lone Star.

Although I didn't want to, I had to admit that going to Dallas appeared to make sense. According to the mosque survey, the Dallas metropolitan area alone is home to about forty mosques, a surprising number of which are newly constructed in the more affluent suburbs north of downtown. Still it felt weird. First, the ostentatious materialism I associate with Dallas made it seem like a city so at odds with Muhammad's message of social equality. Maybe I wouldn't find "real" Islam being practiced in the Big D but some flashy American version where passages in the Qur'an are used to justify a closet full of Louis Vuitton bags. Second, my mind kept going to the brand of fundamental Christianity for which Texas is famous. Dallas, after all, hosts the Pre-Trib Conference, an annual affair in which a big group gathers to happily discuss scenarios in which the mosque on the Temple Mount in Jerusalem will be obliterated so that the rapture and ensuing tribulations may proceed as predicted in the New Testament. What sort of Muslim community could flourish in that environment? But maybe these factors didn't detract from the meaning of what I was doing; perhaps they added to it. Maybe my reluctance was all the more reason to go. I suppose I could have gone on hemming and hawing forever, but I finally recognized the missing puzzle piece sitting before my eyes. It was shaped like Texas.

Jummah

I flew to Dallas and moved in with my grandmother. She still lives in the same general part of town—just north of downtown—as she did when Grandpa was alive. Only she's traded the swanky townhouse for a little unit in a "retirement community." I suppose as far as old folks' homes go, hers is upscale. The building has a Mediterranean feel, with cream-colored stucco exterior, dark wood accents, and lots of archways. Windows look out at gurgling water features surrounded by greenery with a tropical vibe. It all but screams: this is not a last stop on the journey to the grave, it's an exotic holiday!

Grandma's apartment has an extra room with a pull-out sofa. She'd had a helper make the bed and clear a space in the closet for my things. Grandma knew about my project and why I had come to town. I had explained it to her by phone several times, slowly and clearly. Since my last visit, she'd given up driving, though she kept a car in the parking garage for others to use. She kept saying I could use it to drive myself to "synagogues." I never knew if this was an honest slip or wishful thinking. As I would correct her and explain the difference, her eyes always took on a look of distress. I couldn't tell if she was concentrating to hear me or if she didn't like what I was saying. I had two main goals for my time in Dallas: do whatever Grandma wanted and worship at mosques. It occurred to me that the one thing Grandma might want more than anything was for me not to worship at mosques.

The first Friday of my trip, I gave myself an hour to make it to the mosque. *Jummah* prayers were supposed to begin at 1:30, so I left Grandma's at 12:30. It was more time than necessary given the distance, but I was anxious about navigating the roads. I had never been a driver in this city, only a passenger. I studied the street map the night before and wrote out each turn in big letters on my day planner. I wanted to proceed deliberately and cautiously. I didn't want to so much as scratch Grandma's car.

As I set out, I noticed I was a little nauseous. Now that I was behind the wheel, I realized all my worrying about the streets and directions had been a distraction from what I was really nervous about, which was the destination. I had no idea what to expect. Would it be obvious which entrance I should use? Would other women be there? I had selected this particular mosque to start because it had a website with clear information and a recorded phone message specifying the time of prayer. I would have preferred to speak to an actual person, but as I called the mosques on my list, I realized I was more likely to reach voice mail. In most cases I would just need to show up at the appropriate time and hope for the best.

From about a mile away, I spotted the dome. It wasn't huge or fancy, just a simple green-capped cupola at the corner of two main roads in a mostly residential area. I pulled in to the parking lot. The building was situated such that I was able to maneuver the car around its perimeter, observing it from all angles. It wasn't much more than an oversized cube of cream-colored brick uninterrupted by windows. Black security cameras were affixed at each corner, standing out against the blank canvas of the walls. I considered that it might not be a real mosque at all but a brilliant art project providing sociopolitical commentary on being Muslim in Texas.

Mine was the only car so far. I selected a space in front of what appeared to be the main entrance. Though the building had other doors, these were larger and a nearby sign that read "Notice: All Activities Monitored by Video Camera" gave it an air of formality.

As I waited, I arranged the scarf on my head. Growing up, I had always resented what I saw as Dallas's feminine ideal of beauty. One had to be pageant-ready: hair shellacked into a do, figure accentuated, makeup clearly visible on face. I caught my reflection in the rearview mirror. The standard I was trying to live up to now was so far from any of those things. I had to admit it was kind of a relief.

A giant pickup roared into the parking lot. It was a shiny Ford, too new for plates. For an instant I was terrified that I would be witness to a hate crime. I thought about ripping off my hijab and fleeing the scene. With my doors locked and one hand on the key, I watched as a young man got out of the truck. He wandered casually to the mosque entrance. I could tell he meant no harm.

My first official Texas Muslim, and he looked the part: new-but-faded blue jeans and pointy-toed lace-ups that resembled boots. It was a ranch-hand-meets-urban-hipster look.

I got out of the car. "Hello," I called to him.

He was extremely friendly. He told me he was from Pakistan and specialized in import-export. His job was to locate gently used cars and arrange their transport on big ships destined for faraway places. He had cherry-picked his Ford. I asked if he thought other women would come for the prayer service, and he told me normally they did. He pointed out the entrance for women: a separate door near the main doors and another around the corner.

As we chatted, a third car swung into a spot marked reserved and came to rest at our knees.

"It's the imam," my friend said cheerfully.

Through an expanse of windshield, I spied my first imam. He had a beard the color of Ronald McDonald's wig. It was either a dye job gone wrong or an excellent ploy to soften his image. His mouth was set in a no-nonsense expression, but surrounded by all that flaming hair, it was hard not to interpret it as a smile.

The imam unlocked the mosque's front doors, and I waved goodbye to my Pakistani cowboy.

o

Directly inside my entrance was a room for washing. Along one wall was a trough lined in marble tiles. In front of each spigot was a perch for sitting.

I removed my shoes and placed them on shelves for that purpose. I sat at one of the *wadu* stations and turned on the faucet. I let the water trickle on my toes and then I leaned forward and washed my arms and hair line the way Khadija had instructed. I was gentle on my face, hoping to keep on the moisturizer with sunblock I applied earlier. I cranked the towel dispenser and patted dry.

Beyond a set of glass doors sat the ladies' worship area, which was a square of space carved from the larger square of the mosque and cordoned off with frosted-glass walls. Masking tape applied directly to the thick green carpet divided the room into long rows. It wasn't obvious to me which way to face, but I thought the lines were a clue. Back in the washroom, I had plucked a prayer rug from a stack offered by the door. It had a little built in compass in the center with a needle that bounced around. Now I spread it on the floor and plopped on top of it. From my bag, I pulled out the cheat sheets I had used to practice my prayers with Khadija. I arranged them on the floor around me. I needed them as a reference, especially if I would be doing the prayers on my own.

I could tell more men were showing up from the shadows against the frosted walls. The whole point was communal prayers, and I started to feel miffed at being quarantined in this glass box just because I was born female. It took me back to being a little girl on the playground, left out of a game. It made me angry for all the women unfairly passed over for a raise or a promotion. I was getting a little hot under the hijab. Thankfully, an older woman in a beautiful sari walked in. Her presence pacified my blossoming resentment. Suddenly I was glad she and I had our own space without any strange men around.

The woman plucked a plastic chair from against the wall and dragged it to where I was sitting. She smiled at me and pointed to the wall on my left. At first I didn't understand why, and then I realized she was trying to tell me I was facing the wrong direction. I hadn't oriented myself toward Mecca. I was looking some place much less important, possibly toward Albuquerque. I was a little embarrassed given the fundamental nature of this guideline and the compass sewn into my prayer rug, but I shrugged it off and set everything right.

"I'm learning the prayers," I told her, motioning toward the papers.

She grinned and set her chair inches from me. Her head scarf was loose, revealing lovely salt-and-pepper hair pulled back in a bun. "Very good," she said, nodding appreciatively.

More women arrived. One turned on the flat screen that gave us a video feed of the men's section. It focused mostly on the front of the room where the imam was standing, but you could also see men and some boys as they entered the frame and found places to sit on the floor. Once they settled into position, the picture showed just the backs of their heads.

The imam began to speak English mixed with Arabic. The gist of his talk, from the parts I could understand, was about the upcoming Eid holiday commemorating the annual hajj in Mecca. He encouraged all those with means to buy a goat, sheep, or cow for the needy. Those who did so would receive "more reward." I listened closely to see if he would elaborate on the logistics of said purchase and if he was referring to some sort of benefit in an afterlife, but his train of thought was swallowed by a long stream of Arabic.

Women continued to arrive throughout the imam's speech. Many wore colorful saris but others sported the more somber caftans I recognized from home. They would greet one another and find places to sit and chat quietly. Some had small children clinging to the folds of their garments. It reminded me of being on the women's side of the orthodox synagogues I visited in Los Angeles. Privacy afforded us an informality that wasn't apparent on the men's side. Knowing we could see them but they couldn't see us bestowed a bit of advantage. We were like the higher-ups who can watch an interrogation from behind the one-way mirror.

Some of the women who entered skipped the socialization and set about praying. They came in with an air of determination and completed a series of *rakahs* on their own before settling down to listen to the imam. I noticed on the monitor some of the men doing the same. At first I thought I had missed an instruction to begin, but eventually I realized they were either catching up on previous prayers or just doing extras.

Now we stood. A few of the more elderly, including my neighbor, stayed seated but the rest of us came shoulder to shoulder. A couple of women acted as the prayer police and instructed us to fill gaps and move in closer. Everyone, including the seated, arranged and scooted until even the most finicky in the group looked pleased. We were squeezed together too tightly for my papers to be spread in front of me; I gathered, folded, and tucked them away. I'd wing it.

Guided by the imam's voice, we went through the *rakahs* together. The imam narrated long portions for us and then fell silent so we could recite our own parts. When memory failed me, I repeated my favorite short phrases—"*Allah Akbar*" and "*Bismillah*"—again and again or concentrated on the sound of the suras being whispered all around me. I enjoyed the process of synchronized prayer so much that I was disappointed when it came to an end with the second *rakah*. We turned our heads to the left, and then to the right. "Thank you," I whispered in each direction because I felt privileged to have joined this group for worship.

I was in the car about to back out of my parking space when I heard a knock. I turned to see an impressive mustache, handlebar style, in my passenger side window. It belonged to the face of an older gentleman. I pressed the button to make the glass come down. "My wife tells me you are learning Islam." Behind him was my prayer neighbor in her sari.

He asked if I had Eid plans, and I told him I didn't know. I wasn't sure what day Eid was or how it was celebrated.

"Please, may I have your phone number? We would like to invite you."

I wrote my name and cell-phone number on a piece of paper and handed it to him. I explained I was visiting my grandmother in Dallas, that's why I had a weird area code.

I asked his name, and he said something I couldn't quite grasp. I hesitated, and he said, "Please, call me Raj."

o

Just about every night of my stay in Dallas I tried to make it home in time to eat dinner with Grandma, which usually meant getting back by five. Some nights we'd put together something simple like sandwiches and soup in Grandma's little kitchen. A few times we actually cooked from her old recipes; I did the chopping and heavy lifting, while she acted as the brains of the operation. We made dishes I hadn't tasted in more than decade: her herbed meatballs, the yellow squash and tomato casserole, her famous spaghetti. Every third evening or so, we ate downstairs in her facility's "restaurant." The nights we "dined out" were easier in a sense because there was no washing up, but they were a production in their own way.

Grandma has notions about how one should present oneself in public. She never crosses the threshold with less than hair coiffed, makeup flawless, and clothes impeccable. When I was little, I would watch as she readied herself. She had an entire area dedicated to the task, at the heart of which was a mirror ringed in lights with a chair in front like a movie star. She's re-created a similar setup at the old folks' home, only in this new context it seems less privilege and more obligation. It takes her all morning to get ready and most of the evening to undo it. But for whom is she making the effort? She doesn't seem to particularly enjoy the few hours when her appearance is perfect. The energy she once devoted to the tasks she loves most—painting and stitchery—has been consumed by maintenance. Her days are doctor appointments, trips to the pharmacy, and meds swallowed according to schedule. She puts drops in her eyes, hearing aids in her ears, and more pills in piles. Her afternoon nap is a respite from the choppy sea of survival. The only time she seems content, happy even, is first thing in the morning before the jewelry and the outfit and the cream blush when she's reading the newspaper; she drinks her coffee with bare legs sticking out of her nighty and her hair like a fright wig.

When we left her apartment for dinner, Grandma's facade was in place, and I was less her granddaughter than a valet or, perhaps, her handmaiden. As she made her way down the halls with the aid of a walker, I tried to anticipate her needs: jump ahead to hold elevator doors or fall behind to let her through first. The entrance to the restaurant was a logjam of walkers, and we joined the others waiting to be seated, engaged in a bit of group make-believe that this was fine dining.

We usually sat with one of the friends Grandma had made. Except for a longtime divorcee who had never remarried, they are all widowed. Ladies of means, the money they'd been left by dead husbands or parents affords this particular old-age experience, which is undeniably top-of-the-line. Grandpa had been a doctor whose investments paid off, which is how Grandma can live here. The residents have every convenience at their fingertips: cleaners, helpers, drivers. If they need more, there are nurses or aides. When that isn't enough, they can transfer to the assisted-living wing with around-the-clock care. It is down a long hall where things get a lot less fancy. Grandpa went there a few weeks before he died.

Grandma and her friends can barely hear one another. They stick to uncomplicated topics: the status of an ailment, how the day had been, whether the chicken is overcooked. I could never figure out if they'd once had in-depth conversations or if convenience and need was the glue of their bond. They didn't hug and fuss over one another like good girlfriends do. Often they would eat in silence and part ways with no discernable goodbyes.

Ummah

On the days I visited mosques, I never told Grandma what direction I was going. Mostly I headed to neighborhoods north of the city center, which wouldn't have worried her too much. One Friday I went the opposite direction. My destination was not the suburbs south of downtown, an area composed mostly of middle-class African American neighborhoods (and where my mom's parents had lived). I had my sights set on a section of town that sits in the shadow of the skyscrapers, not far from the grounds where the Texas State Fair is held every year. Here, if one is lucky enough to have a home, it is most likely in a small house or apartment building whose exterior is suffering from years of neglect. It's also the location of Mosque Number 48 of the Nation of Islam.

For a lot of people in the United States, the Nation of Islam is the first they were aware of having individuals who identified as Muslim in their midst. Many of us have at least heard about Malcolm X, probably the most famous member of the Nation of Islam ever. Current leader Louis Farrakhan makes national news occasionally. Before I had any real understanding of what it meant to be Muslim, I would buy sweet potato pies from well-dressed Nation of Islam boys at a flea market I frequented in college. Now, I wasn't quite sure how Nation of Islam fit with more mainstream versions of the faith.

When I arrived in Dallas, I called the phone number I had for Mosque Number 48, but it was out of service. I found a website for the place, but most of the pages linked to the national organization with headquarters in Chicago. Online, I learned about "Muhammad's Economic Blueprint," a program in which the small daily donations of many participants are pooled, thereby allowing land to be purchased for farming and urban-renewal projects. I pushed play on a video of Farrakhan explaining the plan: if everyone gives five cents a day, it will add up to $291 million in one year—as long as sixteen million people participate. It's a solid idea in theory, though maybe not realistic. According to some estimates, the Nation of Islam has fewer than a hundred thousand members. Regardless, a theme song starts playing automatically with raps and a refrain—"I got five on it"—so cool I listen twice. There are also links to DVDs of Farrakhan's lectures I can purchase, including one entitled *The Origin of the White Man and the Making of the Devil.*

Specifics regarding Mosque Number 48 were harder to find. I did learn that it had been established in 1968. A street address was provided, but the usual details I had grown accustomed to seeing such as a prominent display of the time of Friday's *jummah* were not in evidence. No mention was made of the five daily prayers, much less a schedule based on local times like so many mosque websites provide. However, I did see a phone number. I checked it against the number I had and found they were the same. I tried it again thinking I might have dialed incorrectly, but I got those familiar three tones and the recorded voice saying "Sorry."

From what I've read and people I've talked with, doubts exist about whether members of Nation of Islam are "true" Muslims. Most of the criticism stems from the fact that the organization doesn't appear to emphasize the five pillars: saying the *shahadah* statement of faith, daily prayers, fasting for Ramadan, the once-in-a-lifetime hajj to Mecca, and giving *zakat* to the less fortunate. I suppose, if true, these are valid complaints—though one might question how closely individuals from other versions of Islam adhere to these tenets. What seems to me more troubling and fundamentally at odds with Muhammad's message is the Nation of Islam's stance on race. White people are forbidden to join, and most of the rhetoric focuses on the financial and spiritual empowerment of African Americans exclusively.

In addition to issues of social justice, Muhammad advocated for the dissolution of tribal affiliations. His vision was of a single *ummah*, or community, made up of individuals bound together by ideals that transcended earthly characteristics such as family ties or skin color or gender or wealth or age. He was able to realize the system he imagined, if only on a small scale, when he cobbled together the five tribes of his adopted hometown of Medina, three of which were Jewish, into a confederation. His was a "supertribe" whose members represented the diversity of the region.

It wasn't until Malcolm X did the hajj that he became aware of this aspect of Muhammad's message. He famously recounts in his autobiography his surprise upon arriving in Mecca to find the full range of skin colors from pale to dark among his fellow Muslims. The experience made Malcolm X see Muhammad's objective in a truer light: to shed individual identities in favor of unity. Not long after his return, he broke ties with the Nation of Islam and was assassinated.

What would I have said if someone had answered the phone at Mosque Number 48? I imagined the conversation might go something like this:

ME: Hello, is your worship service open to the public?

OTHER PERSON: That depends. What color is your skin?

ME: My skin is light.

OTHER PERSON: As in light for a person of color, or . . . ?

ME: White. I'm white. But my hair is black. Hello? Hello?

Instead, I would just show up in person because that was sure to be less awkward. I don't necessarily take offense at the organization's rhetoric.

Nation of Islam dogma may be incompatible with Muhammad's vision but so is the society from which it arose. Many of its members have been denied access to resources based on race for generations. The realization of Muhammad's ideal depends on those with power working to level the playing field for everyone. But what if society is rigged to keep the field uneven? It's difficult to label as unfair a reaction to a biased system.

o

I was surprised to find the mosque so easily, well-marked and on a busy street. I guess part of me was hoping it would be impossible to locate, like some back alley secret society; at the very least, I thought the building might be as defunct as the phone number. But here it was with a prominent sign and even a digital leaderboard flashing information to passers-by. I stopped in front on a Friday just shy of 1:30; at mosques across the city, people were arriving for *jummah*. Number 48's parking lot was empty. I pulled in to a space and let the car idle for several minutes while I watched for signs of life. The only movement was the leaderboard's frantic scrolling: "Sunday General Meeting 10:00 a.m.... Wednesday Night Meeting 8:00 p.m.... Friday Study Group 8:00 p.m." I wondered if they even held worship services or if it was all gatherings of a more functional nature.

After a few minutes I drove out of the lot. I had a back-up plan: a mosque just a few streets away that I knew would be holding congregational prayer. I had called its number earlier in the week and reached a recording confirming the time for *jummah* and inviting me to join. The user-friendly website prominently displayed local prayer times. Under the "History" page its origins were traced back to Nation of Islam's Mosque Number 48. At some point a group had broken off and created this new mosque, which appeared to embrace a more mainstream approach to Islam. I can only imagine Malcolm X was on a similar path when his life was cut short.

The mosque looked to me as if it had once been a single-story house with a big yard. The city had swallowed it up and spit it out. Now the yard was a concrete parking lot and the house had been transformed with additions and a paint job of vaguely Arabian scrollwork. A high iron fence ran the entire perimeter of the property, distinguishing it from the empty lots and boarded-up storefronts.

I parked on the street and put my headscarf in place. Sitting in the car with the engine off, I realized how anxious I felt. Throughout this entire journey from Christianity to Islam, I never set out for a place of worship without experiencing nervousness in my belly. Some of it was due to the logistics: locating the right building, getting myself through the proper entrance, and finding a suitable seat—all without inadvertently offending anyone and, ideally, maintaining a modicum of dignity. The bigger part of my uneasiness had to do with the fear of feeling like an outsider. I worried I wouldn't be welcome—or, worse, treated with contempt.

Today's anxiety had been higher than normal from the get-go. I started to feel it even before I left Grandma's apartment. It's hard enough when what you think makes you suspicious is invisible but quite another thing when your body is wrapped in it. In fact, by the time I was ready to exit the car, I realized the sensations in my chest were bordering on full-blown panic. I closed my eyes and took several deep breaths. I borrowed from my Buddhist experiences and tried to step back to the side of the road where everything was fine. My worries were just thoughts.

I walked around the building and through the first door I saw. It was ajar and led to a little hallway that dead-ended into a bulletin board crowded with notices. From there I could have gone left or I could have gone right. Doors hung in every direction; I felt like a contestant on a game show whose prize hinges on the knob she turns. I heard men's voices coming from one of the options. I didn't have the courage to pick any of them. I busied myself reading the announcements.

A man came from around the corner and paused when he saw me. He wore a white-cotton tunic with matching pants and skullcap. His attire looked exotic against his black skin, but something about the way it came together was uniquely American.

"Can I help you?" he asked, smiling. His pretty teeth matched his outfit.

"I'm here for *jummah*," I said.

"Great!"

His warm demeanor gave me a boost of confidence, and I explained I wasn't Muslim but that I was learning about Islam.

I followed him to one of the doors. "The sanctuary's in here," he said, showing me. The room was large by private-residence standards but modest for a communal gathering space. He pointed to the back,

"That's where the sisters sit. You should go in because it starts soon, but feel free to ask me any questions at the end." Slipping off my shoes and tucking them on a shelf by the door, I thanked him.

Several men were sitting at the front of the room, and a few women were at the back. The people were oriented at a diagonal—proof that the grid of the city doesn't always align to the spiritual. I took my place among the ladies. This was the first I had ever sat in the same room as men during prayer, and I wondered if it would be distracting. One of the men stood and did the call to prayer. There was no niche in the wall at the front like in most mosques, so he cupped his hands and sang the words against his palms, helping the sound fill the room. I suppose I had heard this ritual done before but hadn't fully realized what it was without the visual cue. As men and women continued to arrive, I let the feel of the sturdy floor beneath me ease the remnants of anxiety that still tingled in my limbs.

o

The imam stood to address the room. He sported a trim beard and skullcap. Words didn't just slide out of the imam's mouth and tumble to the floor, they leapt and danced and marched. "People educate their minds, but they don't educate their hearts," he declared. Muhammad's guidance for how leaders are to address gatherings is to "speak from the heart." I noticed that talks given in mosques had a stream-of-consciousness quality to them. They tended to be looser and more spontaneous than speeches I had heard at the worship places of other faiths. This one possessed that same quality but was delivered in an oratory style reminiscent of Martin Luther King Jr. "If you want to change your life, you have to change your heart!" He paused to let that sink in. This congregation perhaps more than any I had visited lived by those words. Every Saturday and Sunday, they operate a program called "Feed Our Neighbors," transforming their parking lot into a food-distribution center. Pictures on the website show the down-and-out crowd waiting in a line stretching up the street. By some estimates, they hand out twenty thousand meals a year. Though far from affluent, they stay true to Muhammad's instruction to help the needy. The imam took a deep breath and scanned the audience with an intense gaze. "Expand the heart . . . and you expand the mind."

By the time we were ready for the communal prayer, a handful of newcomers had shifted the demographics of the room. Before, it had been 100 percent African American; now a small percentage were something else—from various places in the Middle East. I imagined they worked downtown and had found this mosque both convenient and compatible with their needs. As we went through the prayers and my forehead made contact with the floor, I let the last traces of worry melt into the ground.

Our bodies were positioned toward Mecca, but what we were really facing was the little structure in Mecca called the Kaaba. Long before Muhammad was born, the Kaaba had been used as a communal shrine to the various gods worshipped by the different tribes who lived in the region. Muhammad's message of a single *ummah* relied on the unity of the monotheistic one-God concept, and his objective became to bring to the Arabian people this fundamental notion promoted by the Jews and Christians before him. When the idea of monotheism gained enough traction in the region, Muhammad repurposed the Kaaba by tossing out the icons it contained and dedicating it to the one and only Allah.

On my way out of the mosque, I stopped at the information area and picked up a *zakat* form. I thought if I were going to make a charitable donation, one of this mosque's programs would be a worthy recipient. I looked more closely at the form only to discover that what I thought was an appeal for contributions was actually a *zakat* application. This was the first I had seen anything like it. Anyone could take one and request financial assistance. The applicant had to specify why aid was needed, circling from a list of options that included housing, electricity, gas, water, telephone, food, transportation, or other.

"Sister!" someone called. I turned. It was the friendly man in white from earlier; he was addressing *me* as sister. I couldn't help it. Tears sprung to my eyes. "Come back and visit again."

Family

"Your grandma tells me you are Christian." These were the words spoken to me by Judy, Grandma's paid helper who comes once a week to do whatever needs doing. She's a middle-aged woman who is a full-time nanny; she does Grandma's bidding on her day off. Judy and Grandma had just returned from an outing to the doctor. Judy's statement lingered in the air between us: she put it out there, but I wasn't quite ready to receive it. Of all possible characteristics Grandma might have mentioned, this is what she selected? As long as she was borrowing from the realm of fantasy, why not take it all the way? Why not jet-setting socialite or world-renowned orthopedic surgeon?

"Interesting," I said. Maybe Grandma had a point: perhaps I was a Christian whether I chose to be or not. It didn't matter if I accepted Jesus as God. It didn't even matter if I went to church. Some essence that trumps anything I might believe or do has been passed down through generations. I am Christian because as far back as anyone knows, my family has been Christian.

I don't know if it was her getting older or my religious explorations, but since I had been in town, Grandma's Christian identity had cranked up a notch. She acted horrified by the fact that I had never in my life attended an Eastern Orthodox service. "How is that possible?" she asked incredulously. You never took me, I wanted to say.

Now that Grandma was almost ninety, she had a good excuse for never going to church. She said the service started too early and lasted too long. Standing was expected during certain portions of the ceremony, which she could no longer manage. For these reasons I gave up on the idea that she and I would attend a service together. It seemed strange to go without her, so I ditched the notion of going at all. I thought it was ironic that of all the faiths and denominations I had visited, I would be missing the one that was perhaps most closely associated with my family. I made my peace with this fact. Then, early one Sunday morning, Grandma shuffled into my bedroom in her nighty. "Let's go to church today," she said. I looked at her through one squinted eye. I had other plans for that morning, but I wiped them away. If Grandma wanted me to take her to church, by all means, I would do so.

The issue that divides the Orthodox Church from the Catholic Church is reminiscent of the main division within Islam. The Orthodox Church refused the authority of the pope, whom Catholics considered infallible. Orthodox Christians rejected the notion that a person could possess an essence, passed down by blood or some other invisible source of transference, which made his relationship to the divine more profound than that of an ordinary person.

This same idea has been hotly contested among Muslims. After Muhammad's death, a dispute erupted over who should become the next leader of the *ummah*. Some believed Muhammad had intended his successor to be his cousin Ali, who had been a faithful member of the *ummah* from the beginning. No one could deny Ali's loyalty, but others thought Muhammad had specifically wanted to avoid appointing a leader who was related to him by blood. Perhaps he feared his legacy would become like a monarchy, where leaders who ascend based on a birthright are assumed to possess an intangible quality that makes them special. This could threaten the equality among members he worked so hard to establish and inspire a devotion that should be reserved for Allah alone. People in this camp believed Muhammad would want his father-in-law, Abu Bakr, to take over.

The division between these two groups continues to this day, as does the basic question: can a person possess an extraordinary relationship to the divine? Those who might answer "yes" are the Shiites, and they believe their leaders have been endowed with the living spirit of the Prophet. Like the Catholic pope, Shiite leaders at the highest level are thought to be sinless and infallible. Sunnis are those who would disagree. Their leaders are considered religious and political executives. This position is similar to the one held by Eastern Orthodox Christians, who define their priests and bishops as ordinary people occupying extraordinary positions. In keeping with this theme, people in these roles are allowed to marry and have families. Congregants are still encouraged to kiss the hand of the priest or bishop, though in doing so one should keep in mind that it's the office being honored.

But isn't every faith dependent on the idea that a person can have a special relationship to the divine? Christians agree that Jesus was an incarnation of the divine, and every Muslim believes Muhammad brought Allah's words to earth. So perhaps the issue is not a human's ability to channel the divine but whether this quality can exist beyond the originals? Or perhaps the argument is all just a smoke screen for the very human inclination to claim an advantage that lends power and control.

The Greek Church no longer occupies the building I remember visiting as a child. Several years ago, the congregation purchased land just north of downtown and built a new building. The property allowed for a bigger main chapel as well as supplemental structures for social gatherings and classrooms. It also let church leaders mold a fresh identity. They opted not to use a white stucco exterior that is so readily identifiable with Greece. Instead, they used brick in a style more broadly Byzantine: arches and columns and the squat domes that speak to the shared history of a huge region. The strategy seems to be working. Recent years have seen a spike in attendance, filled out by congregants from a wider spectrum of Eastern Orthodoxy.

The main sanctuary may be bigger, but it evokes the same feelings I remember from being a kid standing by myself in the old chapel. Similar red carpeting lines the aisles. Recognizable faces stare down from murals on the ceilings. Even empty and quiet, the room back then had seemed alive. Today it is further animated with movement and sound as Grandma and I slip into a wood pew. The priests and their helpers are revving up around the altar, lighting the candles and stoking the incense. Grandma hands me a pamphlet on the rules and procedures of attending a service she finds tucked into the back of the pew. It spells out the proper way one is to prepare for entering the main chapel: first, by "venerating" an icon and, second, by lighting a candle. It explains that venerating means kissing. Out in the foyer, I had watched others pressing their lips against the glass under which sat a painting of a saint. It says here: "It is not proper to kiss an icon in the face." Thank goodness I skipped it because that's exactly where I would have planted a wet one. Instead I caught up with Grandma, who was making a donation in exchange for two thin candles. She handed one to me. I lit it using the flame of another and then nestled it into the sand of a raised box by the door. Others flickered brightly for those not able to attend today.

The service began. Like Catholicism, it all revolves around the Eucharist or communion. The "Divine Liturgy" contains the steps that prepare the bread and wine for the people and the people for it. Outlined in my rulebook, these include: the Small Entrance, Epistle Reading, Gospel Reading, Sermon, Great Entrance, Priest Censing, and Blessing. As I tried to follow along, I couldn't help but think how, from the perspective of a worshipper, this experience was indistinguishable from a Catholic program. Sure the chapel and other accoutrement were fancier than at the simple small-town Catholic church I had attended, but those are superficial variations. It is the same with Sunnis and Shiites: from the point of view of a worshipper, the differences are negligible. In all my digging I had uncovered exactly two. Shiites are likely to rest their arms at their sides during a portion of the daily prayers when Sunnis are encouraged to hold both hands to their chests. In addition, Shiites are less inclined to use prayer rugs. They opt, instead, to pray directly on clean earth, and if praying inside, they may rest their foreheads on a stone during prostration to represent this earth. The differences are so subtle that Shiites can and do make themselves at home within predominantly Sunni congregations, a necessity especially in the United States, where their numbers are so few.

Of my list of mosques in the Dallas area, only one was exclusively Shiite. It didn't promote itself as such, but I was able to confirm it through online message boards. I found no website, and the phone number kept going to a busy signal. All I had was an address, which indicated a neighborhood northwest of downtown. I set out one afternoon to find the place. I had done this before with another "mosque" on my list, only to be led to a tiny house indistinguishable from all the other tiny houses in a low-income neighborhood. It was either a mistake or this was taking "house of worship" to a whole new level.

I found the Shiite place in a strip mall across from a Loan Star Title Loans. Shiites generally think of their places of worship as "meetinghouses." As such, they tend to lack the more formal elements of a mosque, such as a minaret or a dome. I pulled in to a parking space and tried to imagine what the builders of this structure had intended it to be. A dry cleaner's? A tax preparation service? I doubt they could have imagined this use.

It wasn't shy announcing its purpose. A big maroon awning read "Institute of Quran and Ahlubait." It took me a while to figure out that last word; I finally realized it was a spelling variation of the more common "Ahl al-Bayt," which translates as something like "people of the house," meaning Muhammad's family members. It's a reference to the leaders Shiites esteem for being the Prophet's blood relations.

I tried the door, but it was locked. All the blinds were closed. For now, the building was empty. I got back in the car, thinking what a surprise it was to find this mysterious little outpost of Islam in such a mundane setting. Here in the middle of Texas, next to a taco joint and donut shop, a long-dead Arabian prophet and his family members are actively honored. But the more I thought about it, the more it seemed in keeping with religion in general: that strange domain where divine mystery intersects with the human realm.

Eid

I was sitting on the flimsy mattress folded out from the loveseat in Grandma's extra room when my cell phone rang. It was a local number I didn't recognize.

"Hello?" I answered.

"Corinna?" It was a man's voice.

"Yes?" I replied.

"It's Raj!" It was my mustachioed friend from the first mosque. His enthusiasm was contagious. "Raj!" I cried.

He explained that he was calling on behalf of his family. They would like to invite me to their Eid festivities. They planned to attend the special service at the mosque Wednesday morning and afterward gather at his daughter's home for a meal. Would I like to meet them at the mosque and then caravan back to their place? I told him that sounded excellent.

I had also learned of another Eid celebration, this one arranged by the North Texas Islamic Association, which would be held at the Dallas Convention Center the day before I met Raj and his family. I hadn't officially observed the Eid al-Fitr, the celebratory meal that breaks the fast on the last day of Ramadan, so now I would celebrate double.

When I made my plans to travel to Dallas, I hadn't realized the significance of the Eid al-Adha. I had seen it on my calendar—it was obviously important enough to make it on my mass-produced At-A-Glance monthly planner—but I didn't realize that it is arguably the most significant date of the year for Muslims. That it coincided with my trip was either dumb luck or the hand of Allah.

Aside from the two Eids, Islam has only one other major holiday: Muhammad's birthday—though if and when to observe it is not universally agreed on. Some Muslims opt not to celebrate it, believing its recognition implies a level of devotion that threatens the basic monotheism of the faith. Among those who observe the holiday, there's disagreement about which day to honor. Sunnis generally recognize one date, while Shiites tend to prefer a time several days later. With the Eids, it's different. Everyone gets on the same page—though festivities still might not coincide exactly, most are within hours depending on what country's clock celebrants are observing.

Eid al-Adha is all about the unity of people—and not just of Muslims with one another. It commemorates an incident that appears in the Jewish Torah and Christian Old Testament: when God asks Abraham to sacrifice his son. Only, in the Qur'an the boy is Abraham's son Ishmael (whose mother is Hager) instead of Isaac (whose mother is Sarah). In both cases, God stops Abraham just before carrying out the act and lets him kill a ram instead. Muslims believe that their ancestry can be traced back to Abraham through Ishmael, binding them with

Jews and Christians who both claim this patriarch. Eid al-Adha, or the Feast of the Sacrifice, memorializes the common root of the three major monotheistic faiths. The holiday also coincides with the end of the hajj, so that as the pilgrims gather en masse in Mecca, Muslims are gathering all over the world with them.

As I approached the convention center by car, I could see a few police officers stationed at various pedestrian entrances. I had been conditioned by my time in post-9/11 D.C. to expect heavy security at busy gatherings, especially those involving what might be considered a "hot-button" topic. I thought about the annual Pre-Trib Conference held not far from here and the damage that could be done by one crazed fundamentalist bent on hastening the onset of the rapture. But this show of force didn't appear to be anything more than what you might expect for simple crowd control at a Bon Jovi concert. I wondered if decisions regarding safety measures were dependent on who might be the target of attacks.

Being alone and a little tentative about the situation, I decided I would use the center's official parking garage. I followed the signs to the rear of the building where I stopped at the little parking booth. A single cop stood nearby, but he seemed unconcerned with the likes of me. At the very least I had expected to confront a bomb-sniffing dog. I was prepared for a snout to run the length of my car's undercarriage, maybe be asked to pop open the trunk. I paid and they waved me in nonchalantly.

I snaked my way through the cavernous underground and found an available space near the elevators. It was still a little on the early side; only a smattering of cars were here. I turned off the engine and pulled the scarf from my bag. I had swapped my usual one, which was plain white, for a fancier leopard print. In place of the little safety pin I normally used as a fastener, I had a small rhinestone brooch. These tiny things made me feel all dressed up.

A sedan full of people arrived and parked nearby. I watched as members of a family got out, at least three generations' worth, from little to grown to frail. The women wore saris with dots of sparkle. I wondered if the people at this event would favor a particular nationality. Technically, all were welcome—but in reality how would this play out? Every faith gave lip service to unity, but then most of its members seemed to favor contact with people just like themselves. The women of the family I was watching adjusted the layers of their saris as the men stood patiently. Together they walked to the bank of elevators.

As I made my way to the main floor, I wondered if today's crowd would be drawn mostly from the well-off suburban Muslims who belonged to congregations north of downtown. I had attended *jummah* at two mosques with congregants fitting this description. If Dallas was experiencing a mini-boom in mosque construction, here were excellent examples. Both were big, modern structures that had recently been built. For Friday services, their expansive parking lots were filled with nice cars. Inside, the service was shoulder to shoulder. The women's areas were almost identical: a big room above the main sanctuary, like a balcony but with a wall of clear glass to allow peeking below. From a vantage point on the floor, the view was of the sanctuary's ceiling and, where there were windows to the outside, the tops of trees and power lines and sky. It felt like the Muslim equivalent of visiting a megachurch: big and anonymous, at least from the perspective of a newcomer. No one paid much attention to me. I had grown so accustomed to sticking out that it was a nice change to blend in and go about my business as if I belonged. I worshipped and left, uttering no more than a few pleasantries to random strangers.

o

At the convention center, the elevator doors opened onto a concourse, a big area next to the exhibition space. Groups were happily chatting; giddy kids bounced around. It seemed as if everyone was holding a piece of candy of the "fun size" variety so prevalent around Halloween. Some adults carried bags of the stuff, passing it out to young and old alike.

I stopped at a table being manned by several women in hijab. They welcomed me, explained that the front half of the center was for men while the back half was for women, and handed me a plastic bag for my shoes. Beyond them, the doors were open to the room where the event was taking place. It was huge, large enough to accommodate four basketball courts perhaps, the kind of space that might normally have booths set up in aisles, with hundreds of visitors wandering up and down, collecting brochures of information. Today it was utterly transformed. Big panels of Arabic lettering occupied one end, stretching from wall to wall. The concrete floor was checkered with enormous squares of pristine cardboard, each one cordoned off with tape to prevent shoe-clad trespassing. Slices of exposed concrete created aisles for walking.

If the organizers of this event were expecting enough people to fill the cardboard, they were planning for hundreds, perhaps thousands, of worshippers. All around, people were seated in little groups like picnickers at a park. Compared to the available real estate, their numbers seemed paltry. I doubted the turnout would be as big as hoped.

I selected the swath of cardboard directly behind the men, as close to the front of the room as I could get. I slipped off my shoes, tucked them into the plastic bag, and stepped over the tape. I settled on a spot that gave me a wide berth of personal space.

People entered in a steady stream as I waited. They greeted one another with kisses and took photos together on their phones. I scooted this way and that to accommodate new arrivals. Soon I had nowhere else to go as the women and children crowded in around me. I came face-to-face with a chubby baby in a hijab. I had only ever seen kids at mosques wearing Western-style clothes, and here was a little girl still wobbly on her feet in a special tiny head scarf. I have no idea why dressing tots in grownup clothes has such universal appeal, but my heart melted at the sight of her.

The sermon began. It was about how Allah brings individuals together, how humanity is drawing closer. As if to demonstrate the point, waves of people kept walking through the doors. At some point, I raised my head high enough to see past my nearest neighbors and found that the room was nearly full. The women's side was vibrant with color and style. It included everything from African queens in elaborately folded fabric hats to Persian princesses in sky-high heels; from loose robes to form-fitting designer suits. A covered head was the only common denominator in terms of appearance—and even in this the crowd sported a vast range of styles.

The imam was saying that as we gather today, those of us in this room with others in this country and around the world, we must feel our connection also with everyone who suffers. As he implored us to feel others' need as our own, audience members were passing big plastic boxes for collecting *zakat*. By the time one reached me, it had a mound of bills. I stuffed in a few more dollars before handing it on.

Then it was time for prayer. It took a few moments for us to properly situate ourselves so that our shoulders and arms were in contact. A thousand little whispers and adjustments blended into a sizable drone. When agreement was reached, we began. It was the same series of *rakahs* I had grown accustomed to performing at mosques; only here I was doing them in a crowd much larger than anything I had ever anticipated. It was like I had been learning dance steps in a small classroom for months, and now I was performing them in public as part of a giant flash mob. As a single body, we bowed and kneeled and pressed our foreheads to the ground.

The sheer scale of our synchronized movements made me think of the pictures I had seen of the hajj. They show thousands and thousands of pilgrims wearing the simple garments that erase socioeconomic distinctions. The people walk in circles around the Kaaba, that small structure in Mecca that symbolizes the enormity of an idea: with one God, we are one. Every prayer in Islam is a return to this notion, just as Eid al-Adha is a return to the well from which its shared history flows.

o

The next morning I met Raj and his family at their mosque. It had been the first stop on this Dallas leg of my journey, the one whose walls were a blank canvas for its security cameras; the second time around it felt familiar and not at all daunting. I knew the ropes: what door to enter and which direction to face. When I arrived, many women were present, but Raj's wife wasn't among them. I took a seat on the floor and waited.

My thoughts kept going back to the Eid celebration at the convention center. How had I felt being a part of such a large gathering? For that hour or so, I was united, if only symbolically, not just with everyone in the room but with others engaged in the same activity across the world. When I first saw photos of the hajj, I remember being amazed that all those tiny dots around the Kaaba were people. From the vantage of the photographer's lens, they looked like little bits of something bigger, maybe a single piece of cloth with just minor variations of color and texture. It got me thinking about the irony of unity: you can see it so much more clearly from the outside. At the convention center, I had stitched myself into the fabric of Muslims, an extension of the cloth around the Kaaba, but it didn't necessarily feel how it looked: like we were all the same, like we were one monolithic hunk of humanity. I had blended in and gone through the motions, but I hadn't spoken in depth with anyone. If I had I doubt we would have agreed on all key issues or found that we see the world in the same way. Can we have differences—perhaps even some that are very big—and still be "one"?

Raj's wife appeared and greeted me with a smile and an affectionate hug. She introduced me to her middle-aged daughter and her
granddaughter, who was in her early twenties. They planted kisses on
either of my cheeks. I wasn't sure I deserved such warmth, but I was
happy to receive it. We settled in for the sermon—Raj's wife in her chair
and the rest of us at her feet like she would be giving us a bedtime story.
The flat screens showed the orange-bearded imam and the backs of the
men's heads in the main sanctuary.

The imam's talk was dedicated to an aspect of this holiday I
had yet to focus on: the slaughter of animals. It is customary on this
day to acknowledge Allah's willingness to allow Abraham to sacrifice
a ram in place of his son by killing an animal. In addition, the meat is
to be shared with the needy. For Muslims who are unable to perform
the slaughter personally, services located in the United States or other
countries will do the deed on their behalf and ensure its distribution to
the appropriate parties. Now I understood the flyers I had been seeing
at various mosques the last few weeks that said check a box—goat,
sheep, or cow—and mail a check.

The imam did not spare us the grisly details. He spoke about
the importance of seeing the knife slit the throat, not turning away,
coming face-to-face with the reality of this sacrifice. It reminded me
of the detailed instructions about animal sacrifices that God handed
down to Moses. It brought to mind the gory details from Jesus's story:
the focus on the bloodshed, his wounds, and the lashings. I started to
worry about what was in store once I went home with Raj's family. Just
a few nights earlier, over dinner with my grandmother and me, my great
aunt told us about some old neighbors of hers, recent transplants from
Greece, who kept a "pet" goat in their backyard. Every Easter, the goat
would vanish, replaced by the smell of smoking meat.

o

After the service, I followed Raj's van, filled with his family members,
back to his daughter's house. They seemed lovely, but I had no idea what
to expect. For all I knew I would be the day's ceremonial sacrifice. We
made our way to an upscale subdivision filled with identical-looking brick
homes. Theirs was at the end of a cul-de-sac, the front door dwarfed
by the impressive facade. I parked on the street while Raj stood in the
driveway waiting for me. He reminded me of my Grandpa, who was

always affectionate with me, though I doubted Grandpa would have been as tender with a stranger as Raj. Raj ushered me through the entrance in the garage that led directly to the kitchen.

Inside, the food was ready and the table was set. They insisted I take the head, facing the big picture window looking out to the yard. Through bits and pieces, I had learned that Raj was a retired engineer who dabbled in writing. He and his wife had lived in Texas for close to forty years. Now he beamed with pride as his daughter explained that she and her husband, Abdul, were both doctors. To top it off, his granddaughter, Salma, was currently in medical school. I thought about how envious my grandmother would be—she waged a many-decades-long campaign to convince someone in the family to become a doctor, but not one of her children or grandchildren had been swayed. Here, Raj and his wife were outnumbered by doctors.

Abdul asked what had brought me to their mosque, and Raj said, yes, please tell us. They knew I was learning Islam, so I figured they wanted a longer version. As we ate, I gave it to them. I started at the beginning and explained everything. I had grown up with no religion. I got older and grew curious. Then I moved to a small town and began by going to churches. I worked my way through Christianity, Judaism, and Buddhism. It had taken several years, but I had finally made it to Islam. At home I had done what I could to educate myself. Then I came to Dallas to visit my grandma and worship at mosques.

They nodded but looked confused. I could see them trying to make sense of it. They wanted to know how my experiment would end, where exactly I would land. I didn't know what else to tell them. I was trying to make sense of it too.

Abdul, especially, seemed baffled. He asked if I knew the pillars of Islam. I said them out loud, counting on my fingers: daily prayers, Ramadan, *zakat*, monotheism. That was four. What was the last? "*Sha-hadah*," Abdul said. Of course. The *shahadah*, the statement of faith. He asked if I knew the Islamic view of Jesus. Yes, I answered, he is greatly respected and considered a prophet, similar to Muhammad.

I could sense the question—Did I intend to become Muslim?—on the tip of his tongue. Instead, he switched his approach. "You should become Muslim as soon as possible," he said. What purpose did learning serve unless I planned to convert? I wasn't sure he'd understand that for me, knowledge was having the opposite effect: the more I learned, the less inclined I was to declare myself any one thing. But this hadn't prevented me from developing a deep appreciation, love even, for the ideas and people I met along the way. I recalled Khadija saying she was eager for me to become a Muslim because then she and I would be sisters. I smiled at the sweetness of the sentiment. I wanted to say, "I hope we can be sisters no matter what."

After lunch, Abdul prepared to leave. He had a date with a sharp blade and the throats of two goats. He explained that a farm about an hour's drive offered this service for Muslims in the region. For Eid, its machinery was cleaned under the supervision of an imam. Abdul could select his animals and personally slit their throats, which allowed him adherence to some of the ritual's finer details: he would make sure his knife's tip faced Mecca and he would not turn away from the sight of the animal's blood. The resulting meat would be divided into thirds, Abdul told me. Most importantly, one-third of it would be given to a family that lived on a limited income—a transaction arranged informally through the mosque. His family members would eat one portion, and they would share the final portion with friends, most likely preparing it themselves and inviting friends over to partake. I learned that while it is important that the slaughter occur on Eid, the guidelines about consumption are looser, and the meat might stay in the freezer for weeks.

Once her father was gone, Salma asked if I would be willing to speak with her privately. We sat together on the sofa in the family room off the kitchen. She said she had waited for her father to leave because she didn't want to be disrespectful, but she wanted me to know that she did not necessarily agree 100 percent with his interpretation of what it meant to be a faithful Muslim. Take, for example, the practice of women wearing hijab. "My father believes women should wear a scarf any time they leave their own homes," she told me. "Whereas my mother and I think differently." She explained that she and her mother interpret the Qur'an's passages on the matter more loosely; they read them as referring specifically to Muhammad's wives, whose coverings were a show of discretion around the steady stream of foreign dignitaries and others visiting their house. Salma explained that she and her mom cover their heads while in the mosque, but for busy days at the office or school, they opt to leave the hijab at home.

I nodded. I understood that not all Muslims see eye to eye, despite efforts to reach agreement on even the finest points. After Muhammad's death his closest companions tried to ensure consistency by recording in writings called hadiths the wisdom the Prophet had imparted through his daily habits and personal opinions. Gathered into the Sunnah, this information serves as a practical guide; it's also the inspiration for the name "Sunni." But even with these sources, many topics were never mentioned by Muhammad or his confidants—leaving shades of grey on issues as minor as nail polish. My first night at the mosque back home, my Egyptian acquaintance, Mandisa, caught sight of my painted toenails and explained to me that polish is not allowed in Islam because it acts as a barrier to water during pre-prayer washing. That same night, as I was performing my first-ever communal *rakahs*, I noticed that the woman next to me had a pedicure. I was confused. In my reading I had seen nothing about nail polish; I wanted to get it right before unleashing my bare feet at other mosques. One book had mentioned a hotline available in the United States—1-800-Fatwa—for obtaining rulings by contemporary experts on topics such as these. I dialed the number, but it was no longer dedicated to this purpose. Instead I got a recording about a sweepstakes for a free Caribbean cruise. I decided to err on the side of caution and strip my toenails bare.

As Salma spoke, I noticed her fingernails were tipped magenta. What surprised me about her disclosure wasn't that Muslims could have differences but that such differences might exist within a unit as intimate as husband and wife or dad and daughter without it threatening the familial bond. If ever there were negotiations, it seems they had ceased long ago, and now the family members lived in harmonious dissent. Perhaps this was a lesson for unity on any scale.

"It's important you know that not every Muslim agrees," Salma told me. "I don't cover my head in public, but I don't believe this makes me less devout." On this last point, she was clear: she considered herself faithful. She performed her daily prayers, and she was true to the other pillars. "It's important that we educate ourselves and do what we feel is right for us as individuals." I thanked her for sharing her perspective and silently wondered if voices like hers might help make some aspects of Islam more compatible with contemporary tastes.

o

By the time I was ready to go, Raj and his family had showered me with so many gifts that they also had to give me a shopping bag in which to carry them. I received a beautiful Qur'an, much nicer than the cheap paperback version I had been using. They gave me a box of sweets to share with my grandmother; they were delicious, like extra-rich and dense donut holes. Before his departure, Abdul handed me a jug. It was the shape of a canister one might use for gasoline, but much smaller and made of clear plastic. "It's Zamzam water," he said of the liquid inside. It took a moment for his words to register: I was holding water from Mecca. Aside from the Kaaba, the spring from which this water comes is perhaps the most important site in all of Islamic history. Like Eid itself, its significance is tied to Abraham's son Ishmael. It is said that when Ishmael was an infant and desperate with thirst, the earth gurgled forth at this spot and has offered precious life-sustaining water in abundance ever since. "I brought it back from my hajj," Abdul told me. "You may have it." I couldn't believe this precious item was mine to keep.

After I thanked everyone profusely and promised to stay in touch, Raj walked me outside. At the car I set my bag of gifts down. I felt an overwhelming appreciation for the effort Raj had made to get my phone number that first day. I was grateful to his family for including me in their Eid celebrations and for everything they had taught me. If I was to follow Islamic norms, I would have taken care not to touch Raj. I would have driven away with a wave. But that was all wrong: too formal and not at all indicative of the fondness I felt.

"May I give you a hug?" I asked. I was emboldened by Salma's advice. Each person has to assess guidelines for herself and make judgments about what is and isn't applicable. Raj seemed pleased by my question. "Yes," he answered. He smiled, and I went in for an affectionate squeeze that I believed perfectly fit the situation.

Sufism

While Mecca gets most of the attention for being the birthplace of Islam, it's actually the village of Medina, about two hundred miles away, where Muhammad developed his ideas into a full-fledged faith. In Mecca his message of sweeping social reforms was unwelcome by those whose fortunes depended on the practices he condemned. The wealthy leaders didn't want to give up their lopsided moneylending methods or free their slaves. They certainly had no intention of earmarking a percentage of their incomes for the needy. After more than a decade of failing to convince Mecca's elite of its obligation to care for the most vulnerable members of society, Muhammad decided to relocate to Medina, where he found a more receptive audience.

I can't help but draw parallels between Muhammad's Mecca and my perception of Dallas. Both are commercial centers with vast income disparities, but it's not just that. Muhammad was motivated by the indifference of those around him who hoarded their resources, and I suppose I get this same sense of disinterest when I observe people who not only appear comfortable with inequality but who seem to relish it. All the expensive adornments speak volumes, and not just of the size of one's bank account. Of course, even after relocating to Medina, Muhammad returned to Mecca to visit the precious things he'd left behind: the Kaaba and Zamzam spring and other important sites. Eventually his relationship with the place got less rocky. I suppose the same could be said of me and Dallas. Despite my emotional baggage, I've been drawn back because of my grandmother and others whom I love. Little by little, I'm making peace with the city itself.

If Dallas is my Mecca, Austin is my Medina. When I'm there, everything is less complicated, more laid back. Dallas forces me to swim in the murky lake of my subconscious; Austin is a dip in a crystal-blue swimming hole. I wanted to take advantage of my proximity to Austin to pay a quick visit to the city and my mom before making my way to Washington, D.C., where I'd always imagined this story ending. I was thinking of it as a respite, like a pause at an oasis before continuing on a difficult journey. Austin is about the same distance from Dallas as Medina is from Mecca (two hundred miles). Thankfully my trek via Southwest Airlines was slightly less arduous than taking a camel.

Arriving in Austin signaled that my trip was drawing nearer to its conclusion, which forced me to acknowledge I hadn't yet made proper accommodations to experience a version of Islam that tends to be controversial among traditional Muslims: Sufism. I had put the issue on the back burner at least in part because of Khadija's warning. When I asked what she thought of Sufism, her reply was swift and definitive: "It is not real Islam." She recommended I steer clear of it. It was similar to the reaction I got when I mentioned Kabbalah to some mainstream Jews.

o

So, for the time being, I did as Khadija suggested. Besides, I had my hands full trying to understand regular Islam. Yet I was intrigued by Sufis. The famed poet Rumi was a Sufi. Every faith I had explored boasted similar mystical variations birthed by individuals who cared less for the rules of religion and more for the experience of feeling connected to the divine. In every case the parent faith appeared to be locked in a love-hate relationship with its mysterious little offshoot, engaged in some centuries-long process of dismissal and little-by-little acceptance. When Khadija denied the validity of Sufism, I got the impression she had internalized embarrassment on behalf of the majority of Muslims who are ashamed of the grotesque branch that sprouted from their healthy trunk. But from my perspective, Sufism did not indicate an abnormality. Just the opposite: I found it confirmation that Muslims are no different from anyone else. Within any group of humanity, some will possess these impulses. If anything, Sufism spoke to our shared human nature.

Little details of Sufism reminded me of bits and pieces from other faiths. I read that the name "Sufi" was derived from the Arabic word *suf*, meaning "wool," for the simple garments these individuals preferred to fancier options. This made me think of early Protestants who believed opulent attire was inconsistent with true Christianity and insisted on plain, unadorned clothing. In both cases it was meant as a way to voice concern about the larger society's preoccupation with wealth, which felt like a departure from the core message of faith. I instantly recognized Sufi worship practices like chanting and visualizations as similar to those in Kabbalah and Buddhism, particularly tantric methods, and ditto on the insistence that new students learn from more experienced guides or risk crossing over into dangerous territory. Even significant symbols in Kabbalah and Buddhism like the circle and the ocean made appearances in Sufism. But Sufis also did certain things that struck me as entirely unique. Their chanting might be accompanied by strenuous breathing or thrashing of the head and torso to induce a trancelike state to help separate them from the false reality of the material world. And who hasn't heard at least some mention of the "Whirling Dervishes," those Sufis who spin around and around to represent the movement of the cosmos?

Somehow my inclination to find Sufis in Austin with whom I could worship felt appropriate. Maybe it was Austin's distance from the glitz of Dallas or its reputation for not quite fitting with the rest of Texas. Both Sufis and Austinites specialize in nonconformity; in that way at least, the two seem to go hand in hand. But perhaps this gets closer to the truth: by exploring Sufism some part of me felt like I was betraying Khadija. I thought if I did it spur of the moment and in a location I never imagined as relevant, then it might exist outside the narrative. I see now that in the telling it becomes the story and, at every turn, I've let down somebody.

It wasn't hard to locate a Sufi center in Austin. Its website's pages implied a connection to Islam, invoking Arabic terms and concepts, but nowhere was the relationship overtly stated. It called Sufism "an ancient, practical, and effective school of mysticism based on the teachings of the Prophets." I had assumed that orthodox Muslims were the ones distancing themselves from Sufis. Now I wondered if the feeling was mutual.

The woman who answered the phone sounded surprisingly ordinary as she confirmed the time I should show up Sunday evening. I would be joining a weekly event called a "*Dhikr* Circle." I wasn't sure what we would do in this circle. *Dhikr* means "to remember" and among mainstream Muslims generally refers to a silent reflection or recitation that focuses a person's thoughts on God. With Sufism, *dhikr* takes on a greater range of activity. Depending on the order, *dhikr* may be singing or dancing. It might require feats of stamina and strength. When the Dervishes whirl, that's *dhikr*. I searched the Sufi Center's website to determine what kind of *dhikr* was in store for me.

o

I arrived at the appointed time. The Sufi Center was in a tidy little building near a school that was quiet on a Sunday. The area would have been free from all noise if not for a flock of blackbirds cawing loudly in the trees. I had learned online that today's *dhikr* would be of the vocal variety. The description said we would be joining our hearts, souls, and voices in an ancient Sufi chanting practice.

Inside, the woman I had spoken with on the phone greeted me. Thin and tall, her blond hair was parted in the middle to let her face through. She had two names: the American one her parents had given her and the one she had given herself as an adult, Hayati, which means "life" in Arabic. Hayati explained that first we'd complete the evening prayers and then she would lead the group in repeating names of God. I knew that in Islam Allah is said to have ninety-nine names, some known and some hidden. Each is a noun or an adjective (like "Nourisher" or "All-Wise") that might help a person conceive of the attributes of God. Would we run through the entire list or pick a few? Whatever the case, I planned to just go with it.

More people arrived. They looked to me like a small cross-section of long-time Austinites: white and slightly hippyish open-minded creative types. Maybe they had once been dope-smoking youths, but that was one phase on a long path of soul-searching, the twists and turns of which had somehow landed them here. We gathered in a large room that appeared to take up the majority of the building. It had few furnishings and a beautiful woven rug covered all but the perimeter. Hayati retrieved a small stack of prayer rugs from a closet. I followed her lead, helping her spread them across the larger rug diagonally to face Mecca. The worshippers arranged themselves with men in front. The women pulled scarves out of their bags or lifted them from around their shoulders and draped them over their heads. I grabbed the one I had brought just in case. I was surprised at how conventional this seemed. One of the men played the part of the imam, reciting passages in Arabic. We went through the evening prayers just as we would have in a typical mosque.

After the prayers, we gathered in a circle. Hayati whispered to me that she had selected three names of God. We would focus on one at a time, and I should follow her lead. She began. I think she was saying "Allah" but it sounded like "*Ya . . . a . . . la*," each syllable a burst of breath from her belly. Soon the others joined her. Their eyes were shut tight, and they swayed back and forth. Together their voices sounded like a train leaving the station, "*Ya . . . a . . . la . . . Ya . . . a . . . la . . . Ya . . . a . . . la . . .*" I was embarrassed, but I didn't know what else to do. I closed my eyes and swayed. I was the Little Engine That Could chugging up a hill.

As we chanted in an endless loop, my mind wandered back to a particular afternoon in Dallas. The temperature had been warm, though the sky threatened rain. I decided to leave Grandma's building on foot and walk around the neighborhood. I was eager to get outdoors. In Grandma's building, everything is connected by long hallways. The retirement compound includes beautiful grounds—paths and fountains and exotic plantings—that look enticing. But no one seems to use them. Perhaps at a certain age it is enough to simply imagine walking.

On the day I'm thinking of, I put on old yoga pants and cheap sneakers. I didn't look great, certainly not up to Dallas standards. What did I care? I was going out for some exercise. Grandma's place is surrounded by apartment buildings, so I started making my way around those. After about five minutes, I came to a crowded intersection and a strip mall. It had begun to rain lightly. It was a nice, balmy kind of rain, so I wanted to keep going. The area was not pedestrian friendly.

I hoped to find a quieter street, but I got caught walking along a busy thoroughfare. I kept thinking I'd reach a turnoff up ahead, but everything was blocked. Then the sidewalk stopped, and I found myself walking on the grassy edge next to a freeway. That's when it really started to rain.

There was a shopping mall about a mile ahead. I had a choice: keep going or turn back. I had been out for maybe twenty minutes, so I decided to keep going. The mall could be my destination. I'd walk around inside, and afterward I'd know to avoid this miserable route I'd gotten stuck with. I soldiered on—through the mist sprayed on me from the tires of speeding cars. Eventually I reached a sidewalk and the corner. Just one street to cross and I'd be in the mall parking lot. I waited for the crosswalk signal to show the little man, thankful for this recognition of pedestrians even if I was the only one. I was halfway to the other side when a woman in a snazzy sports car blared her horn at me. She was trying to make a right and apparently my legs were too slow for her.

By the time I made it to the mall, I was seething—and drenched. I was cursing this car-oriented city and all the selfish jerks who lived in it. I entered through the nearest door, which happened to belong to a Neiman Marcus. Inside, my resentment snowballed as I took in the hoity-toity shoppers perusing the racks. Were they staring at me? What, was my T-shirt too damp and ratty? Ugh, these inordinate price tags! Some people in the world had nothing.

I told myself if I just got out to the main part of the mall, I'd calm down. I suppose in a sense, I was right. My rage did dissolve . . . into despair. The mall was teeming with people of all walks of life. They were here for the same reason as the Neiman Marcus–types, though searching for it at lesser price point. I knew I was no different. Our impulse to buy and own things is so strong because possessions help us feel invincible. For a time their permanence is somehow transferrable to us.

I thought about the residents of Grandma's old folks' home. I'm certain some of the ladies in the dining room had once been among Neiman Marcus's best clients. But it was no longer possible to distinguish them from the others. Out of necessity, the finery was gone. Shrunken frames and diminished motor skills had necessitated elastic waistbands and easy pullovers. Even my grandmother, always a stickler for fine fabric, now opted for polyester and acrylic that could be thrown in the washing machine. I didn't know which residents had once worn the best outfits, but I felt I could tell who had made their peace with letting go of those things. Some wore the serene expressions of individuals no longer clinging to the illusion of invulnerability.

Hayati changed our chant to "*Eh...la...la.*" Around and around we went with these new sounds, each an exhalation. Time was not ticking at a steady pace. The bright dots against my eyelids formed patterns that shimmied with my breath. Our chant morphed again. "*Hey...coo-a...la.*" This one sounded hilarious, and I wanted to laugh. It made no sense what we were doing. How was this different from the Pentecostal practice of speaking in tongues? Our mouths were making sounds our minds didn't recognize. Then it was like Muhammad whispering across generations, telling me to just go with it. *Hey...coo-a... la.* Surrender. *Hey...coo-a...la.* Make peace with the bigger picture. *Hey...coo-a...la.* You are not in charge. The patterns behind my lids exploded into chaos, a million points of light shooting in all directions; the entire universe in my eyes.

Jihad

I pictured the Pentagon and me standing near it. I formed this mental image before I even began making my way through Islam, and it grew clearer the further I got. I knew that the building's gaping hole from 9/11 had been patched up and a memorial to the victims had been built. I thought I needed to see these things with my own eyes and that somehow the proximity would help bring closure to the emotional wound those events had caused me. Time and experience had given me a new perspective on certain terms that I once found troubling. In the aftermath of 9/11, I heard people say that the word "Islam" itself means "to submit," implying that the faith is designed to make servants of us all—perhaps with Muslims as our overlords. Now I understood differently. I saw that the submission in question wasn't vis-à-vis another person but something entirely private: a shift in perspective. Islam would have us remember that we are pieces of a vast creation, not the creation itself.

I hoped for a similar realization about the word "jihad." It translated roughly as "holy war," but I had heard two interpretations. The first, the "greater jihad," is an inner struggle. I understood this as the effort each of us must put forth to make peace with the human condition—the one-two punch of life: granted and revoked. Exertion of this kind tends to grow one's capacity to contribute to the greater good. But I'd also heard jihad used to refer to "violence waged on behalf of Islam." Perhaps this was the "lesser" of the two jihads, but it certainly garnered more media attention; in the news, Muslim terrorists are often called "jihadists." I wanted this second version to be a misinterpretation, the result of twisted logic used to justify a selfish agenda.

While digging around for information on the Pentagon's 9/11 memorial, I happened on an article about the multifaith chapel that had been constructed when the building was repaired. Apparently the Pentagon had accommodated a variety of religious services for many years, but never before had a space been specially designated for the purpose. Now the location had been chosen by the nose of an airplane. It was a complicated origami of symbolism: a pocket dedicated to faith within a giant monument to war carved by a shockingly violent act committed in the name of religion. I knew immediately that I needed to attempt to visit the place. Perhaps being there would help me make sense of it. But what were the chances I would be allowed in? Unlike most other places of worship, this one is not open to the public. It's for Pentagon employees, military personnel, and those granted special authorization.

Several weeks after Ramadan, I sent my first message to the Pentagon. I had no special contacts. On the Department of Defense website, I found the email address to the Communications Department. I sent my note to "whom it may concern." Briefly I explained my situation: I had been a D.C.-based employee for the federal government on September 11, 2001; I was now a writer exploring religion; I hoped to be given permission to visit the Pentagon Memorial Chapel. For more than a month, my request bounced around. Public Relations forwarded it to the Office of the Chaplain. Each new contact scooted me along. When my plea came back to the original Communications Department, I had to admit that my chances did not look good. I started again at the beginning, realizing my appeal may never reach a person who could give me the official green light.

So I made my travel plans anyway: Dallas to Austin to D.C. At the very least I'd see that the building had been sealed back up, and I'd walk around the memorial that looked from pictures like an outdoor sculpture garden. That had been the plan before I knew of the chapel. I told myself it would be okay if my request was denied, that whatever happened was meant to be. The story is that which occurs, after all. You can do your best to sway an outcome, but forces greater than you are at play; individual and collective karmas bump and swirl. The future unfolds with a message that might not be easy or fair. I was learning from religion itself: faith is greeting even the most unwelcome events with a level of acceptance.

When I was almost finished with the Dallas portion of my trip, my e-mail request was still traveling in circles. I tried to imagine what being denied access to the Pentagon was meant to teach me. Certainly it was a powerful statement about religion and war. I understood that many people use religion as a means to create divisions between themselves and others, but I had come to see that the absence of such divisions was the one truth to which each religion pointed. The very notion of an "us versus them"—of enemies—is unity's opposite. What could be more emblematic of enemies than the Pentagon? As if to confirm this point, the building itself would not open to my inquiries. Maybe I would go, shake my fist at the Pentagon, and be done with it. I was reaching a place of gratitude for being given this powerful message when the e-mail arrived: I had been granted clearance.

o

My impending trip to the nation's capital had me thinking about the lip service we pay in this country to the "separation of church and state." It's one of the points I've heard used to differentiate our government from those of Muslim countries. The leaders of many Muslim countries claim they are running the state according to the dictates of the Qur'an, or "sharia" law. I've seen this point used to bolster the argument that our world views sit at polar extremes.

But the closer one looks, the more blurry the lines become. The United States can never extract religion from the history of its nation-building. The Qur'an does not provide an exact blueprint for modern government; every Muslim country interprets sharia differently. Lawmakers on both sides seem to have no problem violating their stated ideals to promote their own interests. Americans suddenly thump the Bible, and Muslims reach well beyond anything written in the Qur'an. The division between government and religion is not always clear because both have a similar core objective: caring for the common good. But opinions vary on what this constitutes and how to accomplish it. Americans may see religion as working for this goal theoretically while our government at least attempts to do so practically; for Muslims this distinction is not so important.

The person who had contacted me to say that my request to visit the Pentagon had been approved was a military spokesman. He would be my official escort. We settled on my first Friday in D.C. as the ideal date. He said that would allow me to sit in for a Catholic service in honor of All Saint's Day and the afternoon *jummah* prayers. He told me to give myself an extra hour to make my way through security.

In all my years of using the Metro system when I lived and worked in D.C., I had never once disembarked at the Pentagon. On several occasions I passed that station and went on to the Pentagon City stop, which leads to a shopping mall. But the Pentagon stop had only the military complex above it with nothing but parking lots and freeways beyond. There was no draw for anyone not associated with the armed forces. When I was riding that line, I always wondered about the passengers who got off there, many of whom wore crisp military uniforms. Perhaps they had just flown in from front lines or lonely outposts to make reports to higher-ups. Their fresh-scrubbed facades seemed to invite speculation. What sorrowful sights did those stern expressions conceal?

Now I was joining them. As I exited the subway train, I could sense fellow passengers wondering about me. What would I be doing there? I was not dressed the part: neither military nor typical Washington business attire. I had debated whether to revert to my old pantsuit style for the occasion but decided against it. I had entered a new chapter, so I opted for clothes appropriate to the present. I dressed as I had for the more traditional religious services on this journey, with a patterned skirt to my ankles and a long-sleeve jacket. I was at once too conservative and too casual to fit in.

The Metro exit deposited me above ground just feet from one of the Pentagon's outer walls, too close to gain a sense of the building's size or shape. From this perspective, it looked like any other government building: pale stone adorned with decorative flourishes. I followed signs for visitors, which led to a small structure near one of the main entrances. Inside, a line snaked back and forth, feeding into various checkpoints.

Even as I inched forward with everyone else, I maintained my doubts. I was convinced something would go wrong. I worried that the forms of identification I brought would prove insufficient or my spokesman/escort would fail to meet me. In the months of communicating with various individuals within the Department of Defense, a specific mental picture had taken shape in my imagination: it was of me participating in *jummah* prayers at the Pentagon chapel. I couldn't shake the thought, even as I recognized that almost nothing in this journey had played out as I envisioned it. Instead, some variation or twist I hadn't seen coming unfolded, and I would learn to accept the discrepancy even when it struck me initially as a disappointment. I maintained as light a grip on my expectations as possible. But this particular hope—that I could perform *jummah* at the Pentagon—refused to be dismissed. For this reason I feared a dramatic deviation. I thought even if I managed to get through security and my escort showed up, then something else would go wrong: services would be canceled or, if not that, I wouldn't be invited to witness them, much less participate.

Cautiously optimistic, if a little nervous, I approached the first checkpoint. The man scrutinized my IDs and then turned his laser focus on me. He asked the purpose of my visit. I explained, and he let me through. I waited again for the next probe—this one by x-ray machine. Once again, I passed muster. I was permitted to leave the little security building and make my way through the entrance to the actual Pentagon. Just beyond the doors, I came to a large waiting area that had yet another counter, this one offering the final clearance once a visitor had been united with his or her escort. My contact had explained that he would meet me here.

I joined dozens of other visitors sitting in the chairs provided. I thought, perhaps, this was as far as I would make it; in fact, I was surprised to have made it this far. I took in all the details. The people waiting appeared to be others like me with meetings; a few were well-dressed children, so I thought they might be family members of an employee who had come for an event. We sat adjacent to a small gift shop. Some of the items on sale included Pentagon-shaped refrigerator magnets and ball caps with military logos; there were pink camouflage t-shirts for the ladies. The mood in the room felt light, almost festive. I had to remind myself I was standing in what was probably the planet's most powerful killing command center. Lest anyone forget, a huge emblem on the wall reminded us of our location.

I was genuinely shocked when my guy showed up. We made our way to the last counter. He vouched for me, and they took my picture for a computer-printed badge that I attached to the collar of my jacket. We went through one last checkpoint, and then I was officially inside.

o

My escort and I began to walk. Only then did I get a firsthand sense of the enormity of the building. We walked up corridors lined with offices and down corridors lined with offices. We strode passed cafeterias, a drugstore, and even a florist. We came to a big open atrium that was like a busy intersection with pedestrians going this way and that. We kept going. Even when I thought our destination must be just around the corner, we had farther still to go. Now I saw that an escort was not just a security precaution but a navigational necessity.

Finally, we arrived at the Office of the Chaplain directly across the hall from the chapel. My escort introduced me to the chaplain, a friendly Protestant minister, whose job is to oversee the spiritual needs of Pentagon employees. Each branch of the military also has a head chaplain who leads a squadron of chaplains who provide spiritual guidance to troops. One of the deputies from the chaplain's office agreed to take charge of me, so my escort handed responsibility for me over and said he'd come back later. I thanked him and bade him farewell.

My new escort asked if I was ready. I didn't know for what—but I said I was. We set off again, walking briskly up and down more hallways. As we went, he explained that today's Catholic service would be especially large and would take place in an auditorium, not the chapel. I tried to hide my disappointment. I thought wouldn't that be something to have made it this far and fail even to lay eyes on the Pentagon chapel.

By the time we got to the auditorium, almost every seat was filled. The Pentagon is said to have roughly thirty thousand employees; several hundred had come to honor the individuals throughout history who, according to the Catholic Church, represent the highest embodiment of the faith. The front of the room was transformed into a makeshift altar: a priest in robes, candles, a table set with a chalice. This space was not really a church, and the people present weren't congregants in the traditional sense—presumably they were tithe-paying members elsewhere—yet it was as authentic a place of worship as any I had visited. I marveled at the distance I had come that elements of the ceremony could feel familiar to me: calls and responses, readings from the Bible, communion. I remember agonizing in the beginning over whether to partake in the sacrament. Today, I didn't hesitate. I believed I could approach it with the understanding and intention it deserved. I had earned my stripes.

The service concluded, and my escort introduced me to the priest. A fresh haircut made him look as bare as a new recruit. He agreed to speak with me, and my escort gave him the job of returning me to the office; I was a baton in a chaplain relay. We sat in the now-empty auditorium, and he told me about his years ministering on the front lines in the Middle East. He explained that "ministering" in the military was not necessarily what it sounded like. His job wasn't to preach his beliefs to soldiers but to support their spiritual needs regardless of their religious identifications. Within every large group of soldiers, a spectrum of affiliations might be represented including Christians, Jews, Buddhists, Muslims, and atheists—not to mention the variations within those categories. Given certain constraints—particularly those in war—only one chaplain may be available for all those soldiers. So the situation is likely to arise that a Christian chaplain will make sure that Jewish soldiers have the necessary accommodations to celebrate Passover or that Buddhists soldiers have time to meditate or that Muslim soldiers are given a chance to perform daily prayers or that an atheist soldier be permitted to avoid it all. In one particularly memorable instance, the Catholic priest explained, he had even ministered to a soldier who identified as Wiccan.

Back at the Office of the Chaplain, I was still thinking about what the priest had said. It struck me as radical: the idea that faith leaders would cater to the spiritual needs of people regardless of religious affiliation. I suppose this same scenario may arise in other large public institutions, like prisons. I wondered if religious leaders working in these settings possess some quality that makes them suited to this unconventional approach. Maybe they are more comfortable than most answering questions with a degree of ambiguity, or perhaps they just don't feel the need to voice their convictions. Or perhaps it's less a choice and more a job requirement. As public employees they are no doubt under strict guidelines to avoid any actions that could be construed as discriminatory or intolerant; uninvited proselytizing is likely to rank high on that list. But I think it goes beyond issues of legality. These religious leaders are under no pressure to raise money for salaries or buildings or endowments or whatever else would ensure the institutional longevity of their particular denomination. It might also be that their clientele has unique needs. Chaplains in the military are working with young people whose job description includes not just an ability to kill but a willingness to die. In the task of war, the differences that exist within the group become secondary to the goal of defeating a common enemy. These factors create an atmosphere in which interfaith cooperation seems to thrive. There was so much to learn here that I felt I was swimming in potential lessons because, in a way, isn't everyone on the planet facing the common "enemy" of death? We may or may not go willingly. But go we will.

The Pentagon chaplain himself announced that he was free to meet. I sat opposite him in his office. Out in the waiting area, his mood had seemed jovial and light. Now a storm cloud had rolled in. Even his posture looked to be curving in. He appeared unhappy enough that I considered telling him we didn't have to do this. I hadn't expected a private conversation. I was still amazed I made it through the front door. I had gotten so much, now all I really wanted was to see the chapel.

Neither of us spoke for a moment and then he apologized. He explained that writers made him nervous. Since the chapel's official dedication, journalists had come to do stories that, when printed, never failed to generate a firestorm of criticism. Always, representatives from the general public were outraged that Muslims were allowed to worship in that space. Or someone else was fuming because their particular denomination didn't appear to have a seat at the table. Or another person thought the entire endeavor of adding worship to war was a joke and a travesty.

I tried to assure him that I wasn't *that* kind of writer. I wasn't a reporter, and the story I was working on wasn't journalism—it was personal, more like memoir. At the very least, whatever I was writing was unlikely to appear online in some news publication with an open-access comments section. I told him I sympathized: those comments can be brutal.

He said part of the problem was that people didn't understand the logistics of how faith groups came to worship in the chapel. It wasn't determined by him—or any other Pentagon official, for that matter. The groups are formed by Pentagon employees, and not just military personnel. Anyone who works in the building is eligible: secretaries, cashiers, janitors. Islamic prayers are held in the chapel not for the purpose of making a political or social statement, whatever it might be, but because the Pentagon has Muslim employees who have the same rights as every other employee. Groups that hold weekly prayer services also include Catholic, Anglican, Protestant, Episcopal, Hindu, and Jewish. And those are just the ones that gather in the chapel. Other faith groups meet throughout the building. To be given permission to form, the members must agree to certain ground rules. They cannot speak ill of any other faith or faith group, even in private. They sign a contract agreeing to this. Once a year all the groups are asked to come together to participate in a multifaith service.

The chaplain's demeanor had changed completely—he was back to being relaxed and friendly. He seemed to be thinking out loud: yes, the problem was also one of perception. The chapel had been designed as a space to serve Pentagon employees and, technically, that's how it operated, but this did not account for its symbolic function. The violent events that took place to create the chapel had been a traumatizing, public experience. For this reason people have a sense that the space itself, and all that takes place within it, belongs to everyone.

One of the chaplain's deputies (my second escort of the day) came in and said it was time for both of us to head to the chapel. On our way across the hall, the chaplain explained that we were joining a group of European visitors. These were government administrators from various countries who were attending a conference in D.C.; they had signed up for a visit to the Pentagon chapel. Some of them were Muslim, so the official in charge of Islamic services would be joining to conduct a little question-and-answer session, which would lead directly into *jummah* prayers for those who wished to stay.

At long last, and in fewer than ten steps, I was standing inside the chapel. In some ways, it was an exceptionally ordinary space. The size of perhaps three private offices combined and opened into one big area, it retained elements true to its original use, like industrial-looking carpet and a drop ceiling covered in generic-grade soundproof tiles. Five stained-glass panels offered the only obvious sign of the room's function. All of them had images that spoke to me of patriotism and strength: eagles, American flags, sunbeams, stars. Four served in place of windows, but the fifth was at the front above where an altar might go. The only one with words, it read: United in Memory, September 11, 2001.

I joined the fifteen or so individuals already seated. While the chaplain and Muslim leader greeted each other convivially and then teamed up to answer questions about the chapel's construction and uses, I studied the place. All the furniture was moveable to accommodate different needs. The chaplain and I had entered from the hall, but I noticed a more formal entrance at the back, where a glass door led to something like a foyer and, beyond that, doors to the outside. This must provide easy access for guests invited to special functions such as weddings or memorials; during certain hours, it also allowed visitors who just wanted to see the chapel to have a peek.

I looked at those words: United in Memory. I thought about the oft-used motto, "United We Stand." The unity to which these phrases refer suddenly struck me as so narrow. They implied unity against an enemy such as another country or group of people. The common denominator among every religion I had explored was this: the mindset of an all-encompassing unity. Like soldiers whose differences dissolved in the face of greater concerns, I wondered if humans were capable of forming much broader alliances—uniting, perhaps, against truly universal enemies such as poverty, hunger, illness, greed, hate, and shame.

o

After the question-and-answer session, it was time for *jummah*. The Muslim leader invited me to participate. Within a few minutes, the chairs at the front of the room had been moved and carpets spread on the ground. The chapel was transformed into a little mosque. I fetched my headscarf from my bag. A couple of the men from the European contingent stayed, and more people joined. Most were middle-aged, middle-management types, but some stood out: a young guy in fatigues, an older man whose blue vest suggested cafeteria work, a young woman in hijab. The orientation had shifted: not only were we on the floor, but we were no longer looking toward the front of the room. The other woman and I had our backs against the outer wall of stained-glass panels. The men were only a few feet in front of us. We were all facing the interior of the building.

For months I had imagined doing *jummah* prayers here, and now I was doing them. I thought about what a long and demanding road this project to explore religion had been. I thought how religion should help heal and unite but, more often, is used to hurt and destroy. I thought about the individuals who had died here. I thought about people all around the world killed because of war. As I bent to place my forehead on the floor, my tears dropped on the carpet. I let them fall because it seemed appropriate to leave some tears here.

At the end, everyone was invited to say a few words to the group. When it was my time to speak, I thanked them for allowing me, a non-Muslim, to join today. "I lived in D.C. at the time of 9/11," I told them. "Being here today felt . . ." A sob caught in my throat and I didn't think I could finish. Quickly, I managed, "really good. Thank you."

As we stood to leave, the old man in the blue worker's vest approached me. I thought he might say something. I recognized the look in his eyes: a mixture of sadness and joy that needs no translation. He raised his hand and, without a word, I knew what was being asked. He wanted connection but was unsure how. I looked at the floor, giving him access to the top of my head. He pressed his open palm to my crown. I suppose what he offered was a blessing or healing of sorts; a gesture of love and gratitude, equally. Unspoken, it said everything.

o

Then, just like that, the Pentagon spit me out. After the *jummah* prayers, my original escort had, as promised, returned to fetch me. Again we made our way through the labyrinth of halls and walkways, back to the original entrance I had come through about five hours earlier. I reluctantly surrendered my badge at the exit. Now if I sauntered back in, the security guards would probably tackle me.

The sun was out and the air was crisp. Had it been this beautiful when I went in? It was a perfect fall day, my favorite season when I lived here. Back then I had loved how during this time of year the sky got farther away, and extra blue; the leaves burned brightly and fell, adding a satisfying crunch to my morning commute; Congress came back in session after summer recess and the sidewalks were at full bustle.

The official Pentagon Memorial sat on the other side of the building. I would need to go out and around—two "gons" from where I stood. I set out walking, passed a sea of parked cars and, beyond that, the freeway from which I had peeked at the gaping wound of the building in the days after 9/11. When I came to the section that had been hit, I paused. It looked perfect now, like nothing had happened. I didn't think I would ever find a way to justify the idea of a "lesser" jihad. To kill in the name of peace? To destroy for the sake of unity? No, that didn't make sense no matter what it was called. I didn't want it to make sense. Those actions are not compatible with true religious values as I had come to understand them. But neither is the war machine I was circumventing.

Were they benches? I wasn't sure. The flyer I picked up referred to them as "units," though they were the height and shape usually associated with accommodating the posterior of a weary person or two. They were cantilevered over individual reflecting pools, like small bands of earth had been pulled up to reveal little gurgling springs. Each one—184 in all—was inscribed with a name of a person whose life had been cut short that day. They were arranged by age from youngest (a three-year-old) to oldest (seventy-one) and positioned according to whether the person had been in the building or in the plane. Several had small gifts at their bases; I spotted flowers and a stone engraved with the word *Love*. A handful of other visitors were meandering through the memorial, and it occurred to me that regular civilians now had a good reason to exit at the Pentagon Metro stop.

I thought about sitting on one of the "units," but no one else was. I opted instead for a ledge around the perimeter. I had one last burden I wanted to leave here. I had often thought about the fourth plane—the one that fell out of the sky and landed in a field in Pennsylvania. They say it was bound for D.C. that day, intended for either the White House or the Capitol. The building where I worked was between those two potential targets. It's bothered me for years, thinking how things may have turned out had those passengers not thwarted the hijackers' intentions. It's impossible to say what path of further destruction they saved us from. I just needed to think of that for a moment, offer up an acknowledgment of those lives lost and then set it down like a stone carved with the words *Thank you.*

From this angle I could take in the entire site, all of the benches and the crape myrtle trees interspersed throughout; they hadn't reached full size, but today their leaves burned bright fuchsia. The memorial itself was exceptional, carefully thought out and lovely to look at—though it made me worry that we've become a nation a bit too practiced in building stone monuments to our fallen. Perhaps the most meaningful memorials are less tangible: to take a good hard look at what took place, to accept culpability where necessary, and to work for change. More than anything, what I would be taking away from my visit to the Pentagon were the multifaith efforts. Lots of people talk about building alliances between different faiths, but I'm not sure they're willing to do the work it would take. Here's the drill in all its messy minutiae: curbing the impulse to proselytize or insult; prioritizing needs, not money; focusing on points of agreement. The Pentagon Memorial Chapel itself demands this of its users. So many faith variations forced to work together to share one small space. Is there a more interesting social experiment occurring on the planet? I had expected this to be the darkest corner of my journey and, in a sense, I suppose it had been—but within it I had found a very bright light.

o

For the remainder of my visit to D.C., I spent hours walking, stopping only to eat and drink at familiar haunts or to collapse on a bench at a museum for a restorative moment. The gloom that had settled on every surface, including me, in the weeks after 9/11—and was still there when

I left a year later—was gone. Collectively the city had moved on—being away, I failed to receive the memo. I had tucked my melancholy away for safekeeping. At long last I was gloriously unburdened.

I had only one last bit of unfinished emotional business to which I wanted to attend. The Washington, D.C., apartment from which Christopher Hitchens churned out his anti-religion arguments in the aftermath of 9/11 had been near my apartment. Though at the time I was only vaguely aware of his presence in the neighborhood, I walked past his street every evening on my way to and from the dog park. I continued to take my mutt, Abbey, for her nightly romp: life as usual, my little post-work ritual. Ignoring, at least for the time being, the seismic shift that had torn apart my internal tectonic plates.

In his writing, Hitchens expressed anger at Islam in particular and religion in general. He believed the world would be better off without these beliefs systems, which he said were responsible for 9/11 and other traumatic events throughout history. I understood his sentiments, and I couldn't say I disagreed. But what I felt was more along the lines of sadness and confusion. I didn't know enough to assign blame, and I wasn't sure that even if I did, my finger wouldn't point in a 360 of directions. I suppose it was then that the wanting-to-know-more seeds were planted. Eventually, if I didn't pay its burgeoning fruit some attention, it might mature to the size of a watermelon. My abdomen would grow crowded and uncomfortable as if the warnings were true about what would happen if I swallowed those slippery black pits.

Christopher Hitchens, "antitheist" crusader, had died of cancer in 2011 at the age of sixty-two. I knew he had lived near me, but I wasn't sure exactly which building. Online, I dug up an old video put together by the *Washington Post* in which Hitchens gives a tour of the expansive apartment he shared with his family. He was a Brit by birth, but D.C. was his adopted hometown, and he loved the place fiercely. Perhaps more than anything, we had that in common.

I found his building, a gorgeous and regal structure, the kind of place that has its own name. I had unknowingly passed it on countless walks. I looked up and tried to determine which apartment was his. Based on the views from the windows shown in the video, it was either part or all of a floor at the top. His arguments against religion had been hammered out there.

I leaned against a low wall out front as if I were waiting for someone or something. I felt I needed to give Hitchens his due. Every faith has individuals whom other believers hold in the highest esteem for embodying its main tenets. They might be called saints in Christianity or *tzadik* in Judaism or bodhisattvas in Buddhism or *mu'min* in Islam. I thought among the "no-faith believers," such individuals could be called "hitches" in honor of Hitchens. He had certainly achieved the highest embodiment of the anti-religion belief system. That and the double entendre made it the perfect option. A "hitch" prevents a machine from operating smoothly, and that's what he was and continues to be: grit in the gears of the institution of religion.

In the aftermath of 9/11, I could appreciate much of what Hitchens had to say. He argued that religion was a source of intolerance and violence. Even I knew that to claim otherwise would be to ignore big chunks of the history of every faith, even Buddhism. But just because people have done horrible things in the name of religion, is religion itself bad? I suppose that's the question that burned inside me until I could do the hard work to answer it for myself. Now, after hundreds of hours of worship and study, I finally felt comfortable voicing an opinion. I think faith is as complicated as the experience of being human. It captures a conversation, started by some exceptionally intuitive people—and added to by countless others—about the most profound aspects of being alive. It can help us make peace with having arrived here and the brevity of our life-spans. It reminds us again and again to fully inhabit the moments of our days because finding small ways to do so is how we create the meaning that leads to joy and gratitude. It tells us that the consequences of our actions, both big and small, ripple out into the world so that we must be aware of the legacy we are leaving with the things we do. It points to universal truths: our equality, our connectedness, our responsibility to one another. It would have us expand our alliances to ever-broadening swaths of humanity. Religion is not without its flaws, but to dismiss it outright is to rob oneself of some of the most insightful wisdom available.

I suppose where Hitchens lost me was in his certainty that what he believed was the truth. The line he drew in the sand was as firm as those drawn by fundamentalists who reside within every faith. I understand the impulse to choose sides. There's comfort in clarity: to have the answers, to be right, to know for sure. Who doesn't want to abolish the anxiety of uncertainty?

Still, throughout this religious exploration, nothing turned me off more—and made me want to flee faster—than encountering an individual who insisted that he or she possessed the actual facts. I found these people's explanations too narrow for variations in perception or understanding or even just different styles of saying the same thing. Such strong convictions seem to justify anger at those who do not see or express things in the same way. Their belief built barriers between themselves and others. It shrank alliances instead of expanding them. Religion doesn't breed intolerance, certainty does.

I took one last look at the bank of windows I thought had probably been the ones through which Hitchens had looked. I said a little prayer and then pushed off from the ledge.

Conclusion

After my trip to D.C., I was officially finished with my religious explorations. From the initial visit to the Catholic monastery on an island off the Washington coast to *jummah* prayers at the Pentagon chapel, it had taken roughly four years. I had sung, chanted, meditated, and prostrated along with thousands of others. I had read a stack of books almost to the ceiling in an effort to place the experiences into some context. At times I had felt painfully nervous or confused or left out. Other moments brought unexpected calm, clarity, and connection. I had interacted with people whose lives were utterly unlike my own. I had formed genuine bonds with a few. I was different from the young woman who had started this endeavor—and not just because I crossed the threshold of age forty while chipping away at it. The journey had altered me profoundly. But how? And what did the changes mean?

People presented me with all sorts of questions. They asked what belief system I thought was most true. They wanted to know which version of which faith I liked best. My friends and family had begun asking these questions at the beginning, before I'd even ventured beyond Christianity. I put them off with the reasoning that I couldn't possibly form an opinion until I'd gone all the way through. That reply bought me a few years. But when the end came, I felt I needed even more time. What was I supposed to tell them? I had put in all this information, and now it was my soul's turn to do its mysterious calculations and spit out an answer. Shouldn't it work like that? What was I?

While I waited for the results, I scrambled for some definitive statement that might appease the curious. I decided to explain that, at least for the time being, it was easier to articulate what hadn't appealed to me. I told them I was never turned off by a particular belief system no matter how fanciful or divorced from my understanding of the world. I had no problem with what some might consider "magical" ways of thinking. What I disliked—what made me want to run for the exit—was more a point of view than a form of any faith—and it could be found within every belief system. It made my skin crawl when someone presented what he or she believed as the absolute truth. Such certainty seemed to imply that any other way of conceptualizing the human experience was incorrect, a cancerous abnormality. I most often encountered this conviction within what might be called "fundamental" versions of religion, and it was frequently accompanied by a corresponding "inerrant" holy book. It was by no means limited to Christianity. This same tendency occurs in Judaism and Islam. But it wasn't exclusive to belief in a monotheistic God. I also found it among Buddhists and even atheists. In fact atheists could be the worst offenders. I came across atheists so dismissive of other belief systems that their fervency morphed into its own fanatical fundamentalism.

Such certainty seems a desperate ploy to push away any and all vulnerability. That we can and will experience pain, that's really the only thing we can be certain about. The trick it seems to me is not to grab at certainty for comfort but to find ways to get comfortable in the uncertainty.

More than anything, this attitude seems to function as a source of discord among people. It snubs the one truth each faith shared that felt like it mattered most: the ultimate message of our interconnectedness. No matter what religious road I was on, it seemed to lead back to the idea that we come from, and will eventually return to, a common source. We are parts of a whole. We can be different and still make up a healthy totality. I had long ago given up trying to make sense of how I might define "God." I figured God was too complex a concept and could be imagined an infinite number of ways. I was driving in my car one afternoon not even thinking about any of this stuff when these words popped into my head: God is that which unites us all. Where had it come from? The deep recesses of my subconscious, I suppose. But I think that's the best definition I'll ever have of God.

I also had a deeply personal reason for bristling when I met people whose commitment to faith seemed to depend on theirs being the one "right" answer. Worship is an intimate experience. I never entered a sanctuary without having shed some of the psychological armor I think we all instinctively carry in public. I felt others there had done the same so that we gathered as unguarded versions of ourselves. Mutual exposure forged a kind of kinship. I always pictured what it would be like if I officially belonged to this congregation. I played out the scenario to such a degree that its trajectory continued on in some manner, perhaps in spirit form. Even when I knew that I could never accept the particulars of its worldview as my own, I still felt a sense of loyalty to my imagined co-congregants. I wanted to scold anyone whose belief system's specificity invalidated them. But even as that impulse arose, I realized it was a trap. I couldn't cling too tightly to my disapproval and risk ending up with a viewpoint as staunch as the one to which I was reacting.

o

Midway through my religious explorations, I wrote a short essay about what I was doing and why. I submitted it to the *Los Angeles Times* and it was printed as an article in the Op-Ed section with the subtitle "One of America's growing number of 'Nones' is making it her mission to find out what she might be missing." I had been toying with the idea of starting a blog to chronicle my visits to places of worship. I thought, at the very least, keeping a blog would force me to put fingers to keyboard to capture and help make sense of what I was experiencing. Now, with an introduction coming out in the newspaper, I got the push I needed. The editor said she could print the Web address at the end of the text.

I had a few days to get the site up and running. My plan was to share my experiences in bite-sized bits of six hundred or so words, starting with my visits to Christian places of worship and then working my way through those associated with Judaism, Buddhism, and Islam. In real life I would be several steps ahead of the events I was detailing on my blog, which would give me time to process and present them in a somewhat coherent fashion. However, the blog would eventually catch up, and I would have to release my work in a more spontaneous fashion, a scary thought even if no one was reading.

The day the article appeared was exciting. I watched my blog's page views climb. The story also appeared in the online version of the paper with a live link to my site. I could see the countries of people who were logging on to read more of my story. They were coming from all over the world. I hadn't realized the *Los Angeles Times* audience was so international, but it represented the entire globe.

One of the downsides of having no religious affiliation is the lack of community. A benefit of a blog is the comments section. Anyone can add an opinion. I hoped others like me would reach out, and my blog could provide a little platform for dialogue and connection. In addition, I included a link to my personal e-mail address. I thought some people might have ideas or suggestions they would be more comfortable sharing privately.

Immediately, people began to add remarks at the foot of my entries. Many wanted to share a bit about their own journeys in, out, and around religion. My e-mail inbox began to fill up, too—especially after the article was reprinted in newspapers across the country. I was caught off guard when it popped up in Dallas, Sacramento, Las Vegas, Baltimore, Milwaukee, Atlantic City, and a handful of other cities.

The majority of the individuals writing to me appeared to have a religious affiliation; in fact, they tended to be Christian. Some said they would pray for me. A few said their entire worship group was praying for me. In my secular life, I couldn't recall having anyone say they were praying for me. I thought it sounded nice, like they had placed my name on a gentle breeze. "Thank you," I replied to every last one.

As the numbers who said I was in their prayers climbed, I started to get edgy. I don't mean that metaphorically. I mean my nervous system began to jangle. I felt caffeinated even when I wasn't. I had trouble sleeping. I had heard that praying can be a powerful act: all that thought energy directed at a single source. Now I believed it. I worried that too many people must be praying for me. Then I wondered if they were simply praying too hard. This wasn't my name on a gentle breeze; this was a bolt of electricity to my poor synapses. I wanted to write them back and ask if they'd dial it down a notch. I was exhausted. I passed through a severe grumpy phase. Perhaps all this praying was a bit presumptuous. Was my soul really in such a sorry state?

After a week or two, it dawned on me: I fancied myself a "religious explorer," but that's not necessarily how I was perceived. I had unwittingly become a poster child for the "unchurched," a very public potential convert. One morning I looked in the bathroom mirror and glimpsed what they saw: one of the "Godless" masses who needed saving.

People sent me letters and packages. I got books and expansive thesis statements. I received CDs with sermons on them. I realized that many of the people sending me stuff weren't interested in my story—or any narrative that involved hunting around and poking into different religious trends. They weren't encouraging my exploration so much as hoping to save me the bother. One letter was explicit: once I read the enclosed books, it stated, my desire to explore further would cease. I wondered if I should avoid reading them for fear the sender was right. I didn't want to extinguish my drive.

I laid these offerings on a surface near where I write. Something about my little essay had spoken to strangers and inspired them to affix postage to envelopes. These well-meaning people were sharing with me words and ideas that rang true for them. I committed to reviewing every last item even if it took many months. Who's to say God wasn't giving me a message through some sweet lady living in Albuquerque?

A friendly young minister in Texas sent an hour-long DVD of three confident men, all on the young side of middle age, taking turns explaining Christianity. According to these guys, it boils down to something called the "Doctrine of Imputation." It's all about forming the right relationship with Jesus in the right way.

To understand, they say, we must first accept that we are all criminals bound for the eternal conscious torment of hell. They use an academic metaphor: what we have is a failing grade. Luckily, Jesus lived the perfect life and then died the death we deserve. He has an A+. God, in His mercy, is willing to give us Jesus's grade in place of our own. This switcheroo is something they call "Jesus as our propitiation" and serves as the heart of the Doctrine of Imputation, which can also be called the "Imputation of Jesus Righteousness."

To receive our stellar grade, which apparently is the ultimate goal, an actual transaction must take place. If this transaction is not performed "rightly," they tell viewers, you can't get "Jesus goodness." The men go into complicated stories comparing bonding with Jesus to applying for membership at a country club. I'm more confused than when they started. Not to worry. The men assure me that what the divine has to offer is not something I can earn, nor is it something I can fail to earn.

I watch the DVD twice. The first time I am wide-eyed at the fanciness of the terms and blandness of the metaphors. The second time I try desperately to grasp the meaning behind what they tell me, to see if I could possibly relate to Jesus how they describe. They seem so certain of their interpretation of Christianity, like God has let them in on all the answers and now they have the official cheat sheet. After copious note-taking and ample pondering, I e-mail my synopsis to the friendly minister. He responds that, unfortunately, I still don't quite grasp the proper transaction. I'm left scratching my head. With self-appointed gatekeepers like these, is it any wonder that Christianity's numbers are decreasing?

This project of religious exploration had become a journey and, as such, required forward momentum. But that essential quality of movement also made some people furious. I had commenters chew me out for thinking I could learn anything meaningful in this way. I would never grasp the deep and intangible, they argued. The whole point was to grow roots in one spot, to let a belief system slowly unfurl its hidden truths, to form relationships and community. I could see their point. It was perhaps the best argument against the value of what I was doing. Who didn't want those things? But I felt like this came from people whose reality was vastly different from my own. I belong to a growing segment of the population that doesn't necessarily possess a spiritual blueprint. We have access to vast quantities of information and a huge array of options. Now what? It was a bit like being criticized for being homeless by people tucked under cozy comforters. I don't have a snug bed—that's the point.

Others enjoyed the spirit of investigation up to a point. For some, the moment of disapproval arrived when I came to their par-ticular denomination. They seemed to relish as I poked around other versions of Christianity, jabbing at the various positions. But when it came time for me to enter their spiritual homes, they grew agitated. Suddenly their comments were less positive, more pointed. Some even expressed anger that I could scrutinize and toss aside things they hold so dear. I sympathized. I imagined it felt like they had come home to find their front doors ajar. What did they dislike more: that I had manhandled their precious items or that I had failed to steal them? If I was too brutal for some, others thought I was a spineless pussyfoot. Self-described atheists grew frustrated at what they saw as an overly gentle approach. They wanted me to smash everything to the ground then set fire to the place, watching it burn for good measure. I worried that if I could make people this upset by exploring the United States' most mainstream faith of the United States, how would they respond once I left Christianity for other religions?

Occasionally, brief messages of encouragement were tossed into the mix. These were usually left by commenters who stayed out of the fray but stepped forward long enough to give a quick "keep going" or "thank you." I speculated about these folks—if they had a religious affiliation or if they were Nones like me. I could tell from the blog statistics that those commenting were actually a relatively small percentage of overall viewers. I wondered about this quiet majority. When I felt exhausted or beat down, I let the thought of their presence motivate me. They were out there: open-minded, hungry for information, craving spirituality.

o

After I returned home from Washington, D.C., Khadija e-mailed that her husband had jumped the last hurdle toward his degree and she and her family were leaving. She invited me to their goodbye party. I baked a batch of chocolate chip cookies and dressed in the special bejeweled kaftan Khadija had given me as a gift, but I mistakenly showed up at her apartment without realizing the gathering was at the mosque. I went home thinking I had the day or time wrong, so Khadija and I never got to say goodbye in person. I doubted I'd ever see her again. A few weeks later, she e-mailed that she was back in her country. It was just a short, sweet message, but I could tell from the joyful tone how happy she was to be home. I thought that might be the last I would hear from her, but two months after her first note, she wrote to say another education request had been approved by her government and she was moving again—this time to advance her own schooling. She and her family were packing up and coming back to the United States; of all places, they were headed to Dallas. She said they would stay at least a few months so she could take English classes and hopefully pass certain tests before moving on to a Ph.D. program.

In the months that followed, the comments on my blog began to soften. As I had made my way through the Christian denominations and then on to Judaism and Buddhism, readers who were once feisty or defensive about their point of view calmed down. Whereas in the beginning my forward movement seemed to disturb readers, it appeared to have become a source of comfort. Perhaps they grew to trust that I would not settle prematurely—that I was committed to completing the full journey. When it became clear that each position I explored would be one of many, the comments got less serious and more jovial. Why fight over a single dish when the smorgasbord is so vast? I was adding two or three new blog entries a week. I thought some commenters still believed or hoped I'd be drawn to their particular religious affiliation at the end, but that eventuality was a ways off.

In late winter, Khadija wrote to say she and her family had arrived in Dallas. The roles in her marriage had reversed, and now she was the one spending all her time studying and her husband was the primary caregiver to their little girls. She confided that she was feeling overwhelmed and that she found herself crying almost every day. I responded immediately. "It breaks my heart to know you are going through such a difficult time right now," I wrote. I shared with her what I had learned from my research: Dallas had a vibrant Muslim population. I hoped to reassure her that she wasn't alone. I also wanted her to know how impressed I was with her strength, how tough a person had to be "to go to a foreign country and take difficult tests in a language that is not their native language. I can only imagine the tears I would cry if I were to try to do something similar. But you are preparing to do wonderful things for your country and your family." She responded, "I am always feeling happy when I see you, read your e-mails and I feel this is what is called love."

That spring my grandmother was taken to the hospital unexpectedly. Some sort of infection had caused her to faint. They kept her for several days and flooded her system with antibiotics. When she was released, she was extremely frail. I arranged to fly to Dallas to help settle her back into her apartment and assist with tasks she was too weak to do alone. I e-mailed Khadija that I was coming and I hoped, depending on my grandmother's condition, I could sneak away to visit her, too.

When I arrived, I found Grandma's health deteriorated considerably since my stay the previous fall when I had come to worship at mosques. She needed her walker just to move around the apartment. She wasn't taking her daily trips to the dining room. We ate light meals at her table. But more than her physical decline, her demeanor had shifted. She told me she had had a good life. I considered the real possibility that this might be the last I would see her alive. After dinner, we would play multiple rounds of double solitaire that grew more vicious with each passing evening. I teased her that if she was on her last legs, the least she could do was let me win once in a while. After several days, she announced that she felt strong enough to have lunch downstairs. I thought it was a good sign when she polished off her hamburger and onion rings and then ordered a scoop of rocky road.

Khadija e-mailed me the address of her apartment. I punched the information into my smartphone prepared for it to spit out complicated directions to someplace on the outskirts of Dallas. In fact, her building was in the same general neighborhood as Grandma's retirement home—about five minutes according to the map. I found that strange: these two parts of my life drawn so close. I marveled at how a handful of small coincidences had added up to this unexpected juxtaposition.

I arranged with Khadija to arrive at her place in the early evening on a Friday; Grandma agreed that she could manage dinner on her own. I struggled with what to wear because I hadn't brought my usual ankle-length skirt. It was between a bright green dress that fell at the knee or blue jeans. I debated which was sexier: the outline of my bottom half or bare legs from the knee down. I decided neither but to err on the side of modesty, I'd wear both. It was a terrible outfit to be sure. I was fairly certain that anyone who laid eyes on me would think I was a misguided "fashionista" or insane; perhaps an unfortunate combination of the two. I slipped out before Grandma could see.

On my way to Khadija's I stopped at the drugstore. I wanted to arrive with a few gifts in hand, especially for her girls. It was a week or so before Easter, and the shelves were packed with the commercial trappings of the holiday, egg-shaped doodads and bunnies plastered on every surface. I thought about just grabbing a few items and not worrying about the implications of the imagery. What did eggs and bunnies have to do with Jesus anyway? Weren't they a generic celebration of Spring? Didn't they speak more to the marketing ploys of our culture's most unifying belief system: capitalism? I didn't think Khadija or her kids would take offense, but I decided to avoid the Christian undertones and stick with straight-up consumerism. I had dressed like a clown in an effort to be appropriate, why stop there? I settled on a funny ball with a sticky, stretchy texture and a cheap lightsaber knockoff. They were the only two things I could find that felt not-at-all connected to a messiah rising from his tomb. I also grabbed a little bag of chocolates that were simple squares.

While geographically near Grandma's retirement community, Khadija's apartment was, in another sense, worlds away. No peaceful bubble of opulent landscaping blocked out the city. Her complex was directly adjacent to the freeway, and there was no hiding the busy access road that was essentially its front yard. I initially passed at such a high rate of speed that I had to circle back around and then crank sharp right to career into the parking lot Dukes-of-Hazard style.

This apartment complex was almost as complicated as the old student-housing one: I had to find the right section, building, and stairwell. At last I stood before her door. I felt a wave of self-consciousness about my weird outfit and my uncovered head. I knocked. There was silence on the other side. I stood thinking we had gotten our wires crossed again like the time of her goodbye party. Perhaps we weren't meant to ever see one another again. Then, soundlessly, as if she had been just on the other side the entire time quietly adjusting her head scarf, the knob turned and Khadija was miraculously standing before me.

We hugged and then stood holding each other's elbows as we blinked in disbelief. I had been so consumed with the logistics of arriving that I hadn't considered what I might feel upon seeing Khadija. I had forgotten the overwhelming sense of peace I got from her calm and steady presence. I let a wave of pure joy wash over me.

o

Khadija invited me into the apartment's main room, which was bare save for a folding table and four outdoor chairs. We sat while the girls bobbed around us, distracted for the time being with their new toys. In our last substantive e-mail exchange, she had been sad and unsure of this new phase into which she had dragged her family. We immediately picked up that thread. I wanted to know: how was she holding up? A dramatic shift had taken place. She said she loved Dallas. She adored everything about it: the buildings and the traffic and the heat. I was caught off guard. I had come prepared to provide reassurance that the city wasn't so horrible, really, if she gave it a chance. Khadija said that she and her husband had taken the girls to a mosque—one of the huge new ones—and while they hadn't made any friends yet, they were impressed by the facilities and the congregation. In fact, everywhere she went, she saw other women in hijab. Her new plan was to stay for her Ph.D. program.

Her husband emerged from a bedroom. He greeted me warmly but looked exhausted. He had been on kid duty all day while Khadija was at class. Khadija and I decided we would take out the girls and let her husband have the apartment to himself; poor guy, it was clear he could use the break. We packed the little ones into the family's newly purchased second-hand SUV and, with me at its wheel (Khadija didn't have her license yet), we drove to a nearby strip mall.

Khadija and I had never spent time together in public. Now we were walking side by side through a crowded parking lot toward a busy restaurant. There was no easing into this by degrees: we were out and about in urban America. I couldn't help but consider how we must appear to strangers: Khadija in her somber kaftan and me in this strange concoction of blue jeans and colorful dress. I was fully covered but also decidedly Western looking. I even had on my coolest pair of short black boots. I had purposefully left my hair exposed and free flowing so as not to give the impression—to Khadija or anyone else—that I was officially Muslim. We were an undeniably odd pair. Yet I felt it was also apparent that a level of comfort existed between us, that we shared a genuine intimacy.

We made our way to a Chinese buffet restaurant where she and the girls had eaten on one other occasion; it had been such a special treat that the little ones were bouncing off the walls with excitement to duplicate it. For a set price, it offered an "all you can eat" selection so extensive that it could accommodate the Islamic dietary restrictions called halal. While halal requires that most meat be prepared with special consideration, veggies, dairy, and anything from the ocean is fair game. With a bit of careful choosing and a few consultations with the woman in charge, Khadija and her daughters filled their plates. I tried to avoid pork out of consideration, but all the fried or gooey lumps looked alike, and I'm fairly certain I brought a few small hunks of the stuff back to the table.

I had imagined that after dinner we would take the girls to a park or some outdoor destination where they could run like wild banshees, but by the time we were finished eating it was getting dark. Besides, I didn't know of such a place in the area. I suggested we go to the mall— the same one I had walked to in the rain from Grandma's a few months earlier. The corridors between shops offered plenty of room for romping; they were also peppered with outdoor sculptures, oversized planter boxes, and even a pond to play around. I suppose taking kids there to blow off steam was something of a local tradition; adults had brought me there when I was younger.

In the mall the girls darted around as we walked. I spotted other women in hijab, but their silky scarves and polished outfits made them appear so different from Khadija. They had managed to incorporate a touch of Dallas glamour into their Islam. Khadija's attire made no such compromise. Shrouded head to toe in the same grey fabric, she looked as if he had stepped from a small village in the Middle East onto the shiny floor of the shopping center or wandered in from the desert, as incongruous as a mirage. I wondered if big-city life would change her appearance, especially now that her work would take her outside the home. On several occasions in the past, she and I had spoken about the sacrifices her family was making on behalf of education and because of the instability in her country. I had argued that they were better equipping themselves to make a difference when they went home. I had tried to reassure her with a bit of U.S. history: this country's struggles to form a government after colonization, the Civil War we fought against one another, and the many decades it took to reach a level of somewhat steady functionality. These discussions did seem to provide her a bit of comfort, but they hinged on the idea that she and her husband would ultimately reside in their country. Now I sensed a shift in her thinking, the question of where to settle haunting her, the knowledge sinking in that perhaps her homeland wouldn't be safe in her lifetime. If she stayed in Dallas indefinitely, the changes she experienced could be far more substantial than fashion.

If the future of Khadija's identity was yet to be determined, her kids seemed set on an unstoppable trajectory. In their pink, frilly outfits and sparkly shoes, they were indistinguishable from their American counterparts. Even with no television, the Internet had brought them up to speed on the latest cartoons and characters. As we strolled through the mall, those girls tore into the entrance of an Apple Store so fast I spun, wondering where they'd gone. They beelined for the table of iPads, their little fingers knowing instinctively how to make the games pop up. I doubted whether their adaptation of Western culture could be stopped or even slowed. This train had left the station. We dragged them away, limp and sorrowful, the littlest shrieking her dismay. Yep, I thought, she's an American.

o

As it got later, the crowd at the mall began to thin. Khadija and I alternated between walking arm in arm and then abruptly busting apart to chase down a rogue munchkin. During a period of togetherness, she steered the conversation back to Islam, specifically my own relationship with it. I knew the question was coming: where did I stand? Would I become Muslim? She had posed a similar question early in our acquaintance, though worded differently. "How much do you believe Muhammad?" she had asked a couple weeks into tutoring me. "A lot," I answered because his primary message of social justice spoke to me on a deep level. It was all the little rules and details that developed after Muhammad I wasn't sure about, but at that time I was only beginning to learn what those were. "What percentage?" she asked. I understood what she was getting at: she wanted certainty, some indication that my examination of Islam had a clear goal. For some reason it is laudable to be the kind of tourist who visits new countries to better understand the full range of human experience, but the same impulse is less welcome in religion. Everyone expects you to declare permanent residency or get the heck out. At the time I could only think to answer Khadija's question with a smile and a shrug.

Tonight, I knew I had to be more explicit. Many months had gone by, and I was much more knowledgeable now. I owed her a considerate response. I took a deep breath and told her, at this point, I believed I was as Muslim as I would ever be. She asked what I meant by that. I said that I didn't think I would ever do all the things that most people associate with being Muslim. In other words I couldn't imagine always donning hijab in public or doing all five daily prayers at the right time in the right way or sticking to a halal diet and abstaining from even a sip of alcohol. However, in what I thought of as the most important way, I knew I could be—perhaps already was—a true Muslim. She looked at me quizzically and asked, "What way is that?" So, I explained: honoring humanity as one community—the *ummah*—and supporting the collective's duty to care for its most needy members. I felt more in touch with these ideas in part because Islam provided avenues for acknowledging one's own vulnerability. The trials of Ramadan and all the time spent with my forehead to the ground had brought me to greater realizations of my personal limitations. Yet I had also found comfort and strength in that humbling pose. In yoga it is called "child's pose" because it is a form of surrender. Within it rests keys for unlocking wells of gratitude, joy, and compassion. It was a position I knew I wanted to take as often as possible for the rest of my life.

"The *ummah*," she a said quietly, as if she were remembering something important.

If Khadija was disappointed by what I said, it didn't show. She was surprisingly silent. Perhaps she needed time to consider what my confession meant. Meanwhile, the girls had discovered the area in the mall with a pond surrounded by oversize planter boxes with smooth sides, perfect for scurrying up and then sliding down. I knew because I had done the exact same thing when I was small. The girls flung off their shoes and began hurling themselves into the air. Khadija and I settled on a nearby bench to watch.

As long as I was putting my cards on the table, I had one more I had to show. Khadija knew that I was a writer. I had told her I was chronicling my experiences learning about religion and that I planned to write about Islam too. I would have said more, but she didn't ask, and besides, there wasn't much more to it. Now there was, and I needed to come clean. Not only had I started to tackle Islam on my blog, but I was in talks with a book publisher that could bring my narrative to a wider audience. Also I had found that in the writing process, Khadija had emerged as an important part of the story. I needed to tell her.

Even more than my admission about officially remaining a non-Muslim, I was nervous about this revelation. I worried that she would question my motivation, not just in exploring her faith but in maintaining our friendship. I hoped she would see that my aim was never to harm her or Islam in any way; quite the opposite: I wished to help. I cushioned my disclosure with an abundance of reassurances: that I didn't think she would object to anything I was writing, that I would let her read everything before it was printed, that I believed this story would help people better understand Islam, and that I would most definitely use a made-up name to obscure her identity. This last promise I had already struggled to keep on my blog. I had wracked my brain for a suitable pseudonym that had a similar implication to Khadija. There weren't many female names that carried the same significance as the one belonging to Muhammad's first wife. She is perhaps the most universally beloved woman in all of Islam. I had finally settled on using Fatima, after Muhammad's dear daughter, but even this felt like a compromise.

I would have understood if Khadija had met my disclosure with a bit of defensiveness or a touch of anger. At the least I was prepared to be peppered with questions. Instead, her response was swift and decisive: "You must use my real name," she instructed. At that moment, I knew she was indeed a true embodiment of the woman for whom she was namesake: steady in her belief, unflinching in her dedication. I felt a flood of pure love and admiration and relief. She knew my heart. She trusted me.

o

Back at home, I realized it was time to come to some conclusion. What was I? My spiritual house had been spiraling around this strange cyclone for several years. Now, presumably, the winds were dying down and it was time for it to land . . . but where? I kept asking myself: what do you believe? As I was cooking dinner or walking the dogs or waking up first thing in the morning: what do you believe? Then I would take another approach. Just pick one, I would tell myself. Perhaps it wasn't important what I selected. The goal was to settle in one spot, grow roots, develop, and evolve. I just had to commit to *something*.

Now I was blogging in real time, and I needed to bring the journey to some conclusion. The problem, as I began to see it, was that in selecting one version of one belief system, I was rejecting all the others—or at least that's how it felt. In my imagination, I would make my choice. I would picture signing some official declaration of faith. Trumpets would sound. I now had license to declare myself a practicing such-and-such. But this scenario always made my stomach turn. My mind would wander to the options I wasn't picking, and I would feel queasy at those potential paths I had refused. On some fundamental level, settling down felt wrong. It occurred to me that perhaps my problem was emblematic of the criticisms regularly hurled at today's younger generations. Our disengagement is a sign of some critical flaw manifesting in humankind. An aversion to hard work leaves us craving quick fixes. We want all the answers in our palm for no more effort than the light touch of an index finger. We don't have the patience for deep thinking. We're too blasé and easily bored to struggle—especially with the intangible. I weighed these as possible causes of my indecision, but none seemed an appropriate explanation. In fact it felt like the opposite. I suspected the problem might be too much interest, too much caring.

Nor was my reluctance to pick tied to a newly discovered distaste for religion. On the contrary, I had found pockets of profound insight tucked within each faith. How was I to choose? In becoming a Christian, I could not be a Jew. In Judaism, I was not Muslim. In being Muslim, I gave up Buddhism. I had reached this strange crossroads where not picking among the religions felt like the best way to honor the religions. My not choosing wasn't coming from a place of denial but, rather, a place of acceptance. And if I chose no affiliation, wasn't I also—in a funny way—opting for all of them? It made me think of the symbol of the open circle, so important in mystical traditions like Kabbalah. Represented in everyday parlance as a zero, it implies absence—but at the same time it also suggests receptivity.

In thinking this through, I was reminded of something that had made headlines briefly a couple years earlier. It had been a minor occurrence, no more than a footnote in popular culture, but I had paid attention because it seemed to hint at something bigger. In a live, tele- vised performance from Times Square on New Year's 2012, pop singer CeeLo Green sang John Lennon's classic "Imagine." A great vocalist paired with a fantastic song; lyrics that envision a world healed of conflict and violence. What could go wrong? Nothing—but for one tiny detail. CeeLo changed two words. In his version, "nothing to kill or die for / and no religion too" became "nothing to kill or die for / and all religion's true." Lennon's utopia got tweaked.

Instantly, the Internet lit up with comments. CeeLo received an avalanche of tweets and messages on his Facebook page. Most were voices of displeasure, saying the singer should be ashamed of himself—or worse. *Rolling Stone* magazine ran a brief story about it on its website, which produced a chain of almost six hundred remarks.

Among the more thoughtful commenters were those who specu- lated on what John Lennon meant ("I think 'no religion too' means they are fake! All religions are fake.") or what CeeLo's change implied ("I don't get it. 'All religion's true' seems to be an oxymoron!"). A few voices defended CeeLo. One wrote, "If I'm not mistaken, isn't the meaning of the song to imagine a world without the ideas that separate us . . . If all religion were true wouldn't that mean that all religion exists in harmony where people aren't killing others because of differing beliefs?"

The *Rolling Stone* article characterized those whom CeeLo had outraged as "John Lennon Fans." But was all the fuss really motivated by love for the lost Beatle? I suspected the truth was a bit more complicated. I thought they were more likely people whose distaste for religion had made the song—and in particular that line within it—something of an anthem. Lennon himself had a much softer take on religion. Among his many famous quotes is this: "People always got the image I was an anti-Christ or anti-religion. I'm not. I'm a most religious fellow. I was brought up a Christian and I only now understand some of the things that Christ was saying in those parables." He also said, "I believe that what Jesus and Mohammed and Buddha and all the rest said was right. It's just that the translations have gone wrong."

Almost immediately after the controversy, CeeLo tweeted a mea culpa. Not long after that, he deleted it. In his next public mention of the kerfuffle, he sounded much less sorry. He said he stood by the altered lyric. I thought it was brave what he had done, and I now felt I understood it even better.

The whole point of each belief system I had explored, the motivation of its original thinkers, was to heal—ourselves and the societies in which we live; to help us see that we are a part of something, whole and connected. Yet too often they become another means of discord. Our belief systems keep us feeling special or superior, which are just different ways of feeling isolated. But it's not religion that's torn us apart, because even lack of belief does the trick if clung to with white knuckles. To eliminate the certainty—to take the conviction out of religion—changes everything.

I think more and more people are sensing this, which is why the ranks of the Nones continue to grow. What many of us are saying with our lack of affiliation is that we don't want to take sides. Our stance overlaps with that of agnostics, who also maintain neutrality, though for slightly different reasons. Technically, an agnostic would pick a side if evidence proved which was right. Most Nones aren't interested in who's right. As far as we're concerned, there is no right, only different paths to the final destination. One group claiming the truth at the expense of another is just the sort of thing we're sick of because we see the destruction it's done; used again and again to justify not taking care of one another or, worse, destroying each other. Perhaps Nones are trying something new: not picking sides is the side we're picking. It might even be the most deeply religious decision we will ever make, our way of taking a stand for a more peaceful and loving world. If John Lennon were alive, I like to think he'd be right there with us.

o

Early Christians had a custom of dividing up the day into four blocks of about three hours, each with its own mood and prayers to say. It was actually a practice that historians say was adopted from Judaism as a way to structure and honor the passage of time. I was surprised to see the third portion of the day referred to as the "Hour of None." The None in this instance was derived from the word "nine," referring to the ninth hour of the day, which generally fell at about three in the afternoon and led into evening. But what I found most interesting was how this particular chunk of time was characterized. It was considered the portion of the day when businesses closed for the night and people returned home to bathe and eat. It offered both a break from work and a transition before the last prayers; it played the role a sort of spiritual exhalation. I wondered about the synchronicity of the names—if, culturally speaking, we aren't in our own "Hour of None." Perhaps we've entered something of a pause, a retreat from the normal course of things, an opportunity to reflect and prepare for what comes next.

If we have arrived at such a "time off," then I have the opportunity to consider what to bundle up and smuggle with me into whatever phase awaits. From Judaism I'll take monotheism, which I've come to appreciate as the birthplace of the radical notion that all beings on this planet—human and otherwise—originate from the same source and are, therefore, intrinsically connected. I want to remember the intent of Sabbath—a designated time to surrender productivity—and allow myself to relish the freedom of simply being. I must not forget to take a moment or two each day to focus my thoughts once again on how miraculous it is to be alive, perhaps letting a simple but amazing sight—a cloud formation or a loved one's smile—trigger the thought. I would like to keep the word *Dayenu* on the tip of my tongue, letting it tumble out in those moments when I am suddenly overwhelmed with appreciation or, perhaps more importantly, when I feel slighted or cheated or preoccupied with someone who appears to have it better. *Dayenu!* I have everything I need—more than enough. I must simply tap the deep well of gratitude. Something in my newfound understanding about Judaism has rubbed off on Phil, and he seems more receptive to its lessons—as well as those of other faiths. His Hanukkah amnesia seems to have lifted, and he suddenly can recall how to light the candles.

I refuse to go forward without the story of Jesus tucked close to my heart. Here was a free-thinking rebel of his day who broke with tradition so he could best demonstrate his love and care for others. He lives on as a powerful example: all that is noble and good can exist in a person; the divine can be embodied; we are capable of greater heights of love—for ourselves and others. He would have us eliminate fear as a motivating force. I'll think of the way he died, how exposed he was on that cross; how he literally shared his death with the world, demonstrating that strength is possible even in our most vulnerable moments—perhaps more so in those moments. In my darkest hours, I can rest assured that I am loved because I am not exempt from that most personal message Jesus sent to every single person: I love you. But I must strive with all my might to complete the assignment he left humanity. He was quite clear that our job is to experience joy and to love ourselves and others, two things that one might assume are easy but are perhaps the greatest challenges any of us face.

From Buddhism I'll borrow the daily practice of being aware of "the oneness" to which monotheism points. It shows me how to go beyond recognizing my interconnectedness as an intellectual concept to feeling the truth of it with every fiber of my being. I want to occupy that space of knowing for as often and long as possible, and when I forget, I want to find my way back because great comfort is found there. I can cultivate this sense of well-being, and I can turn around and share it, projecting it into the world where it will manifest in ways too mysterious for my mind to comprehend.

If Buddhism helps me nurture a sense of belonging by focusing inward, then Islam encourages me to fix my gaze outward and translate this unity into duty. It urges me to assume a position—on knees, forehead to the ground—conducive to embracing my own vulnerability so that I am better able to empathize with people in need. Ultimately it would have me transform empathy into action, finding concrete ways to help society's weakest members. Then, as a further challenge, it nudges me to expand the collective to which I identify. It wants me to push beyond the obvious affinities such as nationality, race, socioeconomic status, gender, or religious affiliation to ever-widening circles of humanity. Perhaps, at last, I can arrive to place where I feel beholden to every living creature and the earth itself.

So beautifully do these belief systems seem to complement one another that it's difficult to imagine what anyone could find to fight about or why they might want to waste precious time and energy on an endeavor whose intent seems to be the opposite of perhaps the most important common denominator: gratitude. When one is feeling lucky to be alive, appreciative for each new day, filled with awe at creation, why sow discord in the unity of which we are all a part?

To commit to none, but call on all: what would this look like on day-to-day practical terms? With no official place of worship to call home, my spiritual practices will be mostly self-guided. I can dedicate time each day to meditation and prayer, even if just a few minutes here and there. I will try to utter words of thanks more often, especially first thing in the morning and before eating. This should be easier to remember when I witness something unique like a rainbow or if I travel someplace new, see something I've never seen before.

Annual holidays can provide some structure to my ad-hoc multifaith endeavors. I can imagine participating—in my own way—in the Jewish high holidays of Yom Kippur and Rosh Hashanah. When the days shorten and the weather gets chilly, I'll know to review the previous year. I'll conduct an honest accounting of my behavior, my relationships, how I opted to spend my time. I will make amends, challenge myself to do better, and then release the guilt. As winter trudges forth, I can take some extra time to think about Jesus. I want to remember his example, the care he showed others, the unconditional love he demonstrated. When the days get short, it shouldn't be too much of a stretch for me to think about his death. Such reflections are likely to put me in a somber frame of mind as they will bring up thoughts of my own mortality, but I can look forward to the hopefulness of Easter. This, combined with the triumph of Passover, should rescue me from despair. In the end, life and freedom prevail.

I don't believe I'll ever live through another Ramadan without being transported back to my own experience with the fast. As I write today, it is several days into the next year's Ramadan, and even though I am not officially participating, I can feel the loneliness of my remembered hunger and thirst so acutely it brings tears to my eyes. I can't help but think of everyone around the world abstaining during daylight hours—so much so that I am in alliance mentally if not physically. I feel solidarity with the intent of the fast and with the people for whom going without is not a choice, an affinity that I hope will expand when my multifaith calendar swings back around to Eid al-Adha. From now on when I see this date on my planner, I'll think about that day at the Dallas convention center and remember that the world's most populous belief systems share common roots, bound to one another in collective imagination.

But for how long can I practice my solo patchwork religion before my devotion to it begins to flag and the finer points fade from memory? Maybe I'll have a good reason, like my schedule gets super busy. With no community, no accountability, I can see that a day may arrive when I fail to take the time. The connections I've fostered with my religious endeavors are far-reaching, but they are theoretical. I don't have to come face-to-face with another living soul to practice. Wouldn't some actual companionship on this path do me some good? Some Nones are committed to a place of worship, perhaps even attend regularly, but continue to pledge no allegiance to a particular religion. These Nones appear to have found a balance that doesn't force narrowed loyalties but meets practical needs.

A friend asked recently what I thought my future held, faithfully speaking. I joked that I could continue to make the rounds to various places of worship, A-to-Z, over and over again, circling back so many times that people began to recognize me, perhaps even welcome me—not as a potential convert but for the None I choose to be. It's a daydream that makes me happy. By showing up at the doorsteps of the different houses of worship, hat in hand, I draw the boundaries of my spiritual identity ever larger; it's not just a single dwelling but an entire town, a community both more real and bigger than I ever could have hoped. Perhaps some congregations would come to appreciate me as a little tie that helps connect them to a grander network of worshippers. But how realistic is this vision, really? Could it possibly provide the intimate connections and structure I'll crave, especially as I grow older? As I tiptoe into my golden years, and all the existential issues become more pressing, will my slapdash independence continue to accommodate me? If not, what then?

That winter, as my blog journey began to wind down, I received an invitation to my high school reunion, which would take place in Los Angeles in the spring. It was a big one, and if I went it would be my first. I waffled. But then my dear pal Lisa insisted I attend—and that sealed it. In addition to Lisa and her daughter, Sydney, I would get to check back in with Nina, Deb, and Becky. They had all been essential to this journey, and seeing them once more as I officially wrapped up had a nice symmetry to it.

Once I RSVP'd that I would I be there, I started to get excited. Since my last visit to L.A. when I explored Judaism, my friends and I had stayed in contact, so this time around there wouldn't be any of the heavy reconnecting stuff that comes with too many years of not communicating. It would be just buddies hanging out. In addition I would

285

CONCLUSION

get to return to my high school and catch up with other classmates I hadn't seen since graduation, which seemed appropriate because that setting and the larger community had played a pivotal role in my life back when I was a kid from Texas. It also occurred to me that I could, at long last, accomplish the Yom Kippur custom of *tashlikh*, the tossing of bread crumbs that represent sins or misdeeds into a body of water, which I had failed to perform on my previous visit. When I started the Jewish exploration, I had imagined I would do this when I had access to the vast Pacific Ocean—as opposed to the puny creek that runs through my town. Then I returned home from L.A. and realized I had totally spaced on the task.

By the time I packed my bag to fly to California, I was on the Islam section of my blog. The average number of visitors had stayed fairly consistent in the year and a half since I began, but the tone had changed completely. In the beginning it felt like I had scrawled the word "peace" on a wall in my own home and dozens of strangers had marched in to scratch it out. Now it was mostly a ragtag gang of peaceniks helping me clean up while the white-knucklers were radio silent. I thought perhaps they had stopped following, disgusted by my journey and the phase I was in. But then one or another would randomly pipe up with an observation or thought that sounded downright tolerant. Maybe only those who were a bit more open-minded or curious had stayed with me until the end, but I was okay with that.

Back in Los Angeles, I sat on the bed in my brother's old room deciding what to wear. I counted the months since I had been here last: twenty-four. And how many had it been since I graduated high school? Oh, boy, that number was well over two hundred. I went with a black skirt and a grey top—a little on the fancyish side for California, but not too much. The reunion consisted of a Saturday night dinner and Sunday afternoon picnic, both of which would be held on school grounds. As I headed off from my dad's house, taking the exact same route I used twice a day all those years ago, I felt a little disoriented. Butterflies batted around my belly like the first day of seventh grade. The campus itself had undergone dramatic changes since my days there. An enormous empty field in the back was crowded with new buildings. I had driven past a few times over the years, trying to assess the additions with a swift glance.

Now I made my way from the same old parking lot to the backside of the school, my black pumps clickety-clacking on the pavement. What had been the main school building (really the only substantial structure) during my days here was now just the tip of the iceberg, perhaps no more than a barrier between the street and all the new development. As I walked, I wondered what the school's founder, Shirley, had thought of the growth of her little brainchild. She had died at age ninety-three, just a few months after my trip to explore Judaism. She had been such an important source of encouragement for me during those difficult teen years. She had been a writer, and she told me I was too.

A bunch of people were gathered in a plaza area that connected the old part with the new. I started to feel a little anxious when I couldn't remember what had been in that location before the plaza. An old shed? Would I even recognize the grownup versions of my classmates? I didn't know if this place was too altered to hold any significance for me anymore. I paused at a table of name tags. I didn't want to ruin what existed in my memory as a sacred space, demolished like that poor shed and paved over. But I had to admit the plaza was nice, definitely an upgrade, with pleasant landscaping and places to sit. From across the way, I spotted Deb waving at me. Then, slowly, familiar faces began to emerge, and I knew there was no way to go but forward.

o

"How many you think?" I was showing a plastic baggie of leftover lemon cake to my dad. I wanted him to estimate the number of crumbs because if it didn't seem like enough, I planned to supplement with a few slices of another type of bread.

"Seven thousand?" he said.

I studied the bag closely. The slices had broken up nicely. It was a compact bundle but some pieces were no bigger than grains of sand. I thought seven thousand seemed like an adequate number to cover most of my sins to date.

Near the Santa Monica pier, I found street parking easily but only had change for seventeen minutes on the meter. I would have to make quick work of this task, stay focused as I walked past the old-timey merry-go-round I used to ride. I was meeting Nina for coffee in half an hour. Past the Ferris wheel and the arcade, I kept a brisk pace, weaving around pedestrians, couples hand-in-hand, and families with kids. A long stretch of pier is over sand, so I kept going until I heard the lapping of waves underneath. Crowds thinned, and the pier narrowed. I looked over the railing to assess how far out I was. I wanted the water to be deep enough for fish and for the crumbs to sink out of sight. Farther along I found steps down to a platform especially for fishing. That seemed like a good sign. No one was using it at this hour. Signs posted instructed visitors not to feed birds but mentioned nothing about the fish.

I took out the baggie from my purse and looked around to see if anyone was watching. I was feeling a little iffy. I worried someone might think I was dumping a suspicious substance like cremated remains. Are there rules against that? A little bubble of nervousness formed in my gut. Among the more practical outcomes of this religious exploration are the techniques I've acquired to handle the anxiety that flares up from time to time. Perhaps above any other concern, the return of my old panic attacks had given me the final shove to step foot in places of worship. When I paced around the house in my new hometown and felt the familiar dread percolating, I knew I needed to search for answers in places I had never looked before.

Today I see more clearly the deeper roots of that angst. We all have the knowledge of the incomprehensible odds it took to get here tucked somewhere in our minds and the awareness that our lives as we know them will end. These facts get translated into feelings of inadequacy, fear, and anger. We might even have something convenient to blame for thinking we are not good enough or feeling scared out of our minds or mad as hell, something that happened in our lives or a flaw we think is unique to us. Allow these issues to remain unexamined, and anxiety is perhaps the least of the ills we'll face.

Religions can help us shine a light in these dark corners. They can provide a language, a space, a nudge to put words and images to these ideas. They give us proof that people have struggled with this same stuff for centuries. Afraid of the unknown? Come to your knees. Find strength in accepting your limitations. Remember: countless others have come before you. Feeling unworthy? You are, and have, more than enough. Anxious? Breathe: there is only the present moment. Rest your forehead on the ground: you are an important part of something much bigger than you can comprehend. The influence of our lives ripples out long after our bodies are gone. It might even be helpful to reflect on the transformative powers of faith. Here is a world view in which a negative flips into a positive. Vulnerability becomes strength. It's a paradigm where crippling anxiety or other destructive behaviors might even be interpreted as progress: your "little I" reacting to its diminished importance. So be gentle with yourself.

I watched the bubble of nervousness about my crumb-tossing form and dissipate. "It's just bread," I thought, scooping a handful and tossing it into the water. I imagined each little piece that hit the water as a poor choice or an insensitive action, all the things I had done or failed to do. I was letting go. I looked over the railing to say a final goodbye and realized many of the larger crumbs appeared to be floating. This wasn't how I imagined it. I had pictured them disappearing quickly, sinking like pebbles or gobbled up by hungry fish. Now my sins were bobbing for all to see. I decided to release the remainder of the baggie in one fell swoop, overturn it and give it a good shake. I was sorry for any disappointment I may have caused others in the course of this exploration, people who wanted or believed I would adopt their religious affiliation. I was sorry for the blog readers I had disappointed with my announcement that I would remain a None. In the end I had to accept what I was and do my best to find meaning in it. I hoped they would understand. Maybe Nones have a role to play in the greater story of religion.

As I threw the last of the crumbs, the wind picked up and blew a bunch of them back at me. They coated the front of my shirt and landed around my feet. I tried to brush and kick them away, but that didn't help. They broke into smaller bits and became airborne again. This was not at all the tidy process I had expected. My sins were flying every which way! I was covered in misdeeds! It made me think of something that had happened just a few minutes earlier, as I made my way down the pier. A group of bicyclists were pumping their pedals up the hill that connects the pier to the street. A guy in front of me wanted to give them encouragement. He shouted, "Almost there!" One of the cyclists responded, "Only 3,000 miles to go!" Everyone within earshot laughed at the misunderstanding. The top of the hill wasn't the end of the journey; it had only just begun.

Acknowledgments

I owe a debt of gratitude to every single person I encountered on this journey, only some of whom appear in the pages of this book. Thank you for interacting with me, welcoming me, and teaching me.

I'd like to thank Suzanne Gluck for recognizing the potential of this project; Kirby Kim for guiding me and my work; Wendy Lochner for believing; and everyone at Columbia University Press who contributed to the finished product. I am forever grateful.

A special shout out to: my L.A. gang—Lisa Gunn, Nina Drabkin, Rebecca Rigney, and Debra Loucks—for your grace and friendship; my None pals—Katie, Kelsie, Sueann, and Emily—for your curiosity that encouraged me; and Khadija for your generosity and love.

To all those who helped me take this journey by providing a bed in the cities I visited: Ted and Becky Nicolaou; Erich Gruen and Ann Hasse; Irene Nicolaou; Sally and David Hamilton; Rob and Mariah Litowitz; and Cassie Bates. Thank you for the soft spot to land, both literally and figuratively.

I also want thank all the followers of my blog, *One None Gets Some*, and especially the "merry miners"—Frank, Patti, Merrill, Tim, Walt, and Carmen—whose collective wisdom and ability to engage with one another despite differences inspires me still.

To every member of my big, beautiful extended family, thank you for being a part of my personal story. I love you all.

To Abbey and Athena, my dearly departed mutts, thank you for keeping me company and dreaming while I worked on this manuscript.

Finally, to Phil Gruen: thank for being my center.